HUMAN RIGHTS - TWENTY FIRST CENTURY CHALLENGES

HUMAN RIGHTS-TWENTY FIRST CENTURY CHALLENGES

Edited by

V. N. VISWANATHAN

PUBLICATIONS
KALPAZ PUBLICATIONS
DELHI-110052

Human Rights-Twenty First Century Challenges

Rs. 720

ISBN: 81-7835-658-9

Published in 2009 in India by
Kalpaz Publications
C-30, Satyawati Nagar,
Delhi-110052
E-mail: kalpaz@hotmail.com
Phone : 9212729499

Lasser Type Setting by: Rudra Computer Graphics. Delhi
Printed at : G. Print Process, Delhi

Contents

Preface

A long felt dream of editing the proceedings of a national seminar on "Ethics and Human Values was fulfilled by editing the present book. Ethics and human values are very abstract in nature and quite often moulded by our circumstances. What should be the ethical thing that to be followind in one's own life itself prose a dilema in our minds. Both ethics and values are primordial sentiments that to be nurished by internal and external forces. Ethics and its practics and development have very different historical trajectories in social sciences. On many incidecnes, the practical life nurtured, determines, the ethical content that one must follow. Generally, ethics is considered as the science of describing social conduct and judging its appropriateness. Ethics in connection with human being in this century can be traced from the United Nations Universal Declaration of Human Rights (1948). It can be called as Magna Carta of human values. The outcome of second World War made all of us to pay attention to basic human values. Human being underwent a far reaching misery as a result of programmed genocide and destruction of property. Life values shattered and many ethical norms and practices were under severe constrains. We had forgotten that ethics and basic human values are the foundation for a civilized society. Ethics is a boster of once's own morality and behaviour. There are political and non-political institutions that develop among us, the general and professional ethics.

Poverty today is an unethical situation which compels the State to act in a particular way for its complete eradication. It is a basic human value to put an end to proverty. Inequality, prejudice, racial discrimination, caste consideration, slavery, violence, poverty and gender bias are all signs of human indignity and rejection of values of highest order. World theatre is full of incidences of value conflicts based on social and civilizaional practice. According to Plato, the ethical consideration of an 'Ideal State' is to promote good citizens. It is an integral part of an ideal State. State should act as' Value-Provider'. In fact, State take into consideration the ethics of life which has been germinated and sustained by society at large. Therefore, social institutions have the responsibility of developing the right ethics and values, which later backed by the State. The social science dillema for a very long period has been the use of force for the enforcement of the right ethics and values for the citizens. After all, ethics, human values and morality are not always controlled by law because it hails from our heart and not from our mind. When you are physically harmed, the mind make an instant command to protect yourself and in that event you use force and cause a great damage to your offender. When the same pain caused by a police or State agencies we are in a position to accept it. In the same way when such activity done by an infant, we fail to react, since such impulses are coming from our heart.

Social institutions like clan, tribe, groups, community and religions play a paramount importance in supplying the values and ethics and thus train us to lead a peaceful life. The loss of family system and emergence of nuclear family altogether brings in an entirely new set of values and practices. In short, our behaviours are moulded by our social institutions such as family, schools and religious institutions. Aa Swami Vivekantha said "our great values are nutured by our civilization and we have a duty not only to follow it but to carry forward it to our next generations. Thus, as a human being we have an obligation to germinate the right kind of values in the younger minds.

Respecting the basic rights of others is a value based approach for a peaceful co-existence. Human rights are basic rights of man kind. Protecting the human rights of the people is the modern ethics of "State". Many 'failed State' failed to protect the human rights of its citizens. Modern State system cannot survive when it failed to safeguard the human rights of its citizens. It is for this reason, today, the State not only protects the rights of its people but also fullfil its responsibilities of imparting such values among its citizens.

Indian Universitites, colleges and schools are basic instruments through which basic values are taught to the young minds. The teachers have a great responsibility of citizenship training in inherting the right kinds of values. Through education we can impart the right kind of values. seeking Knowledge should not mere 'fact-finding' exercies but also include moral development. Developing scientific mind is possible only by applying the highest degree of values and morality.

In this 21st century, our values and moral bases are challenged not only by various factors, most importantly by the 'State' itself. Human Rights violations by the State apparatus is an indication of immoral action of the State. Racial profiling by the police is an example unethical policing. Abject proverty and greater inequality are signs of State degrdation. Re-building such shattered states is the prime duty and responsibility of international institutions. The recently evolved Human Rights Council Calls for an Universal values to refine such 'failed states'.

Human Rights values through education is the focus of this book. Besides, it also looks into the various other kinds of challenges faced by modern state system with more specific reference to India.

I am very much indebted to all of my research scholors, faculty members and members of government and non-governmental organisations for their sincere efforts in sharing their knowledge and thus opened the doors for a meaningful debate on Human Rights-21st Century challenges.

Regards

V.N. VISWANATHAN

List of Contributors

1. **V.N. Viswanathan**
Reader in Political Science
Department of Political Science
Presidency College
Chennai- 600005

2. **Dr. R. Baskarasethupathi**
Chief Educational Officer,
Tamil Nadu School Education Department

3. **Johannes (Hans) A. van der Ven**
With PhD Radboud University Nijmegen, the Netherlands and Doctor honoris causa University of Lund, Sweden, occupies the Chair of Comparative Empirical Theology in Nijmegen and the extra-ordinary Chair of Practical Theology at the University of South Africa.

Francis-Vincent Anthony
With Doctorate in Theology at the Salesian Pontifical University (Rome), is Associate professor of Practical Theology in the same university since 1998.

4. **Dr. M. Kaliyaperumal**
Reader and Head
Department of Political Science
Presidency College
Chennai- 600 005

5. **Dr. A. Karuppiah**
Professor of Sociology, Department of Sociology,
University of Madras
Chennai – 600 005

Dr. M. John Sundar
Reader and Former Head
Department of Sociology
Loyola College (Autonomous)
Chennai – 600 034

6. **Dr. V. Prem Sam Ponniah**
Human Rights Activist
No.15, Nancy Street
Purasaiwalkam, Chennai -600 007

7. **R. Subramani**
Lecturer in the Department of Media Sciences
Anna University
Chennai.

8. **Prof. S.P. Guruparan (Retd)**
Department of Political Science
Presidency College
Chennai- 600005

9. **Dr. N. Madavan**
Reader in Political Science
Department of Political Science
Presidency College
Chennai- 600 005

10. **Dr. G. Gowthaman**
Reader in History.
All India Civil Services
Coaching Centre
Govt. of Tamil Nadu
Chennai – 600 040

11. **B.S.Selvakumar**
Lecturer in Political Science
Voorhees College
Vellore-1

12. **Dr. R. P. Pankaja**
Head, Dept. of Sanskrit
M. O. P. Vaishnav College for Women
(Autonomous)
20, IV lane, Nungambakkam High Road
Nungambakkam, Chennai- 600 034

13. **Dr. A. Sethuramasubbiah**
Reader
Tamil Nadu Institute of Lobour Studies
Chennai- 600005

14. **N. Anandhi**
(Advocate, Madras High Court, Madurai Bench)
Dr. S. Suresh Kanan
Faculty, School of Economics
Madurai Kamaraj University
Madurai

15. **G. Subramanian**
Manitham (Human Rights Journal)
Chennai

16. **P. Anathakrishnan**
Vishvodayaa Trust
Madipakkam
Chennai

17. **C. Velayutham**
Lecturer
Department of Media Sciences
Anna University
Chennai

18. **S.Venkasubramanian**
PhD Research Scholar
Department of Political Science
Presidency College
Chennai- 600 005

19. **D.S. Makkalanban**
UGC- SRF, PhD Research Scholar
Department of Political Science
Presidency College
Chennai- 600 005

20. **S. Jayakumar**
Lecturer in Political Science
Government Law College
Chengalpattu
Tamil Nadu

21. **R. Elangovan**
PhD Research Scholar
Department of Political Science
Presidency College
Chennai- 600 005

22. **M. Elavarasi**
M.Phil Research Scholar
Department of Political Science
Presidency College
Chennai- 600 005

Introduction

We learn about our social values by various sources. Values are guiding forces for a good life and for social practices. Imparting right kinds of values to people becomes the most important aspects of social institutions. Our ancient scripts, epics, poems and religious text teaches us the kinds of moral values that one can cherish in their life. Imbibing such values is not only for one's one good but also for the general welfare of the people. All educational institutions are having a great moral responsibility of nurturing such values in the minds of young. Values which accelerate high morality in our life should not only preserve but also passed on next generation. Thus, we, by following positive values trying establish a society with moral quality. Interestingly, human rights are closely associated with values. Following basic human rights are best values practiced or learnt. In the context of development of modern technology and the existence of complex society, it becomes a total neglect of human values. Respecting the rights of others are the best values that we can teach to our future generation. Universalization of rights are becoming an issue in modern world and critics points out that Universal Declaration of Human Rights are Euro-centric and embedded in western philosophy has no meaning for people belonging to eastern hemisphere. One can accept that there exist a vast difference between west and east thinking in various field but one can also see the possibility of universal rights prescribed both in the west and east philosophies. However, the east more concentrated on ethical way life and the west moved towards scientific explorative attempt and evolved more of practical thinking which we encounter in our day to day life practice. The religions of east and west emphasized more on up keeping the noble deeds of respecting the rights of others. Bhavad Gita, the religious text of Hinduism emphasis that a man should do his duties and should not expect its results in terms of benefits. The Holy Quran proclaims that the almighty will come closer to those who care for the poor and the needy people. Christian teaching more concerned about that before God are all equal and treating people unequally itself a creation of the man and it is sin against God.

As stated earlier there is a great responsibility for educational institutions for imparting such values for students. The Education Policy of India 1986 emphatically added that value based education is much needed in order to develop a moral society that respect basic human rights and human dignity. Our aspiration to develop technology must go along with our concern for human values. What is the use of high development in the field of information technology without improving the economic condition of the poor people in India? Extreme poverty in India itself a violation of human rights. Eradication of poverty in India should be our prime concern in coming years. The digital divide and economic disparity are sign of modern human rights violations. There must be ways and means to put forward our efforts in evolving a just society where at least everybody satisfied with minimum need for life and an opportunity to lead a life with dignity. The thinking efforts must appropriately supported by institutional mechanism and also by developing a new breed of human rights culture. Understandably, human rights are cultural approach to resolve the human miseries and difficulties.

The seminar objectives fall within the scope the following:

- to strengthen respect for human rights and fundamental freedom;
- to develop fully the human personality and the sense of its dignity;

- to develop attitudes and behaviours to promote respect for the rights of others;
- to ensure genuine gender equality and equal opportunities for women in all spheres;
- to promote understanding and tolerance among diverse national, ethnic, religious, linguistic and other groups;
- to empower people to participate actively in the life of a free society;
- to promote democracy, development, social justice, communal harmony, solidarity and friendship among nations;
- to further the activities of the UN system, in particular UNESCO, the Office of the UN High Commissioner for Human Rights and UNICEF, aimed at the creation of a culture of peace based upon universal values of human rights, international understanding, tolerance and non-violence.

Education for human rights, should be aimed at full enjoyment of human rights and fundamental freedoms and for that purpose have regards to the following:

- All human rights are universal, indivisible, interrelated and interdependent, and all are essential for the full development of human personality;
- While regional and national particularities are to be borne in mind, it is the duty of States, regardless of their political, civil, economic and cultural systems, to promote and protect all human rights and fundamental freedoms;
- Universal respect for, and observance of, human rights and fundamental freedoms contribute to stability, security and well-being, necessary for socio-economic development;
- Human rights, democracy, peace and development are interdependent and mutually reinforcing;
- Rights of women and girl-child are an inalienable, integral and indivisible part of universal human rights;
- Human rights education should be aimed at the full and equal participation of women in political, civil, economic,

social and cultural life. Awareness towards prevention of gender based -violence, sexual harassment and exploitation should be a component of education programmes;

- Promotion and protection of the rights of the child is a priority and requires dissemination of knowledge of relevant standards. Special efforts are needed to eradicate child labour, child prostitution, and child pornography;
- Special attention should be paid to the rights of persons belonging to various vulnerable groups - national or ethnic, religious and linguistic minorities, indigenous people, refugees and internally displaced persons, migrant workers, persons with HIV/AIDS and other health problems, disabled, and elderly;
- Special attention should be also given to the mobilization of the public opinion againstmajor threats and challenges to human rights: terrorism, organized crime, corruption, trafficking of human beings for exploitative purposes, drug trafficking, violence etc.

The University Grants Commission in its Tenth Plan emphasized the need to conduct seminars and workshop on imparting values through education. It also laid down various reason why value education so important for the future generation. With financial grant from UGC, the Department of Political Science, Presidency College, Chennai conducted a two-Day national seminar on Ethics and Values in education. Human Rights are emerging field universal values that to be followed all in this world. The national seminar was conducted on 29-30, March 2007 and attended by more number of people from academic, government, non-governmental establishments. As far as 107 papers were presented in the seminar and we selected 20 papers which are of original contribution in different fields of human rights. That doesn't mean that the others papers are below our expectations. They also in unique way contributed to the success of the seminar as well far the session discussion that followed the paper presentation in six panels established for that in the course of two days.

As the coordinator of the seminar myself presented a paper titled "Human Values for the Twenty First Century" .It opened a plethora of issues for discussion. The paper on "Human Values for the Twenty First Century" highlighted the emergence of hitherto unknown areas and problems that come into our life and evolve appropriate values for its sustainability. The paper added that a 21st century humanistic ethic requires the scientific basis for the oneness of the human family be accepted and taught internationally, nationally, and locally in classrooms, in families, in religious and secular institutions. On a familial and personal level it becomes incumbent upon every citizen of planet earth to embrace, teach, and practice values that reject violence as a way of solving human problems. The paper also emphasis the equality of the sexes and is important to realize that, despite the implications in the Universal Declaration of Human Rights ,all human life is not enjoying of equal values. The declaration states that all human beings are born free and equal in dignity and rights. They are endowed with reason and conscience and should act towards one another in a spirit of brotherhood. At the end the paper concludes by asserting that for the world of the 21st century, humanistic values must project the vision of a peaceful world in which no man, woman or child, or class of men, women, or children shall live as servants or slaves existing simply to fulfill the whims and wishes and desires of others, a world in which no man or woman or child shall be used as a tool to satisfy the lusts or greed or ambitions of others, a world in which every human life, the life of every man, woman, and child shall be a wanted, welcomed, and esteemed member of the one human family.

The paper by R.Baskarasethupathi highlights the importance of teaching value based education for school children. The author placed a high priority for value based education in our school system. He adds that value education is important for four fold self development programme. That is physical, intellectual, emotional and spiritual self development. The goal of value education in broader sense is to prepare good human beings so that their immense potential can be utilized for the causes of peace social cohesion and environmentally sustain development as well as humanity at large. Indeed many schools in India realized the importance of supplementing of our school education with moral science and to instruct on values that the Indian heritage supported for a long period of time. Character building of young minds much depends on value preaching in school setting through story telling or by portraying drama of great men and women of India.

The article by Johannes A. (Hans) van der Ven – Francis-Vincent Anthony aims at shedding light on the extent to which religion furthers the social integration in secular society, from a civil rights perspective, of people from different traditions and cultures. It seeks to advance a theory of religion's role in the process of social integration in a society whose very core is the separation of religion and state, religious freedom and other civil rights.

After clarifying the models of inter-religious interaction and the possible strategies for social integration, the authors proceed to address two empirical research questions: to what extent do young people, namely, the higher secondary school students in Tamilnadu, India, who comprise the sample, support a lived legal culture of civil rights (part one), and what effects do their religious beliefs and practices have on such a civil rights culture, while controlling for some relevant population characteristics (part two)? The paper ends with a discussion on the salient findings emerging from the empirical analysis with regard to the impact of religion on social integration.

The paper by Dr.M.Kaliyaperumal in 'Human Rights in India- Its Prospective Nature Towards 21st Century', discusses the origin of human rights, the evolution of human rights in various aspects, the infringements of human rights by various organizations and finally suggests how to protect the human rights in coming days in international sphere and in India. The opinions of political and other social scientists are considered as the theme of the paper, trying to throw certain points for valuable suggestions.

Dr.A.Karuppiah and John Sundar provided a well scripted paper on the issues of Children's rights and its violations. Apart from the Child Labour (Prohibition and Regulation) Act, 1986, there are many laws that have the protection and interest of the working children in mind. Some of them are the Factories Act and the Minimum Wages Act, both passed in 1948, the Plantations Labour Act, 1951, the Mines Act, 1952, the Motor Transport Worker's Act, 1961, and the Beedi and Cigar Workers (Conditions of Employment) Act, 1966. The paper reported that over 3,00,000 children who are under the age of 18 work as soldiers for armed rebel forces and even in the government. Documentation of such abuse is evident in countries like Angola, Burma, Colombia, the Democratic Republic of Congo, Liberia, Sudan, and Uganda. Human Rights Watch published more than 13 reports on forced recruitment of under aged children for use in armed conflict. It is one of the worst forms of child labour practiced in the world today. It is an abusive practice and an extremely hazardous form of work to use children as soldiers.

The paper by Sam Ponniah's work on "Human Rights of Scheduled Tribes," is a study of the rights of Tribes in international and national context, focusing on socio, economic and political rights. This paper recounts the present human rights conditions of Scheduled Tribes in India in the very candid fashion providing situational analysis and perspectives with vital statistical information.

The paper presented by R.Subramani argues that Human Rights culture is a way of life and it can create a very cohesive environment to break the traditional misbelieves and misconceptions and help in contributing national values in concurrence with universal human rights values and principles. The world is on the process of redesigning the concept of universality and culture. The diverging views of States on the nature of human rights and the cultural differences of societies should be eliminated through a systematic approach. Human rights culture could be taught as a tool for social change. He argues that education is the only way to build and mould the future generation.

The paper by Prof.S.P.Guruparan depicts the place of humanity in the great work of Saint Thiruvalluvar. His paper titled "Humanity in Thirukkural" focus on the need for all human beings to develop love and affection towards all living things in this universe. According to the author freedom, equality and fraternity will blossom with the fragrance of equal rights when Humanity is based on divinity and rationality. In Thirukkural LOVE and HUMANITY have been given importance along with VIRTUE. One can assert that Thirukkural be considered a treaty on basic life values of Human Kind. Thirukkural with 1330 couplets in Tamil language divided into three parts as 'Arram' 'Porul' and 'Enpam'. In 'Arram' category the poet almost covered all virtues that one must posses to be human. The author rightly stated that we are yet exploit more from the work of Thiruvalluvar to groom our minds and our actions to fellow beings.

Dr.N.Madavan in 'Human Rights Perspective and Media: With Special Reference to Broadcasting' links Human Rights and role of Media. The paper tries:

- to explore the maladies of the human rights violations that have been attracted in the context of the media particularly under broadcasting with special reference to India.
- to define the areas of human rights and limit the boundaries of human rights within the broadcasting arena.
- to provide suitable recommendations from the point of view of incorporating human rights ideals and values in broadcasting arena.

G.Gowtham paper on Human Rights and Bonded Labour discuss about an issue which falls in the category of gross violation of human rights. The author laments that the enactment of the Bonded Labour Abolition Action 1976 had not solved the problem because of the failure of the authorities in invoking the provisions of the Act to put down the evil practice. Steps should be taken to identify the bonded labourers in various parts of the country and initiate legal action against the culprits, who kept the innocents in bondage. The role of NGO's is superb in identifying the bonded labourers. Despite positive laws in the field of bonded lobour the author rightly points out that unless if don't have effective mechanism to implement them, the law will become ineffective.

The paper by B.S.Selva Kumar titled "Right to Clean Environment- with reference to water" is an issue of human right concern today and a burning issue across the nation. The right to environment implies the right to clean or healthy environment. Clean environment has been the pre-requisite to human life and it is universally accepted as a human right. Therefore, right to healthy environment is natural, inalienable and fundamental right of the people. The right to life is another potential instrument of realization of environment right. The United Nations conference remarked that "man is both creature and moulder of his environment which gives him physical sustenance and affords him the opportunity for intellectual, moral, social and spiritual growth. In the long and tortuous evolution of the human race on this planet a stage has been reached when through the rapid acceleration of science and technology, man has acquired the power to transform his environment in countless ways and on an unprecedented scale. Both aspects of man's environment, the natural and the man made, are essential to his well being and to the enjoyment of the basic human rights, even the right to life itself. It is well known fact that in the 21st century, water is the converging and meeting point of the world community. Water is our common present and future. "It is the invaluable heritage of our children. Every effort must be taken to provide water to all without any kind of discrimination.

Dr.R.P.Pankaja dealt with a subject which is not only a right issue but an emotional issue too. At the UN Millennium Summit held in September 2000, the world leaders of the 191 member nations decided to establish time bound measurable goals to combat poverty, hunger, disease, discrimination against women, illiteracy, environment degradation etc... Called the

Millennium Development Goals, hunger and poverty top the list. According to the author the involvement of the civil society is absolutely essential for any policy to be implemented well. If hunger is recognized as a human rights issue, (1) the domestic and international civil societies will have to take an active part. This will create an empowering dimension in the work of the civil society in ensuring a hunger and poverty-free governance as a principle of administration; (2) a political consensus can be achieved on the ways and means of achieving the same; (3) objectivity can be maintained in the implementation of policies relating to fighting hunger and poverty so that resource allocation and targeting of areas and people suffering from extreme poverty is not based on biases and prejudices. This is important for the resources allocated may not reach the beneficiaries.

Dr.A.Sethuramasubbiah a well known academic from Institute of Labour Studies, Government of Tamil Nadu highlighted the problems of child labour in India...He points out that the child labour is attributed mainly to exploitation, discrimination, powerlessness, caste and gender suppersion. There are various attitudinal factors, which are responsible for taking children to hazardous jobs.

N.Anandhi& Dr.S.Suresh Kanan in their paper titled Child Labour and Legal Legilations highlighted the practice of various Indian laws for the protection of children. Both the authors have provided a list of laws that protect the childrens rights both in India and some international instruments wherein India is a signatory nation.

G.Subramanian, an NGO activists predicted the future of Indian children in his paper titled "Child Labour: Indian Prospective". Government has been taking various pro-active measures to tackle this problem. However, considering the magnitude and extent of the problem and that it is essentially a socio-economic problem inextricably linked to poverty and illiteracy, it requires concerted efforts from all sections of the society to make a dent in the problem. India has the world's largest child labourer population.

P.Anathakrishnan paper on "Rights of Disabled Persons- Where Are We in India" very rightly stated that The future work of the disability community has the potential to integrate the resources of "traditional" human rights communities, focusing on political and civil rights and "non-traditional" human rights communities, focusing on economic, social and cultural rights, as well as civil society organizations that have not yet focused on issues concerning persons with disabilities. Together newly emerging disability-sensitized communities would work toward the goal of a society for all in promoting economic, social and cultural rights from a disability perspective, to achieve a society accessible for all.

C.Velayutham in his paper titled "Human Rights Issues and News Media Coverage "Rightly opined that media in India has been involved in highlighting various forms of human rights violation and thus pressurize the government to take appropriate actions. He observes that the media devote very little space for human rights issues, particularly with their market-driven style of functioning in the recent years. They rarely follow up human rights stories, which they report with a greater zeal in the beginning.

S.Venkatasubramanian paper on "Safeguarding Human Rights against Various Future Environmental Threats' is directly related to our rights for environment. Humanity should learn to use the eco-friendly products and controlling themselves from involving in unsustainable activities and injudicious utilization of natural resources. As an individual, every human being must take pledge to do some constructive and regenerative work for saving this earth from its complete destruction of natural resources. They must always use eco-friendly products and involve in various eco-regenerative activities like avoid using polyethylene bags etc. He concludes, by asserting that the government must take a pro-active role in protecting our environment and there by provide inter-generational equity.

D.S.Makkalanban in 'The Role of International Forums in Implementing International Human Rights Laws' explores the importance of human rights, traces the origin of human rights laws in international sphere and how they have been inculcated in international organizations and the role of these organizations. The paper is set with twin objectives:

- Firstly, to explore the historical roots and surface environments that necessitated for establishing international forums and international laws to protect human rights and
- Secondly, to analyze the role of international forums and international laws to promote human rights.

S.Jayakumar in 'Human Rights in Primary Education: The Indian Context' argues the importance of primary education, discusses the loopholes of primary education in Tamil Nadu with illustrative examples. Argues, if there are no Human rights practiced in education – how can one teach human right education among schools and colleges? He observes, unless human rights are observed in educational services, beyond doubt one can expect more of Kumbakkonam incidents in future.

R.Elangovan in 'Atrocities against Dalits' outlines the issues concerned with dalits in particular to Tamil Nadu. He traces the forms of violations by different castes on dalits in Tamil Nadu with examples. Argues for human rights of dalits who have been exploited for centuries together in India. Also provides some remedial measures to uplift the standard of dalits on par with other human beings.

The paper on "Dignity of Dalit Women" by M. Elavarasi place the Dalit Women violated of their rights not because of their caste status but also because of gender. According to Manusmriti, women have no right to education, independence or wealth. It not only justifies the treatment of Dalit women as a sex object, and promotes child marriage but also justifies a number of in cidences of atrocities on women as can be seen in the full verse.

Manusmriti(IX: 94) A man aged thirty years, shall marry a maiden of 12 who pleases him.

Manusmriti IX (3): Her father protects her in childhood her husband protects her in youth, and her sons protect her in old age. A women is never fit for independence even the killing of a Dalit women is justified as a minor offence for the Brahmin's equal to the killing of an animal. If the billing of an untouchable was justified as a minor offense. You can imagine the treatment they received throughout their lives.

1

Human Values for the 21st Century[1]

V.N. Viswanathan

Introduction

The history of human development has been intercepted by various kinds of morality in order to upkeep a society in order. Moral development and ethics in life are found to be the most essential ingredients for peaceful co-existence. What constitute a ethical way of life, we learn by our own experiences and by learning from religious scripts. All religions of the world came into practice to inculcate moral quality in the minds of the people. Beside religion, there are speeches and historical incidents which captured the attention of the world people towards an ethical way of life. The great of work of Saintly poet Thiruvalluvar is full of ethics and morality on different aspects of life. For King, Thiruvalluvar advised as follows:

"The able king gets, stores and guards And spends them for people's safeguards.".

This is considered to be the ethics of good governance.

The objectives of Silappathikaram (one among five great epics of Tamil Literatures) were threefold as made abundantly clear by Elango Adigal, the author in the Pathikam given below:

(1) to emphasize that those in power will be punished if they deviate from righteous principles,

(2) to hail the nobility of chastity in women and

(3) the inevitability of the effects of wrong doings in the previous birth.

The great national epics such as the Ramayana and Mahabratha are a sources of moral and ethical teaching for various stages of life. Every moral preaching and practices are coincided with need of the time and space. The 21st century promises to be a time of scientific and technological growth at a level never before experienced in human history. This growth will either trigger chaos, disruption, war, starvation and disease or will introduce a period of humanistic cooperation, development, progress, and peace. What emerges will depend upon which values are embraced, taught, encouraged, and legislated. It is believed that future moral society much depends upon the kind of moral education that being imparted for the present generations. It is very disrupting to note that market forces develop its own variety of ethics and morality more appropriate for business than for family and society. Of universal value and morality the 20th century has already proclaimed human rights as a cherished ideal that all must develop in their mind and heart. Through politics the future world must conduct good governance through respecting human rights of all people. Democracy, human rights, secularism and freedom are the watch word for the new generation. National boundaries and artificial separation will have no meaning and importance in the international politics if these moral qualities are developed among young minds. Though it look very much ideal, its reality lies in imparting moral and ethical teaching for next generation.

The value choices, which must be deliberately chosen and not left to chance, must be secular, global, and family oriented. The accepted values must be embraced, taught, encouraged, and supported internationally, nationally, locally, and personally. What is proposed here represents some of the value choices, the ethical building blocks, that will enable a world of peace and harmony to come into existence—a world in which human diversity is respected and tolerated and, at the same time, a world in which each individual will be enabled and encouraged to maximize his or her potential, without discrimination and in an atmosphere of freedom. What is required to bring about this idealized world is a democratic, pluralistic society which recognizes the human rights of each individual and in which no man or woman or class of men or women shall be demeaned and treated as mere slaves existing only to fulfill the desires of those who would be their masters; a world in which no man or woman or class of men or women shall be used as tools for the lusts of others, or for the ambitions of others, or for the greed of others, a world in which the life of every man and woman and child shall be recognized and esteemed as a unique and ultimate statement of the evolutionary process and therefore of inestimable value. To achieve and make real, this concept of a world of peace for the 21st century, the following humanistic values provide the basic essentials.

1. Humanistic values for the 21st century must be secular, democratic, and pluralistic

The values must be of the people, for the people, and by the people. They must embrace common moral decencies such as altruism, integrity, freedom, justice, honesty, truthfulness, responsibility, compassion, and must reflect the normative standards human beings discover and develop through living together. Value development must draw upon reason, science, the arts, and must express concern for justice and fairness and concern for the physical and mental well-being of every human being in an effort to maximize individual freedom without limiting the freedom of others.

Humanistic values espouse cooperation and peaceful living and reject the use of violence to settle problems whether the problems be international, national, local, or familial. Humanistic values recognize cultural or religious diversity and individual creativity while rejecting the validity of declarations made by any group alleging spiritual superiority or political autonomy over others. Humanistic values incorporate many of the moral and ethical values espoused by the world's religions, but seek to move beyond particularistic religious belief systems (which often foster separatism) and beyond political agendas (which tend to be local or too narrow) to focus on the full humanity of the person or persons. Obviously, some humanistic values will receive support from religious and political organizations; others will not. For example, the great religions have preached universal brotherhood but, unfortunately, intolerance of other faiths and a spirit of divisiveness have made the implementation of the brotherhood ideal impossible. Narrow, parochial doctrines of salvation have barred those outside of the faith system from fellowship with those within. Humanistic values for the 21st century cannot be so contained and must not be limited by theologies or by deontological ethics that have, over the centuries, encouraged divisiveness and produced violence.

Nor can nationalistic or ethnic teachings and pronouncements that encourage divisiveness and produce violence be permitted to thwart the promulgation of humanistic values. It is clear that the development and emergence of nation-states have freed citizens from foreign domination and have encouraged ethnic and national self-determination. There is no reason why national governments should not play constructive roles in achieving a peaceful world by maintaining systems of law and order that encourage cultural growth and economic prosperity conducive to achieving conditions of internal harmony and enrichment of the lives of those living within their jurisdiction. Unfortunately, some nations-states have violated the rights of their citizens and have engaged in violence to achieve goals. Economic rivalries between nation-states have led to bloodshed and wars. Such battles will not cease until humanistic values are recognized and expressed in world law that is accepted and respected by all countries and supported and enforced on a transnational level

2. Humanistic values for the 21st century must be global

As the first generation in human history to have viewed our planet from outer space, we have been made conscious of the uniqueness of this fragment of cosmic matter which we call "earth" that circles a rather small star (our sun) in an immense universe. So far as we know at this moment, we humans are the only intelligent, rational beings existing anywhere in the cosmos. Statistical estimates suggest that elsewhere planets circling stars may have produced other intelligent life forms, but at this moment we know nothing of these other life forms, despite the claims of those who say they have encountered extra-terrestrial beings. To the best of our knowledge, we are utterly alone in the universe and we are bound together by our habitation on this planet. Our value system must extend beyond national, ethnic, religious, territorial, and racial boundaries. Only a global ethic, a global humanistic value system that embraces the entire world will suffice for the 21st century.

There have been some efforts at regional economic and political cooperation. Pacts and treaties between nations governed by rules of civilized behavior are in existence. But these do not go far enough and balance-of-power politics, economic exploitation, racial strife, and religious bigotry have fostered feelings of hatred and produced violence. The time is at hand for a new vision that will enable the development of political, economic, social, and cultural institutions that will foster peaceful coexistence and cooperation on a worldwide basis. This vision can only become reality through the recognition of a global ethic that acknowledges both responsibilities and duties to the world community.

Because humanistic values are pluralistic, a spirit of tolerance is primary. However, tolerance does not signify the ignoring of patterns of behavior that violate or infringe upon the rights and freedoms of others. Tolerance marks the recognition of the wide variety of human expression and patterns of living; it does not mean closing the eyes to injustice, cruelty, or the dehumanization of persons.

3. Humanistic values for the 21st century must be based on a familial ethic

Anthropological and mitochondrial DNA researches have made clear our evolutionary heritage. As one of the many life forms that have evolved over the millennia, human beings have developed from very simple origins to become the most complex life pattern among all living creatures.

Our best research informs us that human life originated in Africa and from Africa moved to other continents to become the multicultural people we are today. We are all brothers and sisters—children of the same parents. Differences in skin coloration, hair, eye form, and so forth represent the kinds of variations one finds in any family where no two offspring are exactly the same or develop in exactly the same way. Nevertheless, so close are we to one another that blood from one race can be transfused to save the life of someone of a different race. Our body structures, despite minor discrepancies, are the same. Body parts such as heart, lungs, kidneys, liver, and so forth can be transposed between humans without regard to race, nationality, ethnic origins, or other sub-categories of the human family. Therefore, as members of a single family, we must embrace humanistic family values that supersede boundaries, of nation, race, religion, ethnic origin, sexual differences, sexual preferences, and so forth. We must move beyond the outmoded nationalism and separatism that have been taught for centuries and that only serve to breed tension in the human family. The implication that, by belonging to one nation or race or group of people or by embracing a faith system with its particular beliefs, rules, and regulations, somehow separates an individual from or elevates a person above others cannot provide a basis for global familial values. Such membership provides identity solely on the basis of a limited group association which negates responsibility and caring for those outside of the group. Separatism based on ethnicity, nationalism, and religion has bred disaster. The humanistic family ethic, while tolerating and understanding differences in customs, beliefs, and social agendas, embraces an inclusiveness that seeks to rise above religious and political animosities and tensions to emphasize what unites human beings rather than that which separates them. Wherever and whenever ancient moral and separative principles are taught they must be recognized and incorporated as subsections of the broader humanistic family values.

A 21st century humanistic ethic requires that the scientific basis for the oneness of the human family be accepted and taught internationally, nationally, and locally in classrooms, in families, in religious and secular institutions. Moreover, the factual basis for this teaching must supersede all creationist mythologies of human origins generated by earlier non-scientific generations.

At the core of this familial ethic is support for the universal declarations of human rights that embrace all human beings.

4. Humanistic global familial values for the 21st century must embrace a survival ethic

To preserve and honor and reverence the small blue planet "earth" which is our home, all humans must recognize and support an ecological ethic that evolves out of a global family concept. Our view of the earth from space plus research into the interrelationship of ecological factors makes clear that our planet is an independent globe with a single life-support system. There is not one life-support system for Asia and another for the Americas and still another for Africa or Europe—all planet earth life-support systems are the same. There are no national boundaries to our ecosphere. We are one and the earth is our home.

Only fools trash their own homes. Nevertheless, some members of our human family suffer from short-term vision. Their lust for wealth and power expresses little or no concern for human well-being. These persons, and the corporations they represent, are indifferent to what the rape, desecration, and despoiling of forests, land, and waters and the destruction of non-human life forms can mean to the health and security of present and future generations. They trash our home, the earth. In addition, the naive and ill-informed also despoil our environment. Acting on the basis of non-scientific superstitions, ignorant people kill endangered animals for bones, horns, tusks, penises, and other body parts that are supposed to have magical power to enhance sexuality, cure disease, or prolong life. No matter what excuses are given for ecological indifference, international, national, and local education, laws, and counter-controls must be developed as part of a conservation ethic. Individuals or groups of individual must not be permitted to trash our home, the earth. Those who do must be brought to account before courts of law and punished so that their actions become so unprofitable that they will be abandoned.

We are now at a point in history where the establishment of an international environmental monitoring agency is urgently needed. Appropriate standards for the disposal of industrial waste and for the control of toxic emissions must be developed not only to protect the earth's precious resources, but also to preserve a healthy environment for future generations.

5. Humanistic global survival values for the 21st century require that we treat one another as members of a family, which means that we must look out for and care about one another's welfare.

To honour and protect the lives of family members requires commitment to producing a world free from violence, conflict, and power struggles. Statements and pronouncements about the importance and value of human life are not enough. In the words of the ancient Romans, we require: facta non verba: deeds not words-pronouncements must be supported by action.

On an international basis, war and all forms of violent territorial battles and power struggles must be finally and completely outlawed. War has been recognized by military leaders, scientists,philosophers, religious leaders and others as an obsolete way of settling problems. Pacts and treaties promising peace must be supported with the potential for active intervention when agreements are violated and war is threatened. The employment of counter-controls makes the use of violence unprofitable and unsuccessful. In this respect, the United Nations has sometimes been effective but on the other hand has failed cver and over again.

The experiences of World War II taught us the folly to trying to appease or negotiate with power-hungry sociopaths. In 1938, Neville Chamberlain, after seeking to appease Adolph Hitler at the Munich Conference, devised the slogan "Peace in Our Time." The emptiness of Hitler's commitment to peace soon became apparent. There were no counter-controls in place and World War II erupted. The conflict in Bosnia, which could have been contained at its start, was permitted to escalate because the counter controls that were in hand were not immediately employed. NATO and the United Nations failed to live up to their promise of deterring genocide. Time and again after NATO threatened but failed to deliver, the Serbs ignored the threats and continued to slaughter. We know that only when effective counter-controls are put into action immediately that conflict will be contained thereby compelling negotiations. This fact was made clear after the Persian Gulf conflict. When Saddam Hussein's military efforts and radar were unable to locate and repel the American F-117A Stealth Fighters, his efforts to annex Kuwait failed. Later, in October 1994, he once again threatened to move on Kuwait. The deployment of both Stealth Fighters and Stealth Bombers persuaded him to change his plans. Sociopathic, power-hungry people usually prove to be moral cowards and social failures who fear exposure. Counter-controls compel them to observe human rights and conform to international peace efforts.

As a further counter-control, war criminals—those who violate human rights and engage in international conflict—must be brought to trial before the United Nations War Crimes Tribunal and held responsible for their crimes against humanity. When those who employ violence and terrorism discover that the pay-off for their actions will be a demeaning trial in a criminal court, this counter-control serves as a deterrent. Presently, the War Crimes Tribunal is being rendered impotent because of political wrangling.

Counter-controls must be employed nationally-only then will the disruptive and peace threatening efforts of sociopathic terrorists and paramilitary groups be contained. The presence of such controls in America became apparent following the New York Trade Center bombing and the Oklahoma bombing. Those responsible for the violence were quickly apprehended. The perpetrators were recognized, not as heroes but as villains. Counter-controls are also in effect in Japan as revealed in the actions following the subway bombings by members of the Aum Supreme Truth sect. Being caught, tried, and punished makes terrorism unprofitable. Apart from the naive who become the instruments of terrorist groups and who envision themselves as heroes who die for a cause, most terrorists do not want to die. They want to live and bask in the glory of their destructiveness. Counter-controls that pre-doom them to failure through exposure and containment are the most effective barriers to the growth and success of anti-social groups. Therefore each nation must establish counter-control units that cooperate with counter-control groups in other nations to protect citizens from terrorists.

On a familial and personal level it becomes incumbent upon every citizen of planet earth to embrace, teach, and practice values that reject violence as a way of solving human problems. Family members must protect one another, and protection can only develop out of a caring response. When familial disputes arise, violence can never be accepted as a way to resolve the problems. We must begin within the individual family units to reeducate the human family and to redirect aggressive instincts. Child abuse, child abandonment, spouse abuse, and elder abuse are on the rise worldwide. Whether the abuse be verbal, physical, psychological, neglect, or abandonment, those responsible must be held accountable. Through exposure, those who prey upon others or who abuse others lose the security of anonymity and become symbols of human depravity, thereby discouraging others from engaging in such behavior. Places of refuge, where the abused can obtain counseling, shelter, food, and support, must be established and maintained until the people of the world become educated to non-violent ways of settling problems.

6. Humanistic global family values must express concern for the health and well-being of all members of the human family

The first steps have been taken with the introduction of national health insurance programs in all first world countries except the United States and South Africa. Health protection must be extended worldwide. Epidemics can no longer be viewed as local problems but must be seen as menacing all members of the human family. Wars, crop failure, drought, earthquake and storm damage that affect the health and lives of members of the world family in one part of the globe affect us all and call for compassionate and supportive response from family members worldwide. We are one family and in the words of the 17th century British poet, John Donne, we need to remember that:

No man is an Island, intire of itselfe; every man is a peece of the Continent, a part of the maine; if a Clod bee washed away by the sea, Europe is the lesse, as well as if a Promontorie were, as well as if a Mannor of thy friends or of thine own were, any man's death diminishes me, because I am involved in Mankinde: And therefore never send to know for whom the bell tolls, it tolls for thee. (Devotions, XVII)

The first steps have been taken. For example, South Korea set aside past rivalries and memories of war to reach out to family members of North Korea with shipments of food. United Nations peace-keeping forces regularly respond to cries for food and medicine in ravaged countries. Feelings of concern for the well-being of our human family members prompt many of us to respond personally to human need. Such patterns of compassionate family outreach must be part of the value system for the 21st century.

What is equally important are the efforts to close the gaps in international family relationships occasioned by inhumane behavior in the past. For example, Former President Jacque Chirac has publicly acknowledged and apologized for the actions of the Vichy government which, with considerable citizen support, turned Jews over to Germany for deportation to the death camps during World War II. Some 800 Germans went to Holland to apologize to the Dutch for the Nazi invasions. Pope John Paul II apologized for the Roman Catholic Church's complicity in the slave trade and the exploitation of native people throughout the Americas. The Evangelical Lutheran Church in America has repudiated the 1543 anti-Semitic ravings of their founder Martin Luther and acknowledged his contribution to the slaughter of Jews in Nazi Germany. In June, 1995, the Southern Baptist Convention, which came into being during a North-South split over slavery, issued a repudiation of "historic acts of evil" and an apology "to all African-Americans for condoning and/or perpetuating individual and systematic racism in our lifetime." Japanese Prime Minister, Tomichi Murayama, has issued two apologies: the first was to women forced into prostitution to serve Japan's armed forces before and during World War II, and the second was for his nation's deeds during World War II. These acknowledgments and apologies are important recognitions of past inhumane behavior, but something more is needed. What is needed is an accompanying commitment to the present and the future that never again will the nation or the faith system become involved in any behavior or activities or attitudes that violate the civil rights or the human rights of other persons or peoples. Apologies for the past are important polite gestures; commitment to compassionate behavior in the present and in the future is essential.

7. Humanistic global family values demand familial responsibility as we face the problem of population control

We have learned from the past and the present what tragedies can develop when population exceeds/the ability of a nation to provide food, housing, health care, nurturing, and education for all of its members.

It has been estimated that more than 35,000 children die needlessly every day from starvation, malnutrition, and diseases that could easily be controlled. These children are born into families unable to provide the food, clothing, shelter, health needs, comfort, and help required for a meaningful life. Because of where and when they are born, they are the unwanted. Should they mature into adolescence or adulthood, their futures promise to be like those of their parents—characterized by poverty, lack of food, medicines, clothing, shelter, and the necessities for a dignified and purposeful life. We no longer need to breed like animals to assure our survival; our concern must be with quality of life. It is immoral to breed children whose existence will be characterized by want, suffering, and lack of hope.

As we look to future population growth, we know that we are at a point in human history when limits must be placed on the size and growth of our human family. The necessity for these limits must be taught, accepted and practiced internationally, nationally, locally, and individually. To bring children into the human family without the ability or means or intent to support their health, growth, and development is a desecration of family values. Every child should be a wanted child. Nor can there be discrimination on the basis of sex. A female child must be as welcome and acceptable as a male child. Presently, where efforts at population control are legislated, as in the Republic of China, there is good evidence that infant girls are abandoned, or exposed and permitted to die, or are killed, because a male child is preferred. Ancient values based on sex are no longer acceptable. Males and females are of equal worth and cultural or religious patterns of discrimination must be made obsolete through education and through counter-controls.

Even as we emphasize equality of the sexes it is important to realize that, despite the implications in the Universal

Declaration of Human Rights , all human life is not of equal value. The declaration states that

All human beings are born free and equal in dignity and rights. They are endowed with reason and conscience and should act towards one another in a spirit of brotherhood.

This statement is acceptable in a general sense, but it is not accurate. All human beings are not endowed with reason and conscience. Anacephalic infants are born with only functioning lower brain stems that enable them to breathe and their hearts to beat but they lack all cognitive functions and are unable to live beyond a few days. Anacephalic newborns cannot be considered "endowed with reason and conscience," nor should such an infant be considered to be of equal worth to children not so incapacitated. Similarly, a person who has entered a persistent vegetative state has lost the ability to reason and is without conscience. The PVS person cannot be accorded rights equal to those who have the ability to reason and evaluate consequences. In both cases—that of the anacephalic infant and that of the person in a persistent vegetative state—these individuals will never function fully or cognitively as human beings and will forever be completely dependent on others to make life and death decisions. Nevertheless, they are still members of the human family and must be recognized as such. In the language of the Universal Declaration of Human Rights they are to be treated with dignity and accorded whatever rights are in keeping with their needs and dependency situation. Such "acting toward" might not include efforts to prolong their existence. With permission from next-of-kin, guardians, attorneys for health-care, or if the PVS patient has signed an advanced directive, "acting toward" might involve the termination of these lives with a lethal injection and, under proper safeguards and with proper permissions, include the utilization of body parts for the saving of lives of others. By such action, persons who do not have or who have lost the power of reason and conscience can be enabled to make valuable contributions to the welfare of the human family. In all cases and situations, the lives of family members must be honored and protected against abuse.

8. Humanistic values must be taught

It is one thing to propose values, but how are they to become known and adopted? One way is through education. The word "education" comes from the Latin root educare which means "to lead out." As an educator, it is my task to "lead out" (educo: I lead out). "Leading out" involves the dismantling of barriers which impede humanistic ethical growth, while bringing others to a place where new ethical horizons can be seen, recognized, appreciated and approached. Education calls for belief in what is to be shared, commitment to the ideals embraced by humanistic values, and hope for the future. So many are disillusioned and without any belief in the possibility for change. The educational program, which can be instituted as part of curricula in classes ranging from kindergarten to university and also through the public media should include the following.

- The right to personal security and protection.
- The right to personal liberty which includes
- freedom from involuntary servitude or slavery,
- freedom from harassment,
- freedom of thought and conscience,
- freedom of speech and expression,
- moral freedom to express one's values and pursue one's lifestyle so long as it does not harm others or prevent others from exercising their rights.
- the right to privacy which calls for respect for the rights of others concerning
- confidentiality,
- control of one's own body,
- sexual preference and orientation,
- life-stance,
- reproductive freedom within the boundaries

- health care based on informed consent,
- the desire to die with dignity.
- the right to intellectual and cultural freedom which requires a spirit of toleration and understanding with regard to
- the freedom to inquire and engage in research,
- the right to adequate education,
- the right to cultural enrichment,
- the right to express and publish one's views.
- the right to adequate health care.
- freedom from want which means that society must guarantee
- the right and opportunity to work,
- the satisfaction of basic needs when individuals are unable to provide for themselves,
- care for the elderly,
- care for the handicapped,
- the right to adequate leisure and relaxation.
- Economic freedom including
- the right to own property,
- the right to organize,
- protection from fraud.
- Moral equality, which entails equal opportunity and equal access.
- Equal protection under the law which is vital to a free, democratic society, and include
- the right to a fair trial,
- the right to protection from arbitrary arrest or unusual punishment,
- the right to humane treatment.
- The right to democratic participation in government which include
- the right to vote,
- the right of assembly and association.
- the right to hold religious beliefs or not hold religious beliefs.
- The rights of marriage and the family which include
- the right to marry or cohabit,
- the right to divorce,
- family planning,

- the right to bear and the responsibility to raise wanted children,
- child care,
- the right of children and each family member to be protected from abuse and physical or cultural deprivation.

9. Humanistic global family values must be concerned with providing each member of the human family with the means to become involved in meaningful work, employment or efforts designed to promote the well-being of the entire human family.

A meaning-filled life is more than mere existence; it involves purpose, direction, and a sense of belonging. Humanistic family values embrace individual rights to autonomy, dignity, free choice, liberty, fraternity, the pursuit of happiness, and security. Our human family has devised a multitude of different ways to accomplish these goals through law, education, role modeling, as well as through words, acts, and symbols of encouragement and support. Each positive effort must be appreciated and inherent differences tolerated. To establish such values and the ethical standards that protect all human beings for the 21st century we must be prepared to learn from the past, evaluate the present, and project the highest and best that we know into our aspirations for the future. We must examine our values on the basis of international, national, and personal commitments.

What we do now is important. We must, each one of us, pledge ourselves to action in helping to move humankind towards a way of living where the humanistic family ethic overlays the nationalistic, linguistic, religious, and ethnic differences that separate us. We work toward the time when the world will be at peace and human energy will be focused on the needs and well-being of all members of a single family, a time when we will enjoy and celebrate our unique differences while exalting the importance of our human similarities, a time when we will acknowledge the basic human needs that unite us including our mutual concerns for the futures of our children, our grandchildren and our great-grandchildren who constitute the future.

For the world of the 21st century, humanistic values must project the vision of a peaceful world in which no man, woman or child, or class of men, women, or children shall live as servants or slaves existing simply to fulfill the whims and wishes and desires of others, a world in which no man or woman or child shall be used as a tool to satisfy the lusts or greed or ambitions of others, a world in which every human life, the life of every man, woman, and child shall be a wanted, welcomed, and esteemed member of the one human family.

References

Chakraborti, Mohit. *Value Education: Changing Perspectives*. New Delhi: Kanishka Publishers, 1997.

Etzioni, Amitai. *The Monochrome Society*. Princeton, NJ: Princeton University Press, 2001.

Bok, Sissela. *Common Values*. Columbia: University of Missouri Press, 1995.

Kung, Hans, and Karl-Josef Kuschel. *A Global Ethic: The Declaration of the Parliament of the World's Religions*. New York: Continuum, 1993.

Human Values and Beliefs: A Cross-Cultural Sourcebook: Political, Religious, Sexual, and Economic Norms in 43 Societies: Findingsfrom the 1990-1993 World Values Survey. Edited by Ronald Inglehart, Miguel Basanez, and Alejandro Morena. Ann Arbor: University of Michigan Press, 1998

Morrison, Toni. "How Can Values Be Taught in the *University?"<Michigan Quarterly Review,* 40,2 (Spring 2001), 273-278.

Snauwaert, Dale T. *Democracy, Education, and Governance: A Developmental Conception*. Albany: State University of New York Press, 1993.

Isaac, Katherine. *Ralph Nader Presents. Civics for Democracy: A Journey for Teachers and Students*. Project of the Center for Study of Responsive Law and Essential Information. Washington, DC: Essential Books, 1992.

The Journal of Moral Education (UK) See vol. 25, 1 (March 1996): Moral Education from the 20th into the 21st century

Khanna, D.P., *Reforming Human Rights* (New Delhi: Manas Publications, 2000

Kashyap, Subhas Basic constitutional values. Delhi: Ananta. 1994.

Satchidananda, M.K. Ethics, education, Indian unity and culture. Delhi: Ajanta. Xii, 95p. 1991.

2

Value Inculcation for School Students

Dr. R. Baskarasethupathi

Introduction

Value Education in school education is inevitable. School education includes value education as its main component. Making a good society for the Nation is being done in schools. Schools are miniature society and pupil in schools will play various important roles in future society. Value inculcation for school children is essencial and neglection of that process leads to serve problems in society. All Human Rights violation of this century is due to lack of values among public including educated people. In that point of view this article discuss various aspects of value inculcation for school students.

Value Education

India has greater heritage and pride in emphasizing the value education over a long period of time. Religions such as Hinduism, Budhism, Judasim, Islam, Christianity have been major source of value education. Various literates in major languages propagates value education in depth. Vedas, Idhikasas, Puranas provides major literates for value education.

Moral literature enshrined lively in Tamil language. Thirukural in Tamil language one of the greatest source preaching value education in the world which explains value education to greater, deeper, wider extent.

Values

Values are those basic characteristics of human society which set norms for the elements of social control over the individual and modification of his behavior and projected ideal for the members of the society to the shape their life. Value development through school education is not for particular period but throughout the life. Value inculcation in school children will bring discipline and control.

Value Inculcation in school students will mould them with following characteristics:

Group orientation, extensive information sharing and seeking, sense of belongingness, Inter personal relations, Diligence (hard work), perfectionalism, curiosity, Time management, Initiate, Peritistence, concerns for high quality, Decisiveness, commitment to work, efficiency orientation, calculated risk taking, dependability, sense if human, innovation.Value education is important for four fold self development programme. That is physical, intellextual emotional and spiritual self development. The goal of value education in broader sense is to prepare good human beings so that their immense potential can be utilized for the causes of peace social chosen and environmentally sustain development as well as humanity at large.

Swami Vivekananda said that True Education is we want an education which builds character increases strength of mind expands the intellect which equips a person to stand on his own feet.

Mahatma Gandhi also said that the purpose of education is the manifestation of the best existing already in the body mind and sprit of the child.

A comprehensive programe of value inculcation must start at the very earliest stage of school education as a regular part of school's daily routine. The entire educational progress has to be such that the boys and girls of this country are able to know good love good and do good and grow into manually tolerant citizens.

National curriculam framwork for school education also includes and emphasis on value education. Every teacher has to be a teacher of values. Every activity unit interaction must be examined form the view point of value identification inculcation and reinforcement so as to evolve an appropriate strategy for judicious implementation.

Each and every teacher should not hold Co-curricular activities such as NSS, NCC, Yoga, JRC etc., but to lead such activities. Emphasis on value inculcation through various co-curricular activities in around the school such as morning assembly stories and teachings of great prophets, saints major world religious community programmes such as NSS, NCC, JRC, Scouts and Guides etc.

Curriculum in schools has to develop the key qualities like regularity and punctuality, cleanliness, self control, industriousness, sense of duty, desire to serve, responsibility, enterprise, creativity, sensitivity to greater fraternity democratic attitude, and sense of obligation to environmental protection.

Behavioral Characteristics inculcated as value education for students in Institutions:

I. Tender loving relationship

- The Principal personally interacts with students and by and large knows them.
- The Principal is easily approachable and amiable.
- Teachers talk to students softy and with a tone of concern.
- Teachers patiently listen to the students views and problems.

- Students show respect and love for their teachers while talking to them.
- Student freely interact with teachers
- Students help each other in times of problem and convey their problems or difficulties (educational/emotional/ physical) to the teachers.
- The parents are free to visit to the school and interact with principal and teachers.
- Parents Teachers Association (PTA) is constituted in school and regular meetings are organized.
- Programmes are co-curricular activities organised in school have place for parents participation.
- No humiliation students, colleagues and other staff members.
- Guidance and advice is given instead if punishment
- Gender equality is practiced.
- No discrimination on the basis of academic achievement.
- Showing solidarity in times of crisis/emergency in anybody's family
- Mutual respect.
- Respectable words used during communication with each other.
- Everybody respectfully greeting each other in the morning.

II. Punctuality

- Punctuality is maintained in coming to school and other activities.

III. Team work / cooperation

- Students work in team
- Group projects are undertaken.

IV. Social commitment

- The school participates in community programmes like plantation campaign health/ vaccination days, cleaning drive.

- Visits to places like hospitals care centre are organised.
- Takes projects on social problems / issues.
- Quality is maintained in service and production
- Students must understand and committed individually.
- Adulteration in food is against humanity.

V. Sense of belongingness / oneness

- Students do not scribble of rooms and toilets.
- Students do not destroy school property.
- The lights fans and tapes are put off when not in use.
- Encouraging the use of expressions like we and ours in place of I , YOU and Mine Yours.
- Five Universal Values (truth, righteous conduct, peace love and non-violence) are displayed at proper places
- National Anthem, National song and National Symbols are displayed in places of prominence in the school.
- Students handle equipment raw material etc., carefully and gently, (especially deleting with live specimen).

VI. Consciousness about Fundamental Duties and Rights.

- Fundamental Duties and Rights of Indian citizens are displayed neatly and in an attractive manner.
- Teachers non-teaching staff and students are aware of their duties and obligations towards different sections of people or society.

VII. Concern for dignity of others

- Teachers are not reprimanded (rightly or wrongly) in front of others as far as possible.
- Weaknesses of any students are not commented by way of socio-economic status academic achievement non-performance weak- physical / personality trains.
- Everybody talks in a civil and polite manner with each other in school.
- Each others views are respected.
- Giving equal opportunity to all irrespective of good students or showing sub-standard performance in their work.

VIII. Freedom of expressions

- Students are encouraged to ask questions on topics taught in class.
- Teachers readily listen to and help the child understand portions which he / she has not understand
- Teachers and students are not punished for sighting the right reasons for any failure or inability to confirm to rules.
- As far as possible every child is possible encouraged to participate in school programmes according to his / her aptitude and interest.

IX. Abiding by the rules work ethics

- Basic discipline is followed by everyone in the school.
- Basic rules and regulations formulated are followed by all (teachers, students, staff and parents).
- Desirable behavior or extraordinary gestures exhibited by anyone is appreciated recognized and shared with all.
- Abiding Work Ethics / Rules.
- The library has literature related to different religious and culture.
- Chart, Posters, pictures, symbolizing different culture and religious are displayed.
- Visits to historical places or worship of various religions are organized from time to time.
- Cultural activities promoting communal harmony and social cohesion are organized regularly.
- Prayer meditation, Yoga, service (seva) – oriented activities are organised regularly.
- Separate time for reading of value-based literature is provided and students are encouraged to read.
- Students and staff practicing self-development (prayer, meditation, Yoga, reading, reading inspiring. Literature) at home also.
- Farewell ceremony is organised in a decent manner.

- Treating people form different socio-economic background equally and respectfully.
- School assembly is attended by everyone (students, and all the employees)

Modern concepts relating to value educations

Value education is consider as traditional and cultural in nature But it has been developed throught the period of modern world that is in twenty first century also pays greater attention in value education. Even western democracies full liberty oriented countries gives importance to value education. Human resource Development is the modern discipline which includes value education as one of the important philosophy. HRD of the Nation depends the quality of children in the schools. Modern youths creating lot of problems in present day society because of lacking values.

Conclusion

Now a days the most neglected area in schools is value inculcation process It is because of social change of this decade. The teachers quality degraded in this century was the main problem. The teachers quality and altitude of teachers plays vital role in less attention paid for value inculcation. Impact of TV media, and internet communication technology influenced school children and leads to breaking of traditional values. The present need is great effort should be taken to inculcation values for school children It is important to inculcate value education during childhood to teen age period. It is better to teach value education such as obeying Govt. rules as good citizen than to teach algebra or Einstein theory at tender age.

For example obeying traffic rules will save lives and it is vital to everybody in the society. A student not obeying such important laws is useless even those student scores 100 per cent marks.

Value inculcation leads to healthy mind in students. Without value inculcation a brilliant student becoming a doctor or engineer or government official or politician is dangerous to society.

Finally the first and foremost value education for school students must be writing all type of examination honestly .Students must understand scoring less marks is not sin but scoring more marks by malpractice is sin. The teachers must ensure every students are writing examination including class slip test honestly. And that is the best value education for students.

3

Impact of Religion on Social Integration From an Empirical Civil Rights Perspective

Johannes A. (Hans) van der Ven and Francis-Vincent Anthony

This study is meant to shed light on the extent to which religion furthers the social integration in secular society, from a civil rights perspective, of people from different traditions and cultures. It seeks to advance a theory of religion's role in the process of social integration in a society whose very core is the separation of religion and state, religious freedom and other civil rights. Before we proceed we spell out some premises.

Firstly, we accept the existence of communities belonging to diverse religious traditions as given. In other words, religious pluralism is considered a datum, not merely a legitimate principle – hence in our view de facto rather than de jure. This is because of the conflictive nature of present-day religious pluralism, which we shall discuss in due course. De facto pluralism is the starting point, de jure pluralism merely a possible outcome. Otherwise one ends up in a circular argument, taking a possible, desirable result as a premise.[1]

Secondly, taking pluralism as a fact, we focus on the integrative role of religion in secular society. Here we distinguish between three aspects of integration: contact between religious and secular communities, reciprocal influencing between them, and the resulting transformation. The important features of contact are first-hand experience and continuity. The essential characteristics of reciprocal influence are respect, freedom and absence of dominance. The hallmarks of transformation are that it is a dynamic process of change with a relatively stable outcome regarding social, cultural and religious beliefs and practices.[2]

Thirdly, we distinguish between integration and dialogue, especially multireligious and interreligious dialogue. The question is whether multireligious dialogue relates to integration at all, even to the first aspect of contact, because such dialogue mostly entails discussions by representatives of different religions, in which they express their own ideas as well as those of other religions, always in their own terms, without any exchange of perspectives. Interreligious dialogue may actually include exchange of perspectives, which is essential for any real contact, but it does not intrinsically lead to the other two aspects of integration, namely reciprocal influence and transformation.[3]

Fourthly, the aspects of integration mentioned above may occur at three different levels: the level of relations between people from various grassroots religious and secular communities; that of relations between local, national and international religious leaders; and lastly, that of relations between theological participants and representatives of other academic disciplines at scientific conferences. Although contact, reciprocal influence and transformation may take place at all three levels, in the present study we confine ourselves to relations between ordinary people at grassroots level.

Finally we wish to comment on the civil rights perspective from which we approach the question of religion's impact on the process of social integration. International documents on civil rights play a major role, but in this study we refer to them only indirectly. We are not so much concerned with the texts of these documents as with the legal cultures underlying their interpretation and practical application. And within these cultures we are less concerned with the views of legal professionals than with those of ordinary people, for in the long run, certainly in a deliberative democracy, it is ordinary people's convictions that determine the way in which human rights-related legislation and jurisprudence will evolve. Our interest centres on a particular group: youths, who will be the agents and leaders, on whatever level, of society in the near future. In other words, our concern is with the lived legal culture among young people related to lived religions in secular society. Against this background we conducted an empirical study among a group of higher secondary school students in a country known for its lively religious pluralism, where the state constitutionally proclaims itself as fully secular, namely India.[4]

As mentioned already, in this study we explore the following problem: to what extent does religion play a role in the process of social integration in secular society? We concretise the problem in two empirical research questions: to what extent do the higher secondary Indian students we investigated support a lived legal culture of civil rights (part one), and what effects do their religious beliefs and practices have on such a civil rights culture, while controlling for some relevant population characteristics (part two)?

1 Attitudes towards civil rights

The first part of this article focuses on the extent to which the students we investigated contribute to a lived legal culture of civil rights. To answer the question we successively deal with the concept of integration (1.1), strategies of integration (1.2), and the relation between recognition and integration (1.3). We then empirically investigate the attitudes towards civil rights of our research population of higher secondary school students (1.4), and conclude with a discussion of our findings (1.5).

1.1 Integration

Interreligious literature does not really offer a perspective that transcends the process of interreligious dialogue as dialogue, which is seen as an end in itself. The same applies to the religious traditions to which the dialogue partners belong: they tend to restrict the scope of dialogue to the dialogue itself. To overcome this short-sightedness we identify a possible further goal: that of integration.

Interreligious dialogue: an end in itself?

We are not suggesting that interreligious dialogue as an end in itself is worthless. Interreligious dialogue, like all dialogue, is intrinsically good and worthwhile, and need not necessarily be conducted for the sake of anything other than itself. To refresh the reader's memory, in a Platonic view dialogue is epistemological: a way of finding truth, exploring it, disclosing it as a-letheia, that is opening up what was hidden before – a truth that is polysemous yet, for all that, unitary.[5] Husserl's phenomenological conception rests on an ego-logical approach to dialogue: the self precedes dialogue but finds its identity in encounter with the other.[6] Buber sees dialogue as the religious in-between of dialogue partners, I and Thou, which illuminates the ground and mystical depths of the encounter – God.[7] In Levinas' view the other qua other, in her alterity, speaks, reveals her face, and appeals to me not to overpower her but the other way round: to let myself be overpowered by her. Her face reveals the transcendence of infinity and this epiphany calls on me to respond according to Abraham's model: "Here I am" – a response I can only make if I accept the instruction of the other as a teacher of justice and peace.[8]

One could say that inasmuch as interreligious dialogue corresponds to all these aspects – the epistemological truth aspect (Plato), the phenomenological I-aspect (Husserl), the mystical I/Thou-aspect (Buber) and the ethical Thou-aspect (Levinas) – it presages and anticipates peace between religions. Here one thinks of shalom with its Judaic roots, Jesus' blessing extended to peacemakers in the sermon on the mount, Islam's surrender to Allah that includes peace among human beings, Buddhism's compassion for all living beings, and the non-violence of Hinduism.

Interreligious dialogue, interaction and integration

To all these approaches another important dimension needs to be added. The emphasis on the interpersonal nature of dialogue might obscure the reality of society, in which the various religions are situated and which interreligious dialogue cannot and should not disregard or neglect. The empirical facts are that in many present-day societies – Eastern and Western, Northern and Southern – governments, parliaments and institutions, not to mention innumerable citizens, are grappling with the question of a plurality of religious and nonreligious worldviews, especially religious and nonreligious majorities and minorities. We need not expand on that much. Reports of conflicts between supporters of theocratic and secular concepts of the state, conflicts within and between religions, and wrangling between religious and purely humanistic groups fill the columns of the daily press and radio and television programmes. They are literally abuzz with clashes between and within religions, cultures and civilisations in our own and neighbouring countries. How do we deal with this conflictive religious pluralism in such a way that social cohesion and order will not go by the board, to put it negatively, and, in positive terms, integration will be achieved and ensured? In other words, it is important to distinguish between interreligious dialogue and interreligious interaction. The latter does not refer only to constructive and communicative ways in which religions relate to one another in a spirit of mutual support and solidarity, but also to the sphere of neutrality and indifference that may exist between them, the positions of mutual isolation and 'apartheid' that may divide them, and especially the tensions, conflicts, struggles and forms of violence that exist between them. In this perspective the goal of interreligious dialogue refers or should refer to the endeavour – negatively – to push back all these forms of 'hot war' and 'cold war', and – positively – accomplish a step-by-step process of integration.

To clarify the meaning of this positive goal, integration, we compare its substance with that of other non-violent models of interreligious interaction. The framework in figure 1 below comprises two dimensions. The horizontal dimension indicates the extent to which a religious community tries to keep alive and develop its own heritage and identity. The vertical dimension represents the extent to which it engages in relations with other religious and secular communities and expands its heritage and identity. By relating the two dimensions we can construct four ideal types in the Weberian sense: integration, assimilation, separation and marginalisation.[9] The typology includes scales in both dimensions, ranging from positive (+) to negative (-).

Figure 1. Models of Inter-religious Interaction

Maintenance of community's own heritage and identity

+ ?

Relationships (1)
(2)

sought **Integration**
Assimilation

with other (3)
(4)

communities **Separation**
Marginalisation
?

'Integration' in cell 1 refers to the community's striving to keep its own heritage and identity alive and at the same time maintain intensive, lasting contacts with other communities. Here the concept of integration is both broader and narrower than the description we gave at the beginning of this article. It is narrower in that the 'relationships sought with other communities' in this figure only refer to the aforementioned contact aspect, omitting the aspects of reciprocal influence and transformation, to which we return in due course. It is broader in that it includes the dimension of 'maintenance of heritage and identity'. 'Assimilation' in cell 2 also stands for a community's aspiration to develop contacts with other religious and secular communities, but without concern for its own heritage and identity. In the model represented by cell 3, 'separation', this concern is vitally present, but the ambition for enduring contact is lacking. 'Marginalisation' in cell 4 is characterised by the absence of both interest in its own identity and interest in contacts.

The concept of integration can be probed more deeply by analysing it with the aid of the Aristotelian dialectic between the one and the many and between the part and the whole. In our view the dialectic between the one and the many can be approached in terms of the dialectic between the part and the whole. Regarding the one and the many, a population constitutes an integrated whole inasmuch as it is one entity, yet comprising a multiplicity of mutually differing religious and nonreligious groups.[10] How does this multiplicity-in-unity come about? The answer lies in the dialectic between the part and the whole. In this dialectic the part represents the whole and realises the whole by being integrally part of it: the whole exists in its parts and the parts participate in the wholeness of the whole. This means a population forms an integrated whole insofar as the individual religious and nonreligious groups express and actualise the whole in their beliefs and practices. They do so by sharing each other's beliefs and practices while still nurturing their own identity. Such mutual participation is essential, for the wholeness of a population does not transcend the groups; it is not something beyond them that descends on them in a vacuum. It in fact consists in their mutual participation. Wholeness is not overarching but consists in mutual penetration. It is not a canopy but a network. There is no wholeness without participation, no integration without interpenetration.[11]

Integration by participation and interpenetration has several dimensions. There is geographical integration, which seeks to counteract the demeaning segregation of residential areas and promote a proper spatial distribution policy. There is economic integration, aimed at abolishing divisions between rich and poor, and between unskilled and skilled labour based on ethnic and/or religious differences. There is political integration, aimed at having ethnic and religious groups on the underside of society participate fully in deliberative democracy. There is integration in the judicial sphere, aimed at combating criminal overrepresentation in these groups. There is cultural integration, aimed at arresting the proportionally higher dropout rate among pupils from ethnic and religious minorities through a policy of mixed as opposed to segregated schools. Against this backdrop a rhetorical question may be asked: why pursue geographic, economic, political, judicial and cultural integration, yet leave religious segregation and exclusion untouched? Why should we not also engage in and commit ourselves to religious integration through participation and interpenetration? Is religious integration not an important part of social integration?

1.2 Strategies of social integration

Inasmuch as social integration is considered an adequate definition of the goal of interreligious dialogue, the question arises what strategy would best achieve this goal. There are three concepts for such a strategy in circulation that could help us find an answer: tolerance, respect and recognition.

Tolerance

The first is tolerance.[12] At first glance its meaning appears simple and innocuous: other religions are politely tolerated.

But what does 'tolerate' imply? It makes a difference whether one religion represents the majority of the population and the other a minority. In that case the majority tolerates the minority, not the other way round. The minority is tolerated in the sense that it is not massacred or subjected to ethnic cleansing; it is not compelled to convert, either by force or by threats of negative sanctions, nor by religious discrimination. Hence the minority is free to practise its religion, but that freedom is based on tolerance, in this case assent, permission. It is granted a licence that can be withdrawn at any time at the majority's pleasure, as when the Edict of Nantes of 1598 was replaced by the Edict of Fontainebleau in 1685. Such tolerance is not mutual but unilateral, not horizontal but vertical. Thus it makes a difference whether one is looking at a majority-minority situation, or at two or more groups of roughly equal power. In the latter case tolerance amounts to peaceful coexistence, which is largely pragmatic. It is marked by openness to compromise aimed at achieving a viable modus vivendi. Such tolerance is not unilateral but bilateral, not vertical but horizontal. Those who tolerate are tolerated in their turn. It could be a truce between two groups to prevent (further) bloodshed. But it could also entail acceptance of a neutral third party, which sees to it that the two groups treat each other with mutual tolerance. This third party is the constitutional state with its three powers: legislative, administrative and judicial. Adopting a neutral attitude towards all religions, the state passes jointly agreed, impartial laws, administers them impartially and, when there is conflict, adjudicates impartially.[13]

That sounds fine, and one would hope that such tolerance is generally realised. But whether it is a case of majorities and minorities or of two roughly equal groups, it has a socially strategic connotation and undertone, which merely camouflage the underlying religious ethnocentrism. It consists of an attitude of tolerating the other religion as a lesser good while one's own religion is a higher good, or as a lesser evil because war and conflict are considered greater evils. The virtue of patience, a concomitant of this strategy, is that the other is tolerated as a greater or lesser burden. In so doing one may cherish the hope, secretly or openly, that the final judgment at the end of time will settle the score for once and for all, when good will come into its own, on the right hand side, and evil will get its just desserts, on the left hand side.[14]

But can such tolerance really be seen as an appropriate strategy of integration? In other words, is it not at odds with the ethics that religions profess to cherish?

Respect

The second concept proposed as a possible strategy of integration is respect. Respect implies mutual recognition of the dialogue partner as a human person, who is considered in a very real sense to be born free and equal, regardless of differences in gender, colour, culture and religion. Respect means that the partners regard each other as brothers and sisters, because each possesses human dignity as an intrinsic value. They approach one another as autonomous beings that are entitled to live their lives according to their own beliefs, values and norms. What are respected are not the beliefs and rituals but the right of free, equal individuals to hold these views and perform these rituals. Whether or not these convictions and celebrations are part and parcel of their identity is irrelevant. After all, one respects the person – the views and practices are merely tolerated. The respect shown is partial. Interreligious dialogue is often characterised by such partial respect, especially the courtesy dialogue between national and international religious leaders.[15]

Not only religious leaders are prone to showing such respect: the state does the same. To the extent that it accords partial respect, one can distinguish between a secular and a pluralist view. According to the secular view the state treats religions with respect insofar as they confine their activities to the private domain of the individual citizen or group of individual citizens. They are granted religious freedom in this private domain.[16] But it ends there: in the public domain it is taboo. This secular approach is typical of the French and the Turkish state, which has been influenced by French law ever since the Ottoman caliphate and more particularly since the republic of Kemal Ataturk; some groups in the Netherlands, too, seem to be heading that way. According to the pluralist approach religions have the right to enter the public domain, more especially civil society, and express their beliefs and perform their rituals, albeit in a manner that does not infringe the equality of all religions before the law. They are also permitted to conduct missionary activities and practise proper proselytism, where 'proper' implies non-violation of civil liberties.[17] The assumption is that a religion is existentially meaningful to its adherents, since it forms part of their identity. However, adherents are accorded personal respect, whereas their religious beliefs and rituals are merely tolerated.

Again we must ask whether such partial respect – both the private domain and the civil society approach – does justice to religions' self-understanding, ideals and concerns. In concrete terms, what is left of their claims (at least those of some religions) to absoluteness, universality and uniqueness?[18] Even in a pluralist approach where religions' equality before the law is paramount, are these claims not totally abrogated? We must also ask whether such partial respect can be seen as an appropriate strategy for realising integration.

Recognition

The third concept, namely, recognition, may be a better strategy of integration. The proper criterion to assess this would be whether recognition really implies respect not only for the adherents of religions but also for their beliefs and rituals.

The concept of recognition can only be understood against the backdrop of the difference between pre-modern and modern society. In pre-modern society the principle that dominated social relations and interactions was honour.[19] The latter was connected to one's social class and one's position in society on the basis of family or ethnic descent. Hence honour was unequal and class-based. Shame was the consequence of violating honour, be it through one's own behaviour or that of others, which had to be avenged in order to restore it. The transition from pre-modern society to modern society was characterised by the replacement of class-bound honour by the universal equality and dignity of human beings.[20] Equality means that dignity is no longer connected with one's office or function in society – as was the case among the Stoics, Cicero being the exception – but that it is an inherent prerogative of the human being as such: it is intrinsic to each and every person. It is inherent in what makes a human being human – a person's status as a rational and moral agent capable of directing his or her life according to principles. On the basis of this dignity it follows that no human being whosoever may be treated solely as an instrument for another human being's purposes.[21] That would destroy their equal dignity. Equal dignity can only be realised and nurtured if it is mutually recognised. Such recognition is violated if there is non-recognition and/or mis-recognition between the parties.

Non-recognition (and/or misrecognition) leads not only to violations of human dignity, but also to a negative self-image. It leads to self-deprecation, which results in an externally imposed negative identity. These destructive effects can be illustrated by examples from three different sectors of society. Firstly, non-recognition and/or mis-recognition take place through lack of security and love, symbiotic self-interest, dubious, ambivalent affection or neglect between parents in the family. Secondly, they happen through lack of respect in political institutions, as a result of which human rights like freedom of expression, conscience and religion are violated. Lastly, they take place through lack of esteem in social institutions despite the commitment with which one fulfils one's household, professional and civic functions and tasks.[22]

Recognising the others' identity does not refer to a kind of 'hidden self' lurking behind all agency and actions and confined to an intimate, secret sphere, but to convictions which people hold dear and 'sacred' and with which they identify, and to rituals in which they express the existential meaning of these convictions and identification. Their identity is determined by such convictions and rituals, which form the very core of it. Recognition of these convictions and rituals is crucial for their identity. In them they experience their 'ipse-ity', their 'mineness', to use Ricoeur's terms.[23]

On Martha Nussbaum's list of the ten capabilities representing the minimum social entitlements necessary to live a life corresponding to equal human dignity, the fourth one is "to use the senses, to imagine, think and reason – and do these things in a 'truly human way', a way informed and cultivated by an adequate education (...)". This includes the use of religious senses, religious imagination and religious reasoning, as well as free expression of them.[24] In other words, recognising the other person intrinsically implies recognising his or her religious convictions and rituals.

On the basis of the foregoing discussion we conclude that the strategy that best fits integration is not mere tolerance or respect, but recognition, which includes both the dialogue partners as persons and their religious convictions and rituals.

1.3 Recognition and integration in a civil rights perspective

From what we have said so far the link between recognition and human rights should be plain. Human rights can be seen as the elaboration of mutual recognition of human dignity into entitlements. They indicate the conditions to be fulfilled for the realisation of mutual recognition. They are the means of promoting integration.

The choice of human rights is justified for two reasons, one secular, the other religious. The secular reason is that human rights provide a framework for moral and judicial guidelines for national and international social processes, rules that are endorsed by countries around the world as binding, implying that they will be brought to book for any violation thereof. The universal nature of human rights is disputed by Asian and African spokespeople: are they not products of typically Western thought, hence a hegemonic, neo-colonial invention? At all events, more needs to be done by way of pluriform and differentiated interpretation and application of human rights to allow for historical and contextual variation. In the Western legal tradition justice should be administered according to the rule of *epikeia*. This does not entail a one-off exception or exemption from a legal rule, as moral theologians since Suarez have argued. Ever since the reception of Aristotle by Thomas and especially by Albertus Magnus, *epikeia* has meant that in applying any legal rule whatsoever to a concrete situation the contingency and uniqueness of the circumstances should always, without exception, be taken into account and the relevant alternative applications should be weighed up reasonably and fairly.[25] Hence for reasons of national and international stability it is legitimate for non-Western countries to first secure socio-economic rights and treat civil and political rights as secondary to these.[26] The United States has done the reverse: it ratified the international treaty on civil and political rights of 1966, but not the international treaty on socio-economic and cultural rights of the same year.[27] Still, various countries have incorporated human rights into their constitutions and declared themselves accountable for their observance. Therefore human rights can serve as a premise for social integration.

But does that apply to religions as well? Are human rights a self-evident premise for religious integration from their point of view? That brings us to the religious reason for the choice of human rights. Christianity opposed human rights for over a century, the Catholic Church holding out for a century and a half. In all religions at least three groups were and are discernible: those who reject human rights[28] or tolerate them sceptically;[29] those who subscribe to them and then use them opportunistically;[30] and those who embrace human rights as a legitimate condition for the common good life[31] and consider them applicable not only to society at large but to their own religious community as well.[32]

Apart from these historical and contemporary facts there are ample grounds for arguing that religions ought to accept human rights unreservedly as a valid frame of reference for ethics and law. The principal argument follows from what is known as the golden rule, which in diverse forms features in all religions. The literature offers long lists of formulations of this rule, ranging from ancient Egyptian religions to religions that originated in West Asia (Judaism, Christianity, Islam), South Asia (Hinduism and Buddhism) and East Asia (Confucianism). At the most abstract level its negative form reads: "don't do to others what you do not want done to yourself"; the positive version says: "treat others as you wish to be treated".[33] Both versions imply a summons to exchange perspectives. 'I' am called to adopt 'your' perspective, and vice versa. It is interesting that the golden rule is found in all religions, irrespective of place and time of origin. It responds to the innate human capacity to understand other people's feelings, motives, intentions, ideas, beliefs and decisions, but on that basis also to 'reason' and predict their if/then feelings, thoughts and actions. People can 'read' each other's feelings, thoughts and actions and, in so doing, anticipate them. The reciprocity in the golden rule is characterised by symmetry: it puts people on an equal footing. It abrogates the real-life asymmetry of human relations and raises symmetry to an ethical level. It says: you are committed to an exchange of perspectives.[34]

Such a symmetrical exchange of perspectives is to be found in Immanuel Kant's categorical imperative, a universalisation of the golden rule.[35] It reads: "Act in such a way that you always treat humanity, whether in your own person or in the person of any other, never simply as a means, but always at the same time as an end."[36] Treating the self and the other as intrinsically valuable, ends in themselves, is the bedrock of human dignity and, as such, of human rights.[37] Human rights may be seen as an elaboration on human dignity in the sense of a legal explication, generalisation, positivisation and universalisation. That makes human rights a religious duty.

Hence for two reasons – one secular, the other religious – we consider human rights, especially civil rights, a suitable premise for the pursuit of social integration. It does not mean that the realisation of civil rights is a sufficient condition for such integration, but it is a necessary, meaningful and favourable one.[38] We use the word 'condition' in these three senses. Moreover, we confine ourselves to what are known as civil rights, while interpreting their acceptance as a necessary, meaningful and favourable condition of social integration.

1.4 Empirical research into attitudes towards civil rights

In the introduction we pointed out that in this study international documents on human rights play an indirect role. We are not so much concerned, we said, with the texts of these documents as with the legal cultures underlying their interpretation and practical application, that is to say, the legal cultures present among ordinary religious people, especially students, the agents and leaders of future society. To this end we draw on data collected in 2005 in Tamilnadu, India, among 942 higher secondary school students, whom we asked to fill in a questionnaire in the framework of the International Human Rights and Religion Programme. We asked the students to define themselves from a religious perspective, irrespective of their religious upbringing or affiliation. On the basis of their answers we constructed five groups: Christians (305), Muslims (298), Hindus (206), and students who described themselves as religious (102) and nonreligious (31). 6 students did not answer the question. In this part we look for answers to the first concern we formulated at the beginning of this article: to what extent do the students accept civil rights as a necessary, meaningful and favourable condition for their social integration?

To respond to this question we distinguish between secular civil rights and religious civil rights. The first relates to the

Table 1. Means of Attitudes Towards Secular Civil Rights (N= 942)

	Chr	*Mus*	*Hin*	*relig.*	*non-*	*total*	*eta*	*rel.*
Freedom of life style								
1	Our laws should protect a citizen's right to live by any moral standard he/she chooses.	4.2	4.2	4.1	4.3	4.1	4.2	ns
2	Any form of sexual relations between adults should be their individual choice.	3.2	3.2	3.3	3.4	3.7	3.3	ns
Freedom of assembly								
3	Minority groups should be allowed to use town halls to hold protest meetings	3.5	3.6	3.5	3.6	3.7	3.6	ns
4	A cabinet minister should allow his striking officials to meet in a ministerial building.	3.5	3.4	3.3	3.4	3.5	3.4	ns
Freedom of the press								
5	Newspaper columnists should be free to express radical convictions.	4.0	3.8	3.8	4.0	4.3	3.9	.13*
6	TV journalists with radical ideas have a civil right to employment.	3.6	3.6	3.6	3.6	3.7	3.6	ns

Table 1. Means of Attitudes Towards Secular Civil Rights (N= 942)

	Chr	*Mus*	*Hin*	*relig.*	*non-*	*total*	*eta*	*rel.*
Right to privacy								
7	Police searches of private homes without a search warrant are prohibited.	3.6	3.6	3.6	3.8	3.8	3.6	ns
8	The police are only allowed to inspect people's cars under strict legal conditions.	3.4	3.5	3.5	3.6	3.7	3.5	ns

1 = I totally disagree, 5 = I fully agree, ns = non significant; * p d" .05

[Source: reconstruction, elaboration and augmentation of J.A. van der Ven et al. 2004, p.117, n. 15.]

main legal principles underpinning the state, like freedom of lifestyle, freedom of assembly, freedom of the press and freedom of privacy (table 1). The second refers to the main legal principles on which the relation between religion and state is built, like separation of religion and state, freedom of religion, freedom of religious speech and freedom of moral speech (table 2). In order to investigate the students' attitudes to both secular and religious civil rights we took various decisions. We not only made a selection of human rights, especially civil rights, leaving aside rights like the prohibition of discrimination, torture and forced labour; we also selected a number of concrete situations in order to interpret and apply these civil rights and make them relevant and more concrete. We then operationalised these applications in an easily understandable form, with two items for each category. These applications and forms of operationalisation were necessary, otherwise we would have had to use the generalised abstractions from official human rights documents. As a result our empirical findings on the students' attitudes towards civil rights refer only to the actual formulations of the civil rights items, in which we expressed the abstract official formulations in real-life terms. Differently phrased items could have resulted in different positive or negative scores.

After conducting ANOVA analyses – followed, where relevant, by POSTHOC SCHEFFE TESTS – we were able to compile table 1. The second last column gives the means of all students' attitudes towards secular civil rights. The scores in the first five columns are the means of the aforementioned five groups: students who define themselves as Christian, Muslim, Hindu, religious and nonreligious. From this table we see that the students accept secular civil rights as selected, interpreted, applied and operationalised in our questionnaire. General freedom of lifestyle, which refers to the freedom to have one's own moral standards, is most highly rated (item 1: total mean 4.2), whereas freedom of sexual lifestyle is rated least, but almost wholly positively (item 2: total mean 3.3).[39] There is only one item on which the groups differ significantly – freedom of newspaper columnists (item 5: total mean 3.9, eta .13).

But this harmonious picture does not apply to religious civil rights, as is evident in table 2. Only one of these rights – freedom of moral speech – is wholeheartedly accepted by all students: the freedom to have moral discussions in schools (item 15: total mean 3.6) and the freedom to have moral discussion with children in class (item 16: total mean 4.1). We decided to put this right into the category of religious civil rights, because historically and currently religion and morality were and still are viewed as closely connected, at least in ordinary people's minds and especially if they are religious. The students' attitudes towards the other religious civil rights tell a diferent story. The principle of separation of religion and state meets with some ambivalence. Students tend to accept that the issue of euthanasia should be freely decided by politicians (item 9: mean 3.4), but they doubt whether the same applies to abortion (item 10: total mean 3.1). They also express doubt about religious freedom, which historically is closely connected with the principle of separation of religion and state. They agree that politicians should not interfere with religious communities (item 11: total mean 3.8), but they unambiguously reject the notion that prayers in public schools should be forbidden (item 12: total mean 2.3). The students also have doubts about freedom of religious speech, which implies that making fun of both religious people and atheists is allowed. They express reservations about this (item 13: total mean 2.8; item 14: mean 2.6). Only in two instances the groups of students appear to differ significantly: prohibition of prayers in public schools (item 12, eta .13), especially the Christian and Muslim students (Scheffe test, p .021), and the freedom to make fun of religious people (item 13, eta .11).

Overall it appears that the students accept civil rights only partially. They fully subscribe to secular civil rights, but not to religious ones. This is important, for religious civil rights are historically regarded as the touchstone of all civil rights.

Table 2. Means of Attitudes Towards Religious Civil Rights (N= 942)

Chr	*Mus*	*Hin*	*rel.*	*non*	*total*	*eta*	*rel.*
Separation of religion and state							
9 In regard to euthanasia politicians should decide irrespective of any religious leader's will	3.3	3.3	3.4	3.4	3.8	3.4	ns
10 In regard to abortion politicians should take decisions independently of religious leaders	3.1	3.0	3.2	3.3	3.2	3.1	ns
Freedom of religion							
11 Politicians are not allowed to interfere with religious communities	3.9	3.8	3.7	3.9	4.1	3.8	ns
12 Prayers in public schools should be forbidden	2.1	2.5	2.4	2.4	2.7	2.3	.13*
-----------**Freedom of religious speech**							
13 Making fun of religious people in cabarets is a legally protected right.	2.7	2.8	2.9	3.1	3.1	2.8	.11*
14 Making fun of atheists at public meetings is permissible.	2.5	2.6	2.8	2.7	2.8	2.6	ns

Table 2. Means of Attitudes Towards Religious Civil Rights (N= 942)

Chr	*Mus*	*Hin*	*rel.*	*non*	*total*	*eta*	*rel.*
Freedom of moral speech							
15 The community's moral standards should be critically debated in schools.	3.6	3.6	3.5	3.6	3.7	3.6	ns
16 Children should be free to discuss all moral ideas and subjects in schools, no matter what	4.2	4.2	4.0	4.1	4.1	4.1	ns

1 = I totally disagree, 5 = I fully agree; ns = non significant; * p d" .05

[Source: reconstruction, elaboration and augmentation of J.A. van der Ven et al. 2004, p.117, n. 15.]

Hence for these students civil rights are only a partial meaningful and favourable condition for social integration.

1.5 Discussion

Our finding with regard to the first question is that the students wholeheartedly support secular civil rights. This gives a strong indication of their integration with Indian society as far as its basis in the Indian constitution and its civil rights is concerned. The students' attitudes towards religious civil rights reveal a different picture. Only freedom of moral speech is unambiguously supported, whereas the other rights meet with either positively or negatively oriented ambivalence, even rejection.

Let us start with the principle of separation of religion and state. This is accepted by the students as far as euthanasia is concerned, but meets with ambiguity in the case of abortion. They seem to say that politicians should assume responsibility, irrespective of religious leaders' views, in the case of euthanasia, but when it comes to abortion they are usure whether a religious curb should not be put on politicians' powers.

Why is that? A possible answer may lie in the division between public and private spheres. Perhaps the students fear an unconstrained public policy on birth control, including abortion, whereas euthanasia belongs to the intimacy of people's private life, where they are in control. This division between public and private worlds also explains why the students' personal convictions about euthanasia and abortion, irrespective of their beliefs about public policy in that regard, differ.[40] They appear to personally reject euthanasia and more or less accept abortion. Policy-related beliefs and personal convictions do not coincide, public and private do not match.

Secondly, the students are negatively ambivalent about freedom of religious speech, especially making fun of both religious people and atheists. This is counter to Article 19 of the Indian constitution, according to which these activities are not forbidden. The only constraint in comparative constitutional law is on hate speech, and in terms of the British Racial and Religious Hatred Act of 2006 only speech that intentionally incites hatred.[41] This act also specifies that the prohibition of intentional incitement of hatred does not preclude discussion and criticism, expression of antipathy, ridicule or insulting language.[42] None of these is forbidden.

Lastly, religious freedom evokes a varied response. The students wholeheartedly support the idea that politicians should not try to influence religious communities in any way, but reject the idea that prayers in public schools should be forbidden. In this respect they contradict international jurisprudence. Many countries proscribe prayers in public schools, for two reasons: a pluralistic and a secular reason. The first is that adherents of certain religions, such as Jews in the USA, do not want Christian prayers to be said in public schools.[43] The second is that agnostics and atheists object to prayers of whatever kind. They want themselves, and their children, to be exempted from any demands or activity associated with prayer.[44] Prayers in public schools do not comply with the criterion of the erstwhile UN Human Rights Committee, namely that in public schools religion may only feature in a 'neutral and objective way'. Separation of church and state is not the only point at issue. It also concerns the right of parents to raise their children according to their own worldview, which may be Christian (Catholic, Protestant or that of Jehovah's Witnesses, Jewish, Muslim, Hindu, Buddhist, or agnostic/atheistic.[45] One could ask why the students reject the idea that prayers in public schools should be forbidden. A possible explanation might be that they have certain unquestioned religio-centric convictions. They may think that religious students have a right to say prayers at school and that non-religious students should accept it, keep quiet and show tolerance, regardless of their own right to be free from religion – a paradoxical manifestation of an intolerant attitude towards tolerance.

Impact of religion on attitudes towards civil rights

Having discussed the students' attitudes towards both secular and religious civil rights in part one,[46] we proceed to the next question: what are the effects of their religious beliefs and practices on their attitudes towards both secular and religious civil rights?

To answer this question we look at the theoretical implications of the relationship between religion and civil rights (2.1) and then describe the explorative aim of our empirical research (2.2), our expectations for this research (2.3), and the plan of analysis (2.4). We then report the empirical results on effects of our students' religious beliefs and practices on their attitudes towards civil rights (2.5). This second part concludes with a discussion of some salient findings (2.6).

2.1 Religion and civil rights

The question about the effect of religion on attitudes towards civil rights should be seen against the background of the debate between and within theology, religious studies and the social sciences concerning the effects of religious beliefs and practices on political and juridical attitudes in general. Some scholars maintain that religion and modernism, from which the constitutional democratic state stems, have a strained relationship. Historically religious communities protested against the rule of law, separation of powers and human rights – hence an antithesis between theocracy and democracy. Most of them still do, either entirely or partially, and especially in the area of religious rights, where the principles of religious freedom and equality underlying these rights cannot but curtail religious power in these communities, both internally and externally. According to this view, the religious leadership's opposition to democratisation in various parts of world and its hostility, or at any rate insecurity, in the face of an increasingly popular human rights movement are accompanied by a decline in the influence of religion in modern political life and the impact of their beliefs and practices. Religion may still affect people's private lives, so the theory goes, but less so, and it influences modern public life to an ever lesser degree. The fact that the younger generation, especially in Europe, is sceptical about the relation between religion and modernisation in public life may be indicative of such a tendency.[47]

Other scholars, while not denying the declining public influence of religious communities in the modern world outright, add some qualifications. The first concerns differences in social context: tendencies that characterise modern Western, especially European, countries cannot and should not be attributed arbitrarily to countries on other continents, like India, which is profoundly religious. This does not mean that groups in the Indian intelligentsia are not affected by modernisation, which permeates both the political and the religious areas. Our aim is to explore to what extent the process influences these groups, and more especially to what extent our group of students is influenced by it.

The second qualification concerns differences between and within religious traditions and communities. In all religions one finds different factions with different patterns of beliefs and practices. Some religious groups emphasise the importance of conserving their traditions exactly as the founders originally articulated them. Others interpret their traditions contextually in terms of the present situation, allowing for variations in time and space, so as to enhance their social plausibility and relevance.[48]

The third qualification relates to how these traditional and contextual interpretations deal with the dialectical relationship between transcendence and immanence in terms of absolute transcendence, immanent transcendence and absolute immanence. This dialectic is a major issue in all religions, especially the belief in God but also, for Christians, the belief in Jesus, for Muslims the belief in Muhammad, for Hindus the belief in Rama, and for all religious groups their beliefs about the mission of their religious communities and policy on their relations with other religions. Traditional groups generally put the accent on absolute transcendence. Contextual groups tend to favour immanent transcendence in their beliefs and practices, and sometimes adopt an absolute immanent approach.[49]

The fourth and last qualification is that individual people make different choices. Some identify with one of the great religious traditions like Christianity, Islam and Hinduism, which they regard as the cultural embodiment of age-old, sapiential guidelines for authentic relations with God, people, society, nature and the cosmos. Others have no affiliation with or loyalty to these traditions' rules, beliefs and practices. Differences between religions are unimportant to them: they simply regard themselves as 'religious'. Yet others prefer to have nothing to do with any traditions, possibly acknowledging their relevance to other people but not to themselves. They define themselves as 'nonreligious', indicating that for them purely secular or secularist beliefs and values may be important but not religious ones. In our research population the 'religious' and 'nonreligious' groups are, as mentioned already, the smallest (respectively 102 and 31 students) but big enough to be taken into account.

All this complicates the question whether the religious beliefs and practices of our sample of students affect their civil rights attitudes. We do not expect a clear-cut answer: it may range from clearly positive to partly positive, and from partly negative to clearly negative. Much depends on the factors raised in the foregoing qualifications, which may also apply to our research population of young students: intellectual stratum in society and evaluation of individual religions; traditional versus contextual interpretations of beliefs and practices in these religions; choices regarding the dialectic between transcendence and immanence; and lastly, the religious self-definition of individual people.

2.2 Explorative goal of empirical research into religion and civil rights

We mentioned that we have certain expectations about the possible effects of our students' religious beliefs and practices on their civil rights attitudes. The term 'expectations' is important, for it indicates the goal of this part of our study. In the absence of adequate theories and empirical research into the impact of religious beliefs and practices on human rights, especially civil rights (apart from one earlier research project in South Africa[50]), we are not in a position to formulate and test hypotheses, because these have to be deduced from networks of theoretical concepts and validated by empirical investigation. In any case there are as yet no empirical studies of the effects of religion on law, more particularly of religious beliefs and practices on human rights attitudes, since jurists, if and when they do empirical research, restrict themselves to descriptive reports of human rights violations. Important as their work may be, it differs from what we aim to do in our study. Since we cannot build on prior research, we do not formulate hypotheses to be tested empirically, but merely offer well-considered expectations to be explored empirically.

2.3 Expectations

Against this background we formulate some expectations about the effects of religious beliefs and practices on civil rights attitudes among our research population of higher secondary school students. The eleven expectations below may be divided into two groups: expectations referring directly to the students' religious beliefs and practices (expectations 1-4), and expectations relating to population characteristics by which the effects of these beliefs and practices are statistically controlled (expectations 5-11). We start with the first group.

The more the students' religious beliefs are characterised by absolute transcendence, the more likely they are to have a negative effect on their civil rights attitudes. This outcome may be explained by the historical (and actual) objections religions have against human rights, especially civil rights, in the sense of democracy versus theocracy, which is based on a more or less rigid conception of absolute transcendence. The following religious beliefs are associated with absolute transcendence:

theistic beliefs in God, beliefs in Jesus from the perspective of a Christology from above, beliefs in Muhammad's divine revelations, beliefs in Rama's origin from above, and exclusivist and inclusivist interreligious beliefs (expectation 1).

On the other hand, the more religious beliefs are marked by aspects of immanent transcendence, the more likely they are to have a positive effect on the students' civil rights attitudes, since they link religion with this-worldly issues like freedom, equality and solidarity. The following beliefs are associated with immanent transcendence: panentheistic beliefs in God pertaining to the middle ground between absolute transcendence and absolute immanence, beliefs in Jesus from the perspective of a Christology from below, beliefs in Muhammad as a teacher of mysticism and social action, beliefs in Rama as the source of inspiration and solidarity, open-minded beliefs about one's own religious community, and dialogue-oriented interreligious beliefs (expectation 2).

The more religious beliefs reflect aspects of absolute immanence, the more likely they are to have positive effects, since these secular or secular-religious beliefs link up readily with human rights issues. The following beliefs are associated with absolute immanence: pantheistic and metatheistic beliefs in God, humanistic views of Jesus, Muhammad and Rama, and pluralist interreligious beliefs (expectation 3).

As for religious practices, we distinguish between individual and social ones. We expect individual religious practices to have a positive effect on civil rights attitudes, since modernisation leads to similar phenomena in the area of religion and in that of politics and law, namely de-institutionalisation, de-traditionalisation and individualisation. In the area of religion people's religiosity becomes more and more individually oriented, although it should be noted that in Hindu communities (whose culture permeates the general Indian context, including that of Christian and Muslim communities) individual religious practices have always been prevalent. This does not mean that collective conventions and customs are not important in Indian spirituality, but that its main focus was always on personal religious experience and reflection long before modern individualism found its way into India's upper echelons. In the juridico-political area human rights, particularly civil rights, are intrinsically individual. They protect individuals against rules and measures by the state that violate their private sphere and the entitlements they have on the basis of their inalienable human dignity. This does not mean that human rights ignore community life, social cohesion and solidarity, but ultimately loyalty and commitment to any group or collective should stem from personal choice and decision making. Our expectations do not exclude a positive effect of social religious practices on civil rights attitudes, but we expect individual religious practices to have a more positive effect than social religious practices, especially among students who may come from the upper strata of Indian society (expectation 4).

In addition to religious beliefs and practices we formulated some expectations relating to certain population characteristics, which we use to control for the effects of students' beliefs and practices on their civil rights attitudes. First we expect gender to play a key role, because we know from a similar research project on religion and human rights in another modernising, developing country – South Africa – that female students are significantly more supportive of human rights than their male peers (expectation 5).[51]

Ethnicity may also influence students' civil rights attitudes, as we found in the aforementioned project in South Africa. We expect Tamilnadu students whose home language is one of the South Indian languages (75% in our sample) to agree less with civil rights than students who speak some other Indian language at home (25%). We anticipate that the latter, being a minority, will have an ethnic interest in being considered and treated in an atmosphere of equal freedom and free equality (expectation 6).

We also expect students' religious self-definition to influence their attitudes towards civil rights. As noted already, the students were asked to provide such a self-definition. On the basis of their responses the following five groups were constructed: Christian, Muslim, Hindu, religious and nonreligious. For statistical reasons we had to choose a reference category in order to be able to compare these five groups. Since we settled on students who defined themselves as Christians for our reference category, our expectations are formulated in terms of relations between religious and Christian, Muslim and Christian, Hindu and Christian, and nonreligious and Christian. We expect Muslims to be less supportive of civil rights than Christians, since Islam worldwide seems to put great emphasis on the dialectic between transcendence and immanence, inclining to absolute transcendence rather than immanence, let alone absolute immanence. This, we expect, will negatively influence their support for civil rights (see expectation 1). Hindus, we think, will be more positive about civil rights than Christians because of their age-old history of multicultural and multireligious tolerance, respect and recognition. Students defining themselves as religious are expected to support civil rights more strongly than Christians, because their general religious orientation is characterised by an accent on immanent transcendence, even absolute immanence, which can be considered a clear predictor of support for civil rights (see expectations 2 and 3). Students defining themselves as nonreligious are expected to be most supportive of civil rights, because of the aforementioned continuity (see expectation 4) between their purely secular, humanistic self-definition and human rights (expectation 7).

Our next expectation concerns the students' position in the religious landscape, that is their religious socio-geographic location: do they belong to the conservative or liberal wings of their religious tradition, or at least sympathise more with either one or the other? Conservatives prefer a literal, traditional reading of holy books, be it the Bible, the Qur'an or the Vedas. Liberals go for a contextual interpretation, in which they decipher the meaning of these texts in terms of their relevance to people living in a modernising, globalising world where civil rights developments are the order of the day. We expect conservatives to have a negative attitude towards these movements and liberals a positive one (expectation 8).

Some political orientations can also be expected to have more affinity with civil rights, for instance a preference for left and centre left political parties as opposed to centre, centre right or right wing ones. This also applies to frequency of political discussions in the students' homes and the extent to which they consider politics a value (expectation 9).

After the Enlightenment the struggle for human rights, especially civil rights, began to feature more and more prominently on the social and political landscape. Three secular values play a key role in these discussions: family as a value, autonomy as a value and social critique as a value. Strong appreciation of traditional family values has always been seen as indicative of a conservative orientation. Autonomy as a value, centring on individual self-determination, is generally considered a pivotal characteristic of enlightened (including human rights) thought and action. Social critique as a value can be seen as the translation of autonomy into social, collective terms, since it aims at transforming society in the direction of equal freedom and free equality for all citizens in all social strata. Because our students may belong to or be influenced by the upper echelons of Indian society, which may be affected by the spirit of the Enlightenment, we expect these secular values to have some impact: the traditional value of family life a negative impact and the other two – autonomy and social critique – a positive one (expectation 10).[52]

Personality traits may influence our students' civil rights attitudes in a peculiar way. Of the classic four characteristics identified and intensely researched by the Eisenck school (neuroticism, psychoticism, extroversion and social conformism), we expect extroversion to influence a civil rights orientation positively and social conformism to do so negatively, as the latter indicates an inclination to adapt to the social and political status quo, which rejects the challenges implied in civil rights. We also expect neuroticism and psychoticism to have a negative effect, since they inhibit the capacity for pre-reflective perspective and role taking, as well as a proclivity for spontaneous altruism and pro-social behaviour, which are necessary conditions for a human rights attitude (expectation 11).

2.4 Plan of analysis

Here we pay attention to the research design which directs our study, the instruments we use, the statistical analyses we conduct, as well as the sample.

Research design

From the above the research design aims at exploring the impact of the students' religious beliefs and practices on their civil rights attitudes. This impact is controlled for their population characteristics (figure 2).

Figure 2. Research Design

Population characteristics Religious beliefs
Civil rights attitudes
Religious practices

Instruments

The instruments we used to conduct this exploratory study are distinguished into three groups: the civil rights attitudes as the dependent variables, the religious beliefs and practices as the independent variables and the population characteristics.

Dependent variables: civil rights attitudes

The dependent variables are the following civil rights variables (see tables 1 and 2): freedom of *lifestyle* (items 1 and 2), freedom of *assembly* (items 3 and 4), freedom of the *press* (items 5 and 6), right to *privacy* (items 7 and 8), separation of *religion and state* (items 9 and 10), freedom of *religion* (items 11 and 12), freedom of *religious speech* (items 13 and 14), and freedom of *moral speech* (items 15 and16).

Independent variables: religious beliefs and practices

The independent variables relate to the following religious beliefs and practices: *beliefs in God* (theism, individual, social and natural panentheism, deism, pantheism, metatheism); *beliefs concerning Jesus* (Jesus' incarnation, inspiration, liberation, solidarity, and a humanistic view of Jesus); *beliefs concerning Muhammad* (Muhammad's revelatory prophetism, uniqueness, mysticism, Muhammad as a teacher of religious practice, and a humanistic view of Muhammad); *beliefs concerning Rama* (Rama's incarnation, inspiration, liberation, solidarity, and a humanistic view of Rama); *beliefs regarding religious communities* (their prophetism, cultural openness, social inclusiveness, professional orientation, receptiveness to public opinion); *interreligious beliefs* (exclusivism, inclusivism, dialogue, pluralism); *social religious practices* (membership of and participation in a religious community, number of religious friends, religious conversation at home); and *individual religious practices* (reading holy books, especially the Bible, Qur'an, and Vedas, prayer, and religious saliency). [53]

Population characteristics

The population characteristics taken into account are: gender, home language (South Indian and other Indian languages), religious self-definition (Christian, Muslim, Hindu, religious and nonreligious), religious socio-geographic location (traditional or liberal interpretations of Bible, Qur'an, and Vedas), political preference (right, centre right, centre, centre left, and left), political discussion at home, politics as a value, secular values (family, societal critique and autonomy as values), and personality characteristics (neuroticism, psychoticism, extroversion, and lastly the lie scale, interpreted as social conformism).[54]

Statistical procedure

To explore the impact of the students' religious beliefs and practices on their civil rights attitudes, to be controlled for their population characteristics, we conducted a series of regression analyses for each of the 16 civil rights attitudes (see tables 1 and 2). These regression analyses follow a three stage procedure, while using the regression techniques from SPSS for Windows (version 12-1), as well as the regression TEST command from the SPSS-X User's Guide (3rd edition, 1988).

In the first stage the population characteristics are introduced into the regression analysis using the enter method. Next the groups of religious beliefs and practices are inserted according to the test method. This method computes the significance of the R-square changes for each set of religious beliefs (belief in God, Jesus, Muhammad, Rama, religious communities and interreligious interaction) and each group of religious practices (social and individual). The procedure results in some sets of religious beliefs and practices showing a significant R-square change, while others do not. The groups showing a significant R-square change are selected, the others are removed. From the groups of religious beliefs and practices that show a significant R-square change, only those individual variables are selected which yield a significant beta coefficient; the other variables are removed.

In the second stage only the individual variables from the groups of religious beliefs and practices which yield a significant beta coefficient are inserted into the regression equation, together with all population characteristics, this time using the enter procedure only.

In the third stage a special procedure is required to incorporate the students' religious self-definition (Christian, Muslim, Hindu, religious or nonreligious) in the regression analyses. For statistical reasons each of these five religious groups is treated as a dummy variable (values 0 and 1). To compute the effect of each religious group on civil rights attitudes, we decided on Christians as the reference category. The effects of each of the other four groups on civil rights attitudes are computed relative to those of Christians. From these dummy variables a compound variable is constructed covering the religious groups together. This compound variable, i.e. religious self-definition, is inserted into the regression analyses, together with the religious beliefs and practices, selected in the second stage, and all population characteristics, again using the enter procedure only (table 3 and 4).

Sample

As we said earlier, our research population consists of 305 Christians, 298 Muslims, 206 Hindus, 102 religious and 31 nonreligious students, according to their own self-definition, plus 6 students who did not indicate their religious or nonreligious orientation. To be able to make comparisons regarding all the religious beliefs and practices referred to in the expectations we asked all students to answer all items in the questionnaire, including those about Jesus, Muhammad and Rama and about the Bible, the Qur'an and the Vedas.

2.5 Empirical analysis of the effects of religion on civil rights attitudes

We now examine the effects of religious beliefs and practices on the students' civil rights attitudes while controlling for the aforementioned population characteristics.

The results of the regression analyses appear in table 3 (secular civil rights attitudes) and table 4 (religious civil rights attitudes). For comparative purposes only variables with one or more statistically significant beta coefficients (p d" .05) are given in tables 3 and 4. Our verbal report is restricted to the significant (p d" .05) and relevant (beta e" .10) effects shown in tables 3 and 4.

Table 3. Effects of religion on secular human rights (beta coefficients)

Free lifestyle	Free assembly	Free press	Privacy
Item 1 free morals	Item 2 free sex	Item 3 protest	Item 4 strike
Item 5 news papers	Item 6 TV	Item 7 home	Item 8 car

Religious beliefs				
Social panentheism	.11			
Pantheism	-.16			
Metatheism	.13			
Jesus incarnation	.14			
Jesus solidarity	.23			
Muhammad as prophet	.15			
Rama incarnation	.16		-.10	
Prophetic religious communities	.19		.27	
Open religious communities	.11			
Inclusive religious communities			.24	
Religious practices	--	--	-	-
Population characteristics				
Gender-.21	-.14	-.08	-.09	-.16
Language	.10	.		
Religious self-definition	.12	.15		.09
Traditional reading Bible	-.10			
Traditional reading Qur'an	.08	.10		.10
Contextual reading Qur'an	.	.08		-.08
Traditional reading Vedas	-.13	-.10		
Contextual reading Vedas		.12		.10
Political preference	-.08			
Political conversation	.07			
Politics as value			-.08	
Social critique as value	.07			
Autonomy as value.09	.15	.10	.11	.10
Social conformism	.08			
Psychoticism		.08		

Extroversion		.13		
		.08		
N	870	851	844	860
867	866	868	863	
R^2	.10	.14	.10	.12
.13	.04	.07	.06	

p d" .05; variables without any significant beta are not shown in this table.

The first expectation we formulated concerns the negative effect of religious beliefs in absolute transcendence on the students' civil rights attitudes. Tables 3 and 4 show that only belief in an incarnated Rama has a negative effect (on the right to privacy, item 7, beta -.10). The other five transcendent beliefs have a positive effect: belief in an incarnated Jesus on freedom of assembly (item 3, beta .14) and freedom of religious speech (item 13, beta .17), belief in Muhammad's revelatory prophetism on freedom of assembly (item 4, beta .15) and an incarnated Rama on freedom of lifestyle (item 2, beta .16), and belief in inclusivism in interreligious interaction on freedom of religious speech (item 14, beta .20). Thus we find that expectation 1 is not confirmed, with the exception of the negative effect of belief in an incarnated Rama.

We expected religious beliefs marked by immanent transcendence to have a positive effect on civil rights attitudes. In most cases this expectation proved to be correct: social panentheistic belief in God on freedom of lifestyle (item 1, beta .11), Jesus' solidarity on freedom of lifestyle (item 1, beta .23), Rama's liberation on religious freedom (item 12, beta .10), beliefs in prophetic communities on freedom of assembly (item 3, beta .19), on press freedom (item 5, beta .27), on freedom of moral speech (item 15, beta .17), beliefs concerning culturally open communities on freedom of assembly (item 3, beta .11), beliefs regarding socially inclusive communities on freedom of assembly (item 4, beta .24), religious freedom (item 11, beta .11) and freedom of moral speech (item 16, beta .23). Only two beliefs about religious communities have a negative effect: belief in culturally open communities on freedom of religion (item 11, beta -.13) and belief in professional communities on freedom of religious speech (item 14, beta -.11). However, the belief in interreligious dialogue appears to have a positive effect on religious freedom (item 11, beta .11). Thus expectation 2 is mostly confirmed.

Further, we expected secular or secular-religious beliefs marked by absolute immanent traits to have positive effects. This applies to the effect of metatheistic belief in God on freedom of lifestyle (item 1, beta .13), beliefs in Jesus from a humanistic point of view on freedom of religious speech (item 13, beta .19) and in Rama from a humanistic point of view on freedom of moral speech (item 15, beta .14). By contrast pantheistic belief in God has a negative effect on freedom of lifestyle (item 1, beta -.16). Thus expectation 3 is confirmed for the most part, except for the negative effect of pantheistic belief in God.

Remarkably, none of the individual or social religious practices appear to have any relevant or even significant positive effect on civil rights attitudes, either secular or religious. Thus expectation 4 is not confirmed.

As mentioned above, we controlled the effect of religious beliefs and practices for some population characteristics. In the first place we expected gender to have a positive effect on the students' civil rights attitudes. But tables 3 and 4 show that, with one exception, it has only negative effects. It has negative effects on freedom of lifestyle (item 2, beta -.21), assembly (item 4, beta -.14), privacy (item 8, beta -.16), separation of religion and state (item 10, beta -.16), religious freedom (item 12, beta -.19), freedom of religious speech (items 13 and 14, betas -.13 and -.12 respectively), and only one positive effect, namely on freedom of moral speech (item 16, beta .12). Thus expectation 5 is not confirmed.

We expected home language, being an indication of belonging to an ethnic minority, to have some positive effect. It has only one positive effect, namely on freedom of lifestyle (item 2, beta .10). So expectation 6 is only partly confirmed.

Table 4. Effects of religion on religious human rights (beta coefficients

Religion speech | **Religion & state** | **Religious & freedom** | **Moral speech**

Item 9 separate euthanasia Item 10 separate abortion
Item 11 free of religion Item 12 no prayers Item 13
fun of religious Item 14 fun of atheists Item 15 at school
Item 16 in class

Religious beliefs					
Jesus incarnation	.17				
Jesus humanistic view	.19				
Liberation by Rama	.10				
Rama humanistic view	.14				
Prophetic religious communities	.17				
Open religious communities	-.13				
Inclusive religious communities	.11	.23			
Professional religious communities	-.11				
Interreligious inclusivism	.20				
Interreligious dialogue	.11				
Interreligious pluralism	-.09				
Religious practices	-	-	-		
Population characteristics					
Gender	-.16	-.19	-.13	-.12	.12
Religious self-definition	.14	.09	.13	.13	.12
Traditional reading Bible					.09
Contextual reading Bible				.11	
Traditional reading Qur'an	-.12		.08	.08	
Contextual reading Qur'an			.07	.10	
Traditional reading Vedas	-.08		.11	-.09	
Contextual reading Vedas			.08		
Political conversation	-.07			.09	

Politics as value		.08		
Family as value	.09	.10	.11	
Social critique as value	-.08		-.07	
Autonomy as value	.10		-.07	
Social conformism	-.09	.09	-.12	-.10
Neuroticism	-.07			
Psychoticism	.07	.13		
Extroversion	.08	.08		
N	870	860	866	863
862	850	864	867	
R^2	.07	.06	.08	.11
.10	.17	.11	.11	

p d" .05; variables without any significant beta are not shown in this table.

As shown in tables 3 and 4, the students' religious self-definitions have an effect on freedom of lifestyle (item 2, beta .12), the press (item 5, beta .15), separation of religion and state (item 9, beta .14), religious freedom (item 11, beta .13), and freedom of religious speech (items 13 and 14, beta .13 and .12 respectively). Tables 5 and 6 show comparisons between Christians and the other religious groups.

Table 5. Differences in effects of religious self-definition on secular human rights (b coefficients)

Religious self-definition	Free lifestyle Privacy	Free assembly	Free press
Item 1 free morals		Item 2 free sex	Item 3 protest
Item 4 strike	Item 5 news papers	Item 6 TV	Item 7 home
Item 8 car			
Muslim		-.31	-.25

Hindu	
Religious	
Nonreligious	.39

p d" .05; Christians are the reference category

Muslims are less supportive of freedom of lifestyle (item 2, b -.31) and the press (item 5, b -.25), but are more positive about separation of religion and state (item 9, b .33) than Christians. The Hindu and religious categories are more in favour of freedom of religious speech (item 13, b .33 and b .42 respectively) than Christians. The nonreligious group is much more supportive than Christians of freedom of the press (item 5, b .39), separation of religion and state (item 9, b .58) and freedom of religious speech (item 13, b .56). Thus expectation 7 is confirmed.

Table 6. Differences in effects of religious self-definitions on religious human rights (b coefficients)

Religious self-definition	**Religion & state**	**Religion & freedom**	**Religious speech**	**Moral speech**
Item 9 separate euthanasia		Item 10 separate abortion		
Item 11 free of religion		Item 12 no prayers		
Item 13 fun of religious		Item 14 fun of atheists		
Item 15 at school		Item 16 in class		
Muslims	.33			
Hindus		.33		
Religious		.42		
Nonreligious	.58		.56	

p d" .05; Christians are the reference category

As far as traditional and contextual interpretations of holy books are concerned we expected a traditional interpretation to have a negative effect and a contextual interpretation a positive one. Contextual approaches have four and traditional approaches three positive effects, two of which refer to traditional approaches to the Qur'an and one to the Vedas. Contextual interpretations have no negative effects, whereas traditional interpretations have four negative effects. Thus expectation 8 is partly confirmed.

The following group of population characteristics that we inserted into the regression analyses entails three political variables: preference among political parties, frequency of political conversation at home, and the extent to which politics is seen as a value. We expected these to have positive effects. Since this report is confined to significant (p d" .05) and relevant (beta e" .10) effects, there are no positive effects and expectation 9 is not confirmed.

The following population characteristics refer to three values which have played a key role since the Enlightenment: the value of traditional family life, which we expected to have a negative effect, and autonomy and societal critique, both of which were expected to have a positive effect. Contrary to our expectation, traditional family life as a value appears to have a positive effect on separation of religion and state (item 10, beta .10) and on freedom of religious speech (item 14, beta .11). Autonomy as a value has a positive impact on freedom of lifestyle (item 2, beta .15), freedom of the press (item 5, beta .10) and the right to privacy (items 7 and 8, beta .11 and .10 respectively). Thus expectation 10 is confirmed for the most part.[55]

With regard to personality characteristics of our student population, we expected extroversion to have a positive effect, and the other three (social conformism, psychoticism and neuroticism) a negative effect. In fact extroversion has only one positive effect (on freedom of lifestyle, item 2, beta .13). Social conformism does appear to have a negative impact (on freedom of moral speech, items 15 and 16, beta -.12 and -.10

Table 7. Expected and empirically confirmed effects of religious beliefs and practices on civil rights attitudes, controlled for population characteristics

Religious beliefs and characteristics	*population Expected effects*	*Effects practicesand confirmed*	*empirically*	
1. absolute transcendence	negative	no		
2. immanent transcendence	positive	Mostly		
3. absolute immanence	positive	Mostly		
4. individual religious practices	positive	no		
social religious practices	positive	no		
5. gender	positive	no		
6. ethnicity	positive	partly		
7. religious self-definition	positive & negative	Mostly		
8. conservative/liberalholy books	positive &	interpretation	negative	partly
9. political orientations	positive &	negative	no	
10. secular values	positive &	negative	Mostly	
11. personality traits	positive &	negative	Mostly	

respectively). Neuroticism and psychoticism have no significant negative effects.[56] Thus expectation 11 is mostly confirmed.

To sum up: while some expectations are confirmed to some extent, others are not (table 7). The expectations which are most strongly confirmed are expectations 2 and 3 regarding the positive effects of religious beliefs marked by immanent transcendent and absolute immanent orientations, particularly relating to God, Jesus, Muhammad and Rama; beliefs concerning religious communities; and policy-related beliefs on interreligious dialogue. This also applies to expectation 7 about the impact of the students' religious self-definition, which results in the following ranking (in ascending order) of religious groups in terms of their effects on civil rights attitudes: Muslims, Christians, Hindus, religious and nonreligious. Expectation 10 concerning the influence of the students' secular values (traditional family and autonomy) is largely confirmed as well. This also applies to expectation 11 regarding the students' personality traits (extroversion, neuroticism and social conformism). Only partly confirmed are expectation 6 regarding ethnicity (home language is not a perfect predictor), expectation 8 (neither is belonging to or sympathising with the conservative or liberal wing). Unconfirmed are expectation 1 about beliefs characterised by absolute transcendence (they do not always have clearly negative effects), expectation 4 (religious practices do not have any positive effect), expectation 5 (female students generally support civil rights less than their male fellows), and expectation 9 about the students' political orientations (they have no clear impact on civil rights attitudes).

2.6 Discussion

Since it is impossible to reflect on all the outcomes of our research, we focus on a few salient ones. First we consider the limited effects of religion on our students' civil rights attitudes against the broad background of the impact of religion on society in general. Next we deal with the main religious beliefs and the main religious practices in terms of their effects, that is, beliefs concerning religious communities which have the most positive effects, as well as religious practices, both individual and social, which appear to have no effects, positive or otherwise. Lastly we look at the main population characteristic that has a negative effect, namely gender.

Impact of religion on society in general

The effect of religion appears rather limited. This emerges from the relatively low levels of explained variance (R-square), ranging from .04 to .17, the relatively low numbers of significant betas (p d" .05) as well as the relatively low numbers of relevant betas (beta e" .10) regarding the impact of religious beliefs and practices on the students' civil rights attitudes (tables 3 and 4).

The outcome may be linked to the fact that we did not ask our students to indicate what effects they *think* their religiosity has on their attitudes towards civil rights, which is quite common in empirical research; instead we investigated the actual effect. Neither did we ask them to indicate what impact they *want* their religiosity to have on these attitudes – again a common approach – but researched the empirical impact. Nor did we ask them to indicate what effect they think their religiosity *should* have on these attitudes, but concentrated on the actual effect. We did not investigate their thoughts, wants or 'shoulds', but the real effects. What appears from our analyses is that the actual impact of religion on their attitudes towards civil rights is limited.

A further reason for this result may be the way we operationalised the civil rights attitudes in our questionnaire. We did not ask the students to respond to broadly, generally, abstractly formulated values which underlie these civil rights but to concretely formulated norms, connected with concretely formulated situations, to which the civil rights apply. Religion may have strong correlations with values defined in broad terms, that is, on a high level of poly-interpretable ideas, with which different people can easily agree; but when it comes to concrete, sharply delineated norms, that is, on a low level of clear-cut formulations, people easily disagree. In the latter case religion may appear to have less impact than in the former.

Another reason for the result may be that our research deals with the relationship of processes in two different, even separate social domains: the juridico-political domain of civil rights and the religious domain. Evidently higher explanatory levels (indicated by a higher R-square) are found when examining processes in the same domain, for example the effect of democratic attitudes on human rights attitudes or the impact of religious participation on beliefs concerning religious rituals. But when researching processes in two different domains, thus crossing the borders between them (e.g. the juridico-political and religious domains), the impact of processes in one domain on those in the other will appear much lower. This applies particularly inasmuch as the domains are separated through the ongoing process of institutional differentiation, which takes place in the various domains of society according to their own endogenous laws and autonomous mechanisms, obeying their own explicit and implicit codes and proceeding according to their own rules and roles, not those of other domains.[57]

This brings us to the question whether processes in the religious domain influence, or are influenced by, those in other social domains. In the literature scholars approach this question in different ways. From a Marxist perspective religion belongs to the social superstructure of culture, which is determined by the infrastructure of economic processes, while mirroring these processes in a purely ideological way. From a neo-Marxist perspective religion is a life world institution, heavily colonised by economic and political systems, the latter in its turn being heavily colonised by the former.[58] From a Weberian perspective economic (and political) processes are decisive and follow their own course according to their own codes and rules, the only relevant consideration being that worldview systems (including religions) can impede their continuation, progress and pace; hence the sole function of worldview systems is to give the processes in these other domains the go-ahead. In other words, religion has the negative function of not obstructing these processes.[59] Lastly, from a functional, Parsonian perspective religion, being part of culture, helps to direct social processes, especially in the lower domains of society, namely politics and the economy. These lower domains in their turn supply and allocate the resources, without which the higher cultural domains, especially science, ethics, aesthetics, art and religion, cannot exist. In other words, the upper echelons of society give guidance to the lower ones, whereas the latter provide the conditions necessary for the subsistence of the former.[60]

The question is which of these approaches accords best with our empirical findings. Perhaps the Marxist theory goes too far by declaring religion simply a mirroring process, because in that case there should be a one-to-one correspondence between religion and the economy. The neo-Marxist approach affords worthwhile insights which cannot easily be disregarded, namely that religion is dependent on processes in the juridico-political and economic domains and adapts to them rather than the other way round. The Weberian interpretation shows the clearest affinity with our research results, as religious beliefs may obstruct processes in other domains until they give the go-ahead. This could offer the best answer to our question about what religion does and can do to promote what might be seen as both an actual ongoing and a desirable project: the development and continuation worldwide of democratic rule of law, based on universal human rights and the indisputable principle of human dignity. What religion can do is remove obstacles to this project, that is remove hindrances (negative betas) without contributing much to it in a positive way (positive betas). And perhaps the Parsonian approach describes what religious people who wholeheartedly support this democratic process would most like to see happening: support from religious communities and their leaders for this process of freedom and justice, thus setting it free. But on the whole our research does not reflect such a picture.

The main religious beliefs

Having clarified the rather limited effect of religion on the students' civil rights attitudes against the background of religion's impact on society in general, we now focus on two specific aspects of religion that we investigated: the religious beliefs which appear to have the most positive effects and the religious practices which appear to have no effect at all.

Compared to beliefs in God, Jesus, Muhammad and Rama, and interreligious beliefs, those concerning religious communities appear to have the most impact. It is not difficult to guess why. For our student population beliefs in God may be too abstract to be relevant to the concrete, this-worldly affairs to which civil rights refer. For them Jesus, Muhammad and Rama may be too historically distant to be meaningful for the present-day problems that these rights relate to. Similarly, interreligious beliefs may express a policy too remote from their daily interreligious contacts to help resolve the day-to-day issues arising in their multireligious neighbourhoods. In short, in comparison with the abstractness of beliefs in God, the historical distance of beliefs in Jesus, Muhammad and Rama, and the political remoteness of interreligious beliefs, the concrete ways in which religious communities deal with real-life affairs within and between proximate interreligious groups make these communities much more relevant and meaningful. It shows up the abstractness, historical distance and remoteness of beliefs versus the concreteness, actuality and proximity of community role models.

The three characteristics of the religious communities which appear to have the most positive effects are: a prophetic orientation, which directs and guides communities in the direction of equal freedom and social justice in society; an orientation of cultural openness, which refers to receptiveness to cultural innovations in society and working through them critically and constructively;[61] and an orientation of social inclusiveness, in the sense of openness to everybody who may be interested and want to be affiliated and participate in the community. One can also reverse this chain of effects. Insofar as these religious communities are marked by conservatism, which protects a social status quo that lacks freedom and equality, instead of making their critical voice heard prophetically, their effect on civil rights attitudes will be negative. To the extent that they close themselves to the needs, wants and interests of the people – as expressed in the deeper layers of a changing culture – and primarily deal with their own internal affairs, their effects on civil rights attitudes will be no less negative. And as long as they close their doors to outsiders and impose a high threshold for entry and participation, their impact on civil rights attitudes will remain negative. In other words, from the perspective of civil rights the religious communities are challenged to engage in what happens in the minds and hearts of the people, take seriously the questions and problems they grapple with, and commit themselves to helping society to progress towards freedom and justice.

Religious practices

Whereas beliefs concerning religious communities appear to have the most impact on civil rights attitudes, religious practices, both individual and social, show no impact at all. There is no easy explanation – one has to look for one on a more abstract level. On this level the theoretical relationship between religious beliefs and practices may be relevant.

In modern literature beliefs and practices are seen as two of seven aspects of religion, which also has experiential, intellectual, attitudinal, institutional and consequential aspects. In recent literature this list of aspects is reduced to only three: the cognitive (beliefs), practical (ritual) and consequential (moral conduct) aspects,[62] concretised in both institutional and personal forms;[63] or to two, the cognitive (beliefs) and practical (ritual) aspects;[64] or even to just a practical (ritual) aspect,[65] which suggests that ritual practice is considered the core of religion. Does the fact that ritual practice has no effect on civil rights attitudes compromise the meaning and relevance of religion in the area of civil rights in general?

Reversing the question, one might ask: why is it that recent literature devotes so much attention to the aspect of ritual practice? Particularly in the social sciences there is lively discussion about the complex relation between cognitive aspects (beliefs, attitudes) and behaviour. Whereas in the past the accent was on attitudes, in recent decades the emphasis has shifted to behaviour, both ritual and consequential (moral conduct). One reason is that behaviour-focused attention might reduce wishful thinking- and social desirability-driven responses to questionnaire items. Respondents may want, hope for, dream and speculate about all kinds of beliefs and attitudes they find desirable and wish to identify with, but ultimately it is their concrete, concretely observable behaviour that counts. In the area of beliefs people feel at home in the nebulous clouds between heaven and earth, but behaviour is grounded in the rough, gritty soil, the sand and the clay, of everyday life.

Be that as it may, two counter arguments should be mentioned, one statistical, the other empirical. The statistical argument is that factor analyses conducted in various surveys all over the world of the aforementioned five, six or seven aspects of religion did not lead to real consensus on what aspect or aspects might be the most important.[66] Some factor analyses even indicated that the cognitive aspect (beliefs) might constitute the principal or even the exclusive aspect.[67] The empirical argument is that a growing number of people who do believe no longer belong to and participate in religious communities' gatherings and ritual practices. They believe alone and believe only.[68] This insight at least reduces the importance of some elements of what we called social religious practice (social rituals), which leaves the discussion about the relation between religious beliefs and practice open.

The negative effect of gender

Lastly we want to reflect on the most influential population characteristic which emerges from our research, namely gender. Remarkably, although female gender makes a real difference in the area of civil rights, its influence is not positive but negative. This contrasts with the findings of research conducted by one of the authors in another developing country, South Africa, where female students support civil rights more strongly than their male peers.[69]

How do we explain this contrast? We can only speculate. Gender equality is one of the principles of India's constitution, but this has only a gradual effect on the position of women, which is still characterised by submission and suppression. Their situation is reinforced and legitimised by the caste system, which still strongly influences everyday social life in India. What is needed is a process of conscientisation in which female students learn to explore and analyse the situations in which their role patterns prevent them from developing their talents to the full. There is a need for a process of emancipation, in which they learn to overcome the social obstacles that perpetuate discrimination and prevent them from growing and flourishing. What is required is solidarity among women and men alike, in order to launch a struggle for gender equality, using legal instruments, including civil rights, to transform society in that respect. If there is one project religious communities should engage in wholeheartedly it is the process of conscientisation, emancipation and solidarity that will enable women to live the life to which they are entitled on the basis of their equal human dignity.

Conclusion

So what have we learnt from our research? In the first place, the students we investigated show greater support for secular civil rights than for religious civil rights. As mentioned, this lesser support for religious civil rights conflicts with international human rights interpretation and jurisprudence. Secondly, we investigated the effects of their religious beliefs and practices on their attitudes towards civil rights, while controlling for some population characteristics. We found that the effects are limited, and that beliefs in God, Jesus, Muhammad and Rama and the various interreligious beliefs have less impact than those concerning religious communities. The latter are more influential, especially those regarding prophetic, culturally open and socially inclusive communities. Remarkably, the students' religious practices, both individual and social, have no impact at all, that is zero effect. We also found that the population characteristic with the greatest impact compared with all other population characteristics and even all other independent variables is gender. Its impact is almost entirely negative.

All this leads to a question frequently asked in recent times: do human rights need God?[70] On the basis of our research we may rephrase the question: do civil rights need religion? In the strict sense of the word civil rights do not need religion for legitimation, but in a Weberian sense religion may give the go-ahead and contribute to a social civil rights campaign, especially on behalf of those who suffer most from the lack of equal freedom and free equality.

Lastly, we may rephrase the problem stated at the beginning of this article: does social integration need religion? Again, strictly speaking, the answer is no as far the legitimation of integration is concerned, but in a Weberian perspective it may give the go-ahead and promote it step by step, not only as a necessary condition, but also as a meaningful and favourable condition. This applies particularly to the social integration of women. Here religious communities can contribute actively to the process of conscientisation, emancipation and solidarity that will enable women to live the life they are entitled to on the basis of the core principle of equal human dignity.

End Notes:

1. Valkenberg, P. 2006. Sharing Lights On the Way to God. Muslim-Christian Dialogue and Theology in the Context of Abrahamic Partnership. Amsterdam/New York: Rodopi, 150-162, 197.

2. Sam, D. 2006. Acculturation: conceptual background and core components. D. Sam & J. Beryy (Eds.). *The Cambridge Handbook of Acculturation Psychology* (p. 11-26). Cambridge: Cambridge University Press, 14-17
3. Van der Ven, J.A. 2006. A Chapter in Public Theology from the perspective of Human Rights *Journal of Religion* 86(2006)3, 412-441.
4. Devasahayam, J.R. 2007. *Human Dignity in Indian Secularism and in Christianity*. PhD Diss. Radboud University Nijmegen.
5. Heidegger, M. 1993. *Sein und Zeit*. Tübingen: Max Niemeyer Verlag.
6. Theunissen, M. 1965. Der Andere. Studien zur Sozialontologie der Gegenwart. Berlin: De Gruyter.
7. Buber, M. 1977. *Ich und Du*. Heidelberg: Lambert Schneider.
8. Levinas, E. 1969. *Totality and Infinity*. Pittsburgh: Duquesne University Press. Cf. Ricoeur, P. 2005. *The Course of Recognition*. Cambridge: Harvard University Press, 157ff.
9. Berry, J. 2006. Contexts of Acculturation. D. Sam & J. Beryy (Eds.). *The Cambridge Handbook of Acculturation Psychology* (p. 27-42). Cambridge: Cambridge University Press., 34-35.
10. Aristotle 1984. *The Complete Works of Aristotle*. The Revised Oxford Translation. Edited by Johanthan Barnes. Princeton: Princeton University Press, 1054a20ff.
11. Aristotle, ibidem, 210a16, 1023b29.
12. Zagorin, P. 2003. *How the Idea of Religious Tolerancc Came to the West*. Princeton; Princeton University Press.
13. Forst, R. 2003. *Toleranz im Konflikt*. Frankfurt: Suhrkamp, 42-45.
14. Ibidem, 53-69.
15. For example, *Dominus Jesus* 2000.
16. Religious freedom is an individual, not a collective right.
17. Taylor, P. 2005 *Freedom of Religion*, Cambridge: Cambridge University Press, 67-70.
18. Masuzawa, T. 2005. *The Invention of World Religions*. Chicago: University of Chicago Press.

19. Taylor, C. 1989. *Sources of the self. The making of the modern identity*. Cambridge: Harvard University Press.
20. Berger P. 1983. The concept of shame. S. Hauwerwas. *Changing perspectives in moral philosophy* (172-180). Notre Dame: Notre dame University Press.
21. Kant, I. 1964. *Groundwork of the Metaphysics of Morals*. New Yor: Harper & Row
22. Honneth, A. 1994. Kampf um Anerkennung. Zur moralischen Grammatik sozialer Konflikte. Frankfurt: Suhrkamp.
23. Ricoeur, P., o.c., 69-149.
24. Nussbaum, M. 2006. *Frontiers of Justice. Disability, Nationality, Species Membership*. Cambridge: Harvard University Press, 76.
25. Wils, J.-P. 2006. *Nachsicht. Studien zu einer ethisch-hermeneutischen Basiskategorie.* Paderborn: Schöningh.
26. Nussbaum, o.c., 288-289, even though we know that certain dictatorial regimes use this argument as a pretext to maintain the status quo.
27. The two treaties, which originally constituted a single treaty, were eventually separated to prevent refusal to ratify socio-economic and cultural rights from blocking ratification of civil and political rights as well.
28. E.g. Pius VI, Pius VII, Gregory XVI, Pius IX.
29. E.g. Leo XIII.
30. E.g. Leo XIII, Pius XI: Dondeyne, A. 1962. *Geloof en wereld.* Antwerpen: Patmos.
31. Agius E., Chircop L (Eds.). 1998. *Caring for Future generations. Jewish, Christian and islamic Perspectives*. Twickenham: Adamantine Press; Baderin, M. 2005. *International Human Rights and Islamic Law*. Oxford: Oxford University Press; Bucar, E., Barnett, B. 2005. *Does Human Rights Need God?* Grand Rapids: Eerdmans; Runzo, J. 2003. *Human Rights and Responsibilities in the World Religions*. Oxford: Oneworld; Van der Vyver, J.D. & Witte, J. (Eds.) *Religious human rights in global perspective. Legal perspectives* .The Hague: Nijhoff; Witte, J., Van der Vyver, J.D. (Eds.) *Religious human rights in global perspective. Religious perspectives* (pp. 121–141). The Hague:

Nijhoff; Witte, J. Alexander, F. (Eds.). 2006. *The Teachings of Modern Christianity on Law, Politics and Human Nature*. Vol. I-II. New York: Columbia University Press.

32. For the history of the codification and reception of human rights in the Catholic and Protestant traditions, see: Van der Ven, J.A. Dreyer, J.S., Pieterse H.J.C. 2004. *Is There a God of Human Rights?* Leiden: Brill, 213ff., 243ff., 245ff.; 247ff.
33. Dihle, A. 1962, *Die goldene Regel.* Göttingen: Vandenhoeck & Ruprecht, p. 80-82.
34. Ricoeur, P. 1994. Entre philosophie et théologie I: La Règle d'Or en question (273-280). *Lectures 3*. Paris: Deuil.
35. Ricoeur, P. 1992. *Oneself as Another*. Chicago: Chicago University Press.
36. I. Kant, o.c., 96.
37. Nussbaum, o.c., 70, 74, interprets human dignity in terms of human beings as ends in themselves, which applies to each and every person and thus forms the intuitive basis of human rights. This interpretation of human dignity requires an *impartial* approach to others, according to Nussbaum 12, 37.
38. Weber M. 1980. *Wirtschaft und Geselschaft*. Tübingen: Mohr, 5-6; Kalberg S. 2001. *Einführung in die historisch-vergleichende Soziologie Max Webers*. Wiesbaden: Westdeutscher Verlag, 202ff.
39. Means in this study are interpreted as follows: strongly disagree 1.00-1.79, disagree 1.80-2.59, neither agree nor disagree 2.60-3.39, agree 3.40-4.19, strongly agree 4.20-5.00.
40. Here we refer to other parts of our survey research not reported in this article so far.
41. Art. 29B, 29C, 29D, 29E, 29F, 29G. Neither the International Covenant on Civil and Political Rights (1966), article 20, nor the International Convention on the Elimination of all Forms of racial Discrimination (1966), article 4, mentions *intentional* incitement, only incitement (Lerner, N. 1996. Religious Human Rights under the United Nations. Van der Vyver, J.D. & Witte, J. (Eds.) *Religious human rights in global perspective. Legal perspectives* (79-134).The Hague: Nijhoff, 93).

42. Art. 29J: "Nothing in this Part shall be read or given effect in a way which prohibits or restricts discussion, criticism or expressions of antipathy, dislike, ridicule, insult or abuse of particular religions or the beliefs or practices of their adherents, or of any other belief system or the beliefs or practices of its adherents, or proselytising or urging adherents of a different religion or belief system to cease practising their religion or belief system." The criterion of hate speech is not lack of tolerance or respect nor insults but, according to long-standing jurisprudence, as noted, (intentional) incitement of hatred (P. Taylor, o.c., 77-84).
43. Cotler, I. 1996. Jewish NGOs and Religious Human Rights: A Case Study. Witte, J., Van der Vyver, J.D. (Eds.) Religious human rights in global perspective. Religious perspectives (pp. 235-294). The Hague: Nijhoff.
44. Ravitch, F. 1999 School Prayer and Discrimination, Boston 1999; Ravitch, F. 2000. A Crack in the Wall: Pluralism, Prayer, and Pain in the Public Schools. S. Feldman (Ed.), Law and Religion (p.296-315). New York: New York University Press. Witte, J. 2005. Religion and the American constitutional experiment. Essential rights and liberties. Second Edition. Boulder: Westview.
45. Cotler, o.c., 250.
46. Part one of the article was published in the previous issue of Salesianum.
47. Ziebertz, H.-G., Kalbheim B., Riegel U. 2003. Religiöse Signaturen heute. Ein religionspädagogischer Beitrag zur empirischen Jugendforschung. Freiburg: Herder, 61-86.
48. Halman, L., Riis, O. 2003. *Religion in Secularizing Society*. Leiden: Brill.
49. Van der Ven, J.A. 1998. God Reinvented? A Theological Search in Texts and Tables. Leiden: Brill.
50. Van der Ven J.A., Dreyer, J.S., Pieterse, H.J.C., o.c.
51. Ibidem, 585.
52. Israel, J. 2001. *Radical Enlightenment. Philosophy in the Making of Modernity 1650-1750.* Oxford: Oxford University Press; Israel,

J. 2006. *Enlightenment Contested. Philosophy, Modernity and the Emancipation of Man 1670-1752*. Oxford: Oxford University Press.

53. All religious scales, constructed from two or three items, were inspected for their reliability (alpha e" .60). Only one scale does not satisfy this criterion, i.e. individual panentheism constructed from two items (alpha .48).

54. The three secular values scales (Eisinga 2002) and the four personality scales (Francis 2007) stem from internationally validated instruments, but do not meet the reliability criterion (secular values: alpha .47, .19, .40; personality scales: alpha .57, .19, .37, .56). Nevertheless we keep them for comparative reasons in the framework of the cross-cultural program 'Human Rights and Religion'. But this fact has to be taken into account in relation to the interpretation of some outcomes in the analyses below. This especially applies to the value of societal critique and the personality trait of psychoticism (see note 54 and 55).

55. The impact of societal critique, mentioned in note 53, is not relevant (beta < .10).

56. The impact of psychoticism, mentioned in note 53, on the freedom of religious speech (beta .13) is not important because of the low alpha of the scale.

57. Luhmann, N. 1990. *Die Wissenschaft der Gesellschaft*. Frankfurt: Suhrkamp; Luhmann, N. 1997. *Die Gesellschaft der Gesellschaft I-II*. Frankfurt: Suhrkamp.

58. Habermas, J. 1982. *Theorie des kommunikativen Handelns I–II*. Frankfurt: Suhrkamp; Habermas, J. 1993 Faktizität und Geltung. Beiträge zur Diskurstheorie des Rechts und des demokratischen Rechtsstaats. Frankfurt: Suhrkamp.

59. Weber, M. 1920/1978. *Gesammelte Aufsätze zur Religionssoziologie*. Tübingen: Mohr, 252.

60. Parsons, T. 1953. *Working Papers in the Theory of Action*. Glencoe: The Free Press; Parsons, T. 1959. *Structure and Process in Modern Societies*. Glencoe: The Free Press; Williamson, O. 2000. The New Institutional Economics: Taking Stock, Looking Ahead. *Journal of Economic Literature* 38(2000)595-613; Sakwa, M.

2006. Bible and Povery in Kenya. An Empirical Exploration. PhD Dissertation Radboud University Nijmegen, 90.

61. The negative beta (-.13) of cultural openness in relation to religious freedom, which prohibits politicians interfering with religious communities (item 11), may be interpreted as expressing openness to politicians' cultural convictions regarding the position and role of these communities in modern society.
62. Jacobsohn G. 2003. *The wheel of law. India's secularism in comparative constitutional context.* Princeton : Princeton University Press, 31-48.
63. On the basis of Stark and Glock's proposal one of the authors, together with two colleagues, worked out a framework of religious practice that comprises cognitive, normative (consequential) and expressive (ritual) systems in both institutional and personal forms: Anthony, F.V., Herrmans C., Sterkens C. 2007. Religious practice and religious socialization: comparative research among Christian, Muslim and Hindu students in Tamilnadu, India. *Journal of Empirical Theology,* 20 (2007) 100-128.
64. Pals, D. 1996. *Seven Theories of Religion.* New York: Oxford University Press, 270, 282-283.
65. Asad, T. 1993. Genealogies of Religion. Baltimore: The John Hopkins University Press, 27-54.
66. Wulff, D. 1997. *Psychology of Religion.* New York: Wiley, 208-219.
67. Felling, A., Peters, J., Schreuder O. 1987. *Religion im Vergleich.* Frankfurt: Lang.
68. Davie, G. 2002. *Europe: The Exceptional Case.* London.
69. Van der Ven, J.A. et al. 2004, o.c., 585.
70. Bucar, E., Barnett, B. 2005. *Does Human Rights Need God?* Grand Rapids: Eerdmans.

4

Human Rights in India Its prospective nature towards 21st Century

M. Kaliyapermal

Introduction

The theory and practice of Human Rights in India and in International level are discussed in its various spectrum by ths Social scientists. The subject of Human Rights has been widely talked about in India and aborad in the early sixties of the last century by various Committees, Commissions, study- groups. Observing authorities have been taken up the matter and gave their ways and means and also the future plans to safeguard the Human Rights for the days to come. This paper analyse the origin of Human Rights, the evolution of Human Rights, in various aspects, the infringments of Human Rights by various organised agencies and finally how to project the Human Rights in the coming days is also suggested for opinion of the future generation. The opinions of the political and other social scientists are considered as the theme of this paper, trying to throw certain points for valuable suggestions.

The origin of the Human Rights

Ever since the "State" was formed, the "Government" had given assurance to the people to protect their Human Rights within the frame work of their rules regulations and social values.

Perhaps this might have been the practice during the hey days of the Greek Civilisation. Following the Greek, the Romans the Phoneisions have left various suggestion in their classical civilization of Human Rights. Even in the Artha Sasthra, Kautilya prescribed certain rights for human beings in their professional spheres. The earliest Sagam Literature of the Tamil People had many poetic expression of the then people. Human Rights towards the state and vice versa. In the early South Indian Sociological ethics, the Cholas and Vijayanagara rulers had the minimum level of Human Rights for the artisans and professional Guild and in inscriptions such rights are indicated as called Kula Dharma an Vardhaga Dharma. As long as the prescribed rules and regulations are practically followed by the people the respective government had assured their Human Rights in their limited sphere within a narrow space. Therefore the medieval and modern India was not ignorant of the human rights and its various dimensions.

Human Rights in India
In European flavour

When the western nation had contracted the Oriental land, we are instructed a new meaning and vision of the Human Rights in larger scope. Perhaps it was the India Company people brought the sociological principles of the human rights. The earlier western though it Indian came across with reference to Human Rights through the book of John Locke (1632-1704) entitled "The Two treatise on Government" where in he said,

"As long the state had control over the people. It must protect the people their life, speech, religion, desire, profession etc., and any encrochment by other agency must be immediately prevented by the organised government".

Perhaps this was the greater aim of the established Government. The similar views was infact pronounced by Thiruvalluvar in a particular chapter on duty of the Government and if the king does not protect the people then it is not a state, but a forest where tigers live.

Following John Lcke, perhaps the most comprehensive meaning o the Human Rights has been given by the French traveller in the United States in the middle of the 18th century. In his famous book Democracy in America. French Traveller Alex De Toqueville had given the success of democracy and even in the republican tendency mainly depend upon the efforts of the government to protect the Human Rights within the jurisdiction. Unless or otherwise there is no sense in calling a Government as Democratic one. Most probably, Thomas Jefferson who was the high priest of democracy and believed to be the Ghost author of the Federalist Paper was the first persoin who put it Human Rights in the declaration of American Independence in 1776. Even in his first message to the Congress be declared.

"I have sworn upon the alter of God to raise external hostility against every form of tyranny over the mind of men."

In the declaration of Independence he said Man is given the right of life, liberty and pursuit of happiness. These three rights are sent by God as they are not be separated from human being. Therefore the word inalienable rights. Even the French Declaration of Human Rights of man in 1789 declared the Concept of Liberty Equality and Frertinity, as three pillars of Human Rights, which were subsequently equated with democratic principles.

In 1945, the United Nation Charter in its many articles had given complete protection for Human Rights particularly Article 1. The Human Right in language and religion, Article 13, the protection of fundamental freedom, Article 55, the protection of race, language and religion etc. The universal Declaration of Human Right by UNO on December 10, 1948 had doubtedly with much clarity, had given 30 articles to protect the Human Rights.

Human Rights in India

As already related the Human Rights protection by the organised Government with empires was not fully unknown to India. Even the Sanskrit vedas pronounced certain in seperable rights to the people. In South India during the medieval period the great emperor Krishnadevaraya in his famous book Principles of the Government. "Amutha Malthya" had devoted a chapter that the primary duty of every government is the protection of the human rights of the people within his empire. Moreover he has also insisted the human rights and duties towards the state and they were the two sides of the coin without which a successful government cannot be administered. Even in Akbarnama. There is a chapter on Human Rights in the Quranic Standard. It was followed until Aurangazeb period upto 1648 A.D.,

When the western democratic principle of Anglo – Saxon Government had contact with India, the introduction of various government of India Act and in 1950 we have the present constitution which in III chapter had very comprehensive aspect of Human Fundamental Rights. No constitution of the world has given so much enlightment and comprehensive expressions as the Indian constitution has it, on Human Rights. But the Human Rights are subjected to easy separation to the emergency provision. In the past fifty years the working of the present Indian Constitution had undoubtedly proved that the human rights mainly remained. But on the other hand from the late sixties down to 2000 in Tamil Nadu. Orissa, Bihar, Madhya Pradesh and very recently the killing of the Pandits in Kashmir and kidnapping of a children by the gang of people to make the boys and girls as beggers in Metropolitan areas of clear and classical evidences that human rights both theory and practice became both inhuman and unhuman. The police Report submitted to the Govt of India about the activities of Tihar Jail NewDelhi, in 1998. The underground dons of Mumbai, the highly sophisticated, the redliht mafias of greater metropolies are the dear evidences in India of the gross violation and very spirit of the Human Rights is dismandelled by the authorities concerned and the most barbarious dhadhas.

Every day the Indian Newspapers are reporting the constitutionally enshrined human rights in all walks of life are crumbling both day and nights in the court and outside on public and private places and the development of scientific devices such as mulitimedias, cellualar phones RDX bombs, rifles are the clear villians of the sacred human rights not only Indian 's and in International citizens.

The author of the present article wants to draw the attention of the audience by citing two examples that happend after independence and only two incidents here to note that mear law in paper, interpretation in the court, various regulations by the police and administrative tribunes, vigilance departments and various -branches of secret services are mere waste unless the great English Philasopher and Orator Edmund Burke once pronouned "Only one thing that can change the whole humanity is actually the change the whole humanity is actually the change of heart". The problem must be assessed and analysed in the subconcious mind and therefore a physcologi-eal approach is more viable thatn a constitutional ora legal approach to make Human Rights stand straight.

The first incident which is worthy of note here is the Kilvenmani massacre of Tanjore District and the final judgement given in that case and secondly the author want to evoke your imagination the frequent genocide in Bihar and Orissa where the tribal people are frequently killed like small birds in the name of the caste. Where is th.e human rights and the tentackles of the great law? Where are the custodians, who are paid by the Government to Uphold the Human Rights theory?

In 1968, the then sitting M.P. in Lok Sabha by name L. Ilayaperumal was assaigned to study the social status and treatment of the Tribal people and schedule caste people in India. He had submitted the report in 1968 in the Parliament subsequently called L. Ilayaperumal Commission Report. When the Report was under discussion in the same session of the Lok Sabha, the Report given by Vikram Sarabai the great scientist and the Report given by Homee babha were also considered in Lok Sabha. One member of the Parliament very sarcastically remarked the happenings the following words, he said, "in India we have a simultanious growth in the one hand, classical barbarious tendency on the other hand the hightech scientific development I do not know when the two ends will meet or may not meet.[6s] Therefore the Human Rights with reference to India are only passing dangerous cross road.

Conclusion:

The paper lightly touched the origin and the development Human Rights from the classical civilisation down to the 20th century. In India the Human Rights was popularised and protected by the successive monachs. However it had its own failures and success. The introduction of the western political principles made the human rights as the legal statue and various agencies have been created to give the new life and a meaning to the human life. But it is very unfortunate the more attention that we are paying, the greater care we are nourishing, we received only less dividend. Has not there a solution? The only solution is that the Great Mahatma once said,

"For many social problems and evils in India which eroded the very deep of the Indian Culture the immediate solution is a spontanious brain wash all rational change of mind ".

This is possible not today, tomorrow sometimes in future and we are waiting for the day where there will be no exploitation, at this points only Jesus Christ, Mahatma Gandhi and Karl Marx they look a single focal point for the welfare of the Universal humanity. On that day the Human Rights will be more meaningful pregnant with the greater message to the world.

References

1. Dr. Dunnings, Political Philosophy, Asian publication, New Delhi, 1974, edition, vol.ll, see the Essay on John Locke, pp.55-56.
2. See 39th Athikaram of Tirukkural.
3. Alex De Tocqueville Democracy in America translated in English by Dr. Beard. Penyulvania University, Indian edition of 1970, Vikas Publication, New Delhi, See chapter IV Book IV.

4. L.D. White, The Jeffersonians, Random House, New York, (Reprint) 1972. p.57.
5. N. Venkaramaniya (Trans) Amutha Mallithiya of Krishna Devaraya (Kannada). Mysore, 1968, Canto 12-13.
6. Dr.S. Quershi, The Multal structure and principles of Government, Kitab Mahal, Allahabad, 1945 edition, Chapter III.
7. G. Huge, Life and Times of Edmund Burke, Blackie & sons, London, 1982, Chapter on the speeches of Edmund Burke in the Parliament, P.152.
8. Louis Fisher, The Mahatma Gandhi, Blackie & Sons, New Delhi, reprint of the book 1932, interview with Gandhi at Sabarmati Ashram indicated in the IV chapter, p.84.

5

Children's Rights: Investing in Future

A. Karuppiah & M. John Sundar

Introduction

To guarantee the human rights of children is to invest in the future. Children's rights are the building blocks for a solid human rights culture, the basis for securing human rights for future generations. As human beings, children are entitled to all the rights guaranteed by the Universal Declaration of Human Rights (UDHR) and the various treaties that have developed from it. But children also need special protection and care. They must be able to depend on the adult world to take care of them, to defend their rights and to help them to develop and realize their potential. Governments pay almost universal lip service to this ideal, yet have signally failed to ensure that the rights of children are respected.

Children suffer many of the same human rights abuses as adults, but may also be targeted simply because they are dependent and vulnerable. Children are tortured and mistreated by state officials; they are detained, lawfully or arbitrarily, often in appalling conditions; in some countries they are subjected to the death penalty. Countless thousands are killed or maimed in armed conflicts; many more have fled their homes to become refugees. Children forced by poverty or abuse to live on the streets are sometimes detained, attacked and even killed in the name of social cleansing. Many millions of children work at exploitative or hazardous jobs, or are the victims of child trafficking and forced prostitution. Because children are "easy targets", they are sometimes threatened, beaten or raped in order to punish family members who are not so accessible.

The international community has long recognized the need to protect children from such abuses. The 1959 UN Declaration of the Rights of the Child set out 10 principles which provided a powerful moral framework for children's rights, but which were not legally enforceable. The Convention on the Rights of the Child (CRC) was adopted by the UN General Assembly in 1989, and entered into force the following year. Since then, the CRC has been ratified by every single UN member state in the world, except Somalia — which has had no central government able to do so for many years — and the United States of America (USA).

The CRC elaborates rights according to the special needs and perspectives of the child. It is the only human rights treaty that covers the full spectrum of civil, political, economic, social and cultural rights, stressing their indivisible and interdependent relationship. By virtue of its comprehensive nature and near-universal ratification, the CRC stands as a landmark for the international consensus on the basic principles of the universality and indivisibility of all human rights.

According to the CRC, every human being under the age of eighteen is a child, unless majority is attained earlier under national law. This stipulation poses important challenges for the application of the CRC, especially in countries where the age of majority is linked to puberty, often different for boys and girls. Under the CRC, all states are required to establish a minimum age of criminal responsibility, which according to The Beijing Rules1, should "not be fixed at too low an age level, bearing in mind the facts of emotional, mental and intellectual maturity". And even though a state may set the age of criminal responsibility below 18, the rights in the CRC still apply, especially those governing the child's treatment at the hands of law enforcement and judicial authorities.

One of the guiding principles of the CRC is that the "best interests of the child" should be a primary consideration in all decisions or procedures related to the child. Children have the right to be heard and to have their own opinions on matters affecting them taken into account, "in accordance with the age and maturity of the child". Very young children rely on others to express their views and protect their best interests; as they grow older, they become more and more able to speak for themselves and to engage in decision-making on their own behalf.

It is up to governments to ensure that all children enjoy their rights. No child should suffer discrimination. The rights of the CRC apply regardless of "race, colour, sex, language, religion, political or other opinion, national, ethnic or social origin, property, disability, birth or other status". The essential message is equality of opportunity. Girls should be given the same opportunities as boys. Poor children, disabled children, refugee children, children of indigenous or minority groups should have the same rights as all others, the same opportunities to learn, to grow, to enjoy an adequate standard of living.

Categories of Rights

The rights contained in the CRC fall into four broad categories:

- **subsistence rights:** including the rights to food, shelter and health care;
- **development rights:** which allow children to reach their fullest potential, including education and freedom of thought, conscience and religion;
- **protection rights:** such as the right to life, and to protection from abuse, neglect or exploitation;

- **participation rights:** which allow children to take an active role in community and political life.

One of the key differences between the CRC and other treaties is that it recognizes that rights must be actively promoted if they are going to be enforced. People who know their rights are better able to claim them, and Article 42 imposes a responsibility on governments to make the CRC widely known to adults and children alike.

The CRC deals not just with child rights, but with the responsibility of the child to respect the rights of others in their family and community. It recognizes that all children should be able to grow up in a happy and loving family environment, and stipulates that the family has a duty to help children understand both their rights and their responsibilities, in order to prepare them to live "in the spirit of peace, dignity, tolerance, freedom, equality and solidarity".

While the CRC emphasizes that the family is the natural environment for nurturing the child, it places the primary obligation on the state to protect children from all forms of abuse, neglect and exploitation, even where these are not carried out directly by state agents. In this way, the CRC challenges the traditional perception that states are not responsible for abuses committed within the family or the community. Domestic violence, bonded child labour or child prostitution, for instance, are usually perpetrated by private individuals, but governments can be held accountable for failing in their responsibility to protect children from such abuses.

Implementation of the CRC is overseen by the Committee on the Rights of the Child. The Committee comprises 10 experts "of high moral standing and recognized competence in the field".2 They are elected by secret ballot of all state parties to the CRC, each of which may nominate one national expert. Because the CRC is so wide-ranging, covering social policy as well as law, the Committee usually includes people from a wide variety of professional backgrounds, such as human rights and international law, juvenile justice, social work, medicine, journalism and governmental and non-governmental work.

Governments are obliged to report to the Committee within two years of the treaty coming into effect in their country, specifying the steps taken to bring national laws, policy and practice into line with the principles of the CRC. The Committee examines the facts and hears a wide range of evidence relevant to the government's report, often from non-governmental organizations (NGOs), and meets with each government to discuss its child rights record. The Committee advises governments on the implementation of the CRC, and engages them in substantive policy discussions on the resolution of specific children's rights issues. At the end of the process, the Committee adopts "concluding observations", which provide a series of recommendations on how states can improve their implementation of the provisions of the CRC. Governments must submit progress reports every five years.

The only regional treaty on children's human rights, the African Charter on the Rights and Welfare of the Child (the African Children's Charter), was adopted by the Organization of African Unity in 1990. The African Children's Charter is rooted in other human rights treaties, such as the UDHR and CRC, but it emerges out of the social and cultural values of Africa, including those relating to family, community and society. In some respects, the African Children's Charter strengthens the protections afforded by the CRC: it stipulates that everyone below the age of eighteen is a child, without exception; it enjoins states parties not to recruit children to military service; and internally displaced children are accorded the same rights as refugees. In addition, the African Children's Charter seeks to eliminate harmful social and cultural practices, in particular those that are discriminatory or that put the health of the child at risk.

Child Labour As Against Children's Rights

The definition of child labour varies. In the dictionary, child labour is defined as physical or mental work, especially hard or exploitative work, forced upon children. Commonly, child labour can be understood as the work done by children who are under the age of 15, or 14 in certain backward or developing countries. It includes any type of work that damages, restricts or risks the children's physical or mental growth. It has not only to do with the hampering with the physical and mental growth of the children working, but also their emotional, social and spiritual growth as well. It is common knowledge that when one speaks of child labour, one means work that is intolerable or harmful to children. It means work that denies the child to play or to go to school like his more fortunate peers. But this does not mean that it can be taken for granted that all work is harmful to children. Safe work in the right proportion may help instill a sense of responsibility in children and also help them learn new skills.

The ILO (International Labour Organization) estimates the number of child labourers in the world today to be around 250 million children who are between the ages of 5 and 14, more than half of them working full time. Child labour presents problems dealing, not only with exploitation, but also poverty, child starvation and malnutrition, social and economic structure, education and also the status of women in society. The ILO estimates that 61 percent of the world's child labour occurs in Asia, 32 percent in Africa and 7 percent in Latin America.

Children are beaten, confined and restricted to their work places, not even given permission to visit or go back to their families at their will. The children are forced to work for long hours every day of the week, in highly congested little rooms, as in the case of rug looms in India, or made to work in dangerous environments of machinery and chemicals causing alarming side effects like arthritis, eye damage, lung disease and stunted growth.

Child Labour In India

Child Labour, in India, has to do more with the rural areas than the urban areas. Usually, about 90 percent of the children working in the rural areas work in the field of agriculture and agriculture related activities. In both the rural and urban areas, the informal or unorganized sectors, like small shops and small pieces of cultivation lands, account for most of the child labour happening in the area.

The poverty line in the Indian context means a basic distinction between people in India who can afford the basic amount of food calories necessary for life everyday, and those who can't. Those who can are said to be above the poverty line and those who can't, are said to be under it. Those states that have a larger population living under the poverty line have more incidence of child labour. Due to the high child labour incidence in these states, naturally more children drop out of school to go to work. The amount of child labour happening in an area also integrally depends on the social and economic development and mindset of the people living in that particular area. The attitudes of parents in the context of the socio-economic development in the area, also accounts for the number of child labourers in the area. The number of children working in India, according to the 1991 census, was about 11.28 million.

Apart from the Child Labour (Prohibition and Regulation) Act, 1986, there are many laws that have the protection and interest of the working children in mind. Some of them are the Factories Act and the Minimum Wages Act, both passed in 1948, the Plantations Labour Act, 1951, the Mines Act, 1952, the Motor Transport Worker's Act, 1961, and the Beedi and Cigar Workers (Conditions of Employment) Act, 1966.

In order to pay attention to the situation, the government of India's Labour Ministry also appointed a 16 member committee. The chairman of the committee was Shri M.S. Gurupadaswamy. The report of the committee states that *"Extreme poverty, lack of opportunity for gainful employment and intermittency of income and low standards of living are the main reasons for the prevalence of child labour. Though it is possible to identify the child labour in the organized sector, which forms a miniscule of the total child labour, the problem relates mainly to the unorganized sector where utmost attention needs to be paid. The problem is universal, but in our case, it is more crucial."I*

This now brings us to the question of what the labouring children are doing in terms of work and how important they are to their families who rely on them for financial support. The 1981 census of India said that child labor occurs in nine industrial divisions. They are cultivation, agricultural labour, livestock (also including forestry, fishing and plantation), construction, trade and commerce, transportation, storage, communication, and other services. In accordance with the industrial division, it was observed that the majority of the children working in the rural sector, 84.29 percent, work in cultivation and agricultural labour. In the urban sector, 39.16 percent of the urban child labourers work in manufacturing, processing, servicing and repairs.

Child labour is an integral source of income for poor families below the poverty line. The ILO conducted a study and found that *"Children's work was considered essential to maintaining the economic level of households, either in the form of work for wages, of help in household enterprises or of household chores in order to free adult household members for economic activity elsewhere."* In the study, it was also found that, in many cases, 34 to 37 percent of the household's total income was contributed to, by children going to work. This concludes that the child labourer's income is essential to the livelihood of a poor family. We cannot blame the parents of these children for being compelled to send their children to work as these families have no other alternate sources of income. The poor Indian families have no proper welfare systems as the west does, nor do they have easy access to loans.

The ILO's studies show that children are paid less than their adult counterparts for the same type of work. Child labourers are used mostly because owners find them to be easily exploitable. Adult workers have the sense to form unions and demand their work's worth as their salary. Children are young and do not understand the meaning of forming unions or asking for more wages. Those that do, are manipulated and severely beaten, thus suppressing their cry for justice by using physical force on them. Also because of this, other children learn from examples of what happened to their peers, that they shouldn't rebel or the suffering that their peers went through will come to them.

Bonded Child Labour

Bonded labour means that a family takes a debt from a landowner or a moneylender and agrees to repay the debt by sending their children to work off the debt to the lender. These lenders charge such high rates of interest that the child isn't even able to work off the debt in his life time and the debt is passed on from generation to generation. This means that if a child could not work off his family's debt in his lifetime, his child would work for the lender after him and his child after him generation after generation as the debt grows bigger and bigger due to the accumulation of high rates of interests to be paid back.

Bonded labour has been outlawed by the 1956 United Nations Supplementary Convention on the Abolition of Slavery, the Slave Trade, and Institutions and Practices Similar to Slavery.

Bonded labour is mostly prevalent in the rural sector in the fields of agriculture and domestic work. Millions of child labourers work as bonded labourers in India alone. As documented in the *Human Rights Watch 2003 report, Small Change: Bonded Child Labour in India's Silk Industry,* and *1996 report, The Small Hands of Slavery: Bonded Child Labour in India.* A number of bonded labourers are subject to severe physical, emotional and sexual abuse, as cited in the *July 1995 Human Rights Watch report, Contemporary Forms of Slavery in Pakistan.*

Domestic Work

People don't even consider domestic labour to be a part of child labour. These children who work in domestic households alone, are hidden from the scrutiny of the public and their lives are controlled by their employers. Often domestic working children are of the age wherein they don't know what to do when they are verbally, physically or emotionally abused. Due to the amount of work given to them, they are forced to quit school in order to spend more time on doing household chores for their employers. Since these children are hidden away in the privacy of homes, they are particularly vulnerable to sexual abuse. They may be fired for small mistakes they may commit, losing not only their jobs and place of residence, but their daily sustenance as well.

The ILO has estimated that more girls work as domestic labour than any other form of child labour. But even though this is the case, they receive no protection or attention what so ever. The government laws often pay less attention to the basic labour rights of domestic workers. The condition of these domestic workers in private houses are rarely looked into, and there are very few programs that address the issue of child domestic labour.

Child Soldiers

Over 3,00,000 children who are under the age of 18 work as soldiers for armed rebel forces and even the government. Documentation of such abuse is evident in countries like Angola, Burma, Colombia, the Democratic Republic of Congo, Liberia, Sudan, and Uganda. Human Rights Watch published more than 13 reports on forced recruitment of under aged children for use in armed conflict. It is one of the worst forms of child labour practiced in the world today. It is an abusive practice and an extremely hazardous form of work to use children as soldiers.

It is estimated that there are around 1,20,000 child soldiers in Africa, accounting for half the total of the child soldiers in the world today. In Uganda, children make up around 90 percent of the Lord's Resistance Army (LRA), an armed opposition group, mostly between the ages of 13 to 16. Usually, child soldiers are of the ages between 15 and 18 but some are recruited as early as the tender age of 10 itself. The girls who are forced into combat face the added torture of sexual slavery. Almost 100 percent of the girls that escaped from the LRA had sexually transmitted diseases.

Poverty and lack of education draw many children to becoming soldiers. In Afghanistan, where few children have access to education, the percentage of child soldiers has increased from 30 percent to about 45 percent in recent years. Children are forced to commit atrocities against their loved ones, thus rendering them homeless, so they can concentrate fully on fighting the war.

Trafficking of Children

The recruitment, transportation, transfer, harboring or receipt of a child, for the purpose of sexual or labour exploitation, forced labour or slavery is the definition of the term child trafficking. It is estimated that over a million children get cheated and trafficked every year. They are given false promises of education, jobs and professional training and are transported within the country or to other countries for exploitative labour, sexual abuse and so on.

Both girls and boys are trafficked. The boys are used for hard labour in the agricultural fields and the girls are made to do domestic work, thus making them subject to physical, emotional and sexual abuse. Child trafficking is prohibited under international law as a practice similar to slavery and as one of the worst forms of child labour.

Conclusion

No magic word or deed can end the atrocities endured by child labourers. Solutions to child labour were discussed in the papers prepared by the UNICEF for an International Conference in 1997.They found solutions in '*education, social awareness and activism, the removal and rehabilitation of children who are labourers, legislation and proper enforcement of those laws.'* The government must make proper financial commitment to the cause of education of the child labourers by making primary education free and compulsory. In Malawi, in 1994, primary education was made free and compulsory. The enrollment increased roughly by 50 percent over the year. The new student were more females than males. Though our country is a developing country, we do have enough finance to make primary education free and compulsory. It is only a question of budgeting.

With the children, who would have otherwise been working, enrolled in school, their adult relatives will have no other choice but to go back to work and take on the pressure of supporting the family financially. They, being more sensible than children, can start trade unions and demand good wages for the work they put in. They can demand acceptable environments to work in, acceptable hours of work and a day off every week.

The children of today who do not work come to know of the atrocities of child labour through social awareness. They are the educated generation that will bring justice to their peers of the other terrible world of child labour, eventually.

The children who are currently working, must be moved from the dangerous environments they are exposed to and taken to rehabilitation centres so that physical, emotional and mental rehabilitation can be provided to them along with the care they deserve. Rehabilitation together with education will ensure that these children never return to work again as long as they are children. A liberated child with no options will find himself in an even more dangerous situation than the one he was liberated from. State run rehabilitation centres are an expensive affair. They may require professionals like doctors, lawyers, educators and sometimes even police protection. But we must compare this cost to the cost of losing the coming generations of children to lives of servitude and ignorance. The latter will definitely seem a higher price to pay.

References

1. Ali, A. 1980, *Health and genetic problems,* The Newsletter, Govt. of India, New Delhi, Ministry of Home Affairs.
2. Census of India, 1971. *Female age at marriage*, Series 1, Paper 4.
3. Census of India, 1991. Paper-1 of 1992: *Final population totals.* Census Commissioner of India. New Delhi.
4. D'Souza Philomena, 2005. *Trafficking of Asian women,*New leader, August, Chennai.
5. Kumar Ram, 1990. *Women health Development and Administration*, New Delhi: Deep & Deep publications.
6. Mukta Mital, 1995. *Women in India- Today and Tomorrow*, India: Anmol Publications PVT LTD, New Delhi – 110002.
7. Sardadevi, October 1911, *A women's movement,* The modern Review, : 343
8. Singh K.S, 1994. *The Scheduled tribes*, New Delhi: Oxford Univesity Express.
9. Vir Dhara, Kamlesh Mahajan. 1996. *Indian women*, Delhi: New Academic Publishers.

www.UNICEF.com
www.childrightscharter.com
www.childlabour.com
www.ILO.org
www.childlabour:the situation.com

6

Human Rights of Scheduled Tribes

V. Prem Sam Ponniah

The human rights are inherent and intrinsic of human beings and its recognition is as old as the human civilization. The concept of human rights was the issue of the concept of non-discrimination on the basis of race, colour, creed, sex, age, class, language, national, origin and political belief. Human rights should be a matter of concerns to all of us especially, to the poor and disadvantaged people. What was happening in practice is that the human rights of marginalized people have been systematically ignored and downgraded. The present paper focuses on how far the concepts of human rights are applicable to marginalized and underprivileged people, especially, to the Scheduled Tribes.

This paper makes an attempt to look into the rights of Tribes in the perspective of human rights concepts, because the Tribes are more vulnerable and susceptible to various human rights violations. Although for many years victimized, Tribes are increasingly raising their voices to draw attention to their situation on a national and international level, but their voices are hardly heard and heeded to.

Definition and Meaning of Tribes

In the international context, Tribes are termed as Indigenous People. The term "Indigenous" is derived from the Latin word "indigena", meaning "native".[1] The expression has come to designate persons who had been variously, named Aboriginals, Indians, Tribal people, Natives, Minorities, Earth People, First People, and even the Fourth World. The term has found a considerable degree of contemporary acceptance, but there is still controversy about the groups to which it is properly applicable.[2]

According to dictionary meaning Tribes are defined as "a group of people of the same race and sharing the same language, religion, customs, etc, often led by a CHIEF". [3] In Indian Context, there are ten accepted parameters to define the Tribes, which includes: Unique art and Culture; Dependency on the Forest; Hunting / Gathering and Collection of Minor Forest Produce (MFP); Group Living; Traditional Lifestyle; Conservation Practices; Group Ownership; Traditional Worship; Activities related to traditional Knowledge; and Joint decision Making and Action.[4] The crucial factor in the definition of Tribes is their original inhabitation of the land on which, they have lived from time immemorial.[5]

The Tribes face unique threats to their human rights. Almost always outnumbered in the country, where their ancestors were the first inhabitants, Tribes face threats to their culture, their traditions, their political autonomy, and often their very lives.

Human Rights of Tribes in the International Perspectives

The world population of Indigenous peoples (Tribes) is gathered in more than 4,500 different ethnic and cultural groups, [6] they numbered between 250 to 300 million, or upward to 600 million if the distinct people of Africa are included. Taking this figures into consideration, indigenous people comprises between 5% - 10% of the world's population and can be found in every continent.[7] Therefore, the human rights issues concerning Tribes are very important.

Unless in the past, however, today's Tribes have some International Organizations to defend their rights, The UN, with its tradition of defense of human rights, has been at the forefront of defending Tribal right. The roots of the UN's support for Tribes human rights can be found in the United Nations Universal Declaration of Human Rights (1948). Article15 (1), states, "Everyone has the right to nationality," and Article 27, demand specific cultural protection, it states, "Everyone has the right to freely participate in the cultural life of the community, to enjoy the arts and to share in scientific advancement and its benefits".[8]

The two important conventions that emphasis the Tribes (Indigenous people) rights are:

(i) ILO: Indigenous and Tribal People Convention, 1989 and

(ii) UN Draft Declaration on the Rights of Indigenous People.

In emphasizing the importance of human rights for these groups, the United Nations declared the year 1993 as the year of Indigenous People and 9th August as International day of Indigenous People. The United Nations also declared 1994-2004 to be the International Decade of the World's Indigenous people.[9]

The general problem / issues faced by indigenous people (tribes) world wide

Despite variations in the specific political and historical circumstances surrounding non-dominant native population, nearly all-Tribal groups share a common set of problems. Common threats / problems concerning the plight of Tribes include: Environmental Degradation, Deforestation, Tourism, Weapons testing, Militarization, Cultural breakdown, Colonization, Invasion, Mining projects and a host of other ills. Although for many years victimized, Tribes are increasingly raising their voice to draw attention to their problems on National and International levels.

The Indigenous people (Tribal) all over the world, generally long for the four basic needs, namely the need for

(a) Cultural Protection;
(b) Recognition of Land Claims / Ownership;
(c) Recognition of Individual, Economic and Social (Welfare) Rights and
(d) Political Autonomy.

(a) Cultural Protection

Tribes are usually non-dominant minority groups. Often they are unable to live according to their cultural traditions, especially, when their traditions clash with those of the dominant groups of the society. Their cultural concerns include: religious freedom, subsistence economic activities, dress, diet, education, communal, "ownership" of goods,[10] indigenous technology and medicine.

The struggle for indigenous people's human rights, they were often labeled as "savages", "Natives" and, more kindly, "Tribal people." All these labels were offensive, because they implied that these groups were primitive and uncivilized. These labels are a form of racism, which is an attack on the human rights of its victims. Indigenous people went to great extent to prove to the world that their cultures are not less civilized, but simply different.[11]

(b) Recognition of Land Claims

A central element of the demand of the Tribes is the right to possess their traditional land and its resources. There is no legal system in the world explicitly excluding, Tribes from enjoying the right of ownership. Their claim for their ancestral lands, cannot be fully appropriated without understanding the spiritual link between Tribes and Mother Earth."[12]

The pressing problem faced by Tribes, is loss of land. In most cases they have been evicted from the land, they originally possessed. They were then displaced and relocated in reserved places situated on small patches of often-barren land.[13] Their attempts to recover their lost lands through legislation or legal action, have met with little success. Especially, when these lands may be rich in mineral resources, the State is reluctant to grant large areas of land to Tribes seeking to establish a limited form of self-Government in these areas.[14]

(c) Individual, Economic and Social (Welfare) Rights:

It becomes increasingly very clear that operationally and in actual practice that there should be a greater emphasis on basic human rights which are crucial for human survival. First and foremost, the individual is entitled to a certain amount of food, clothing, shelter, medical care and other necessaries of life, and further has right to enjoy and participate in spiritual, intellectual and cultural activities. These are elementary vital rights, which can be called subsistence rights or survival rights. .[15]

Tribes are currently the victims of discrimination and are denied essential amenities and legitimate rights by their respective States. Moreover, even when Tribes gain access to social programmes are able to have their individual legal rights enforced, they often find that these programmes and laws do not adequately address their people. For example, the educational needs of Tribal people are seldom met by the State systems that do not teach their indigenous languages or impart education in their language.[16]

(d) Political Autonomy.

Of all the human rights that might be accorded to Tribes, the right of self-determination[17] is perhaps the most important one. Indigenous people with the right to self-determination can create their own Governments, protect their own societies, and treat other Governments on something approaching an equal basis.[18] Not surprisingly, most Government's are reluctant to grant the indigenous people living within their borders these basic human rights.

The Human Rights of Tribes in India

The Government of India reports that there are 577 Scheduled Tribe communities and around 6,77,58,380 Tribes live in the country that forms over 8.08% of the total Indian population. According to the Anthropological Survey of India under the people of India project, 461 Tribal (Adivasi / Indigenous) communities have been identified all over the country.[19]

The Indian Constitution imbibed the spirit of Universal Declaration of Human Rights, which is fully reflected in its Preamble and is elaborated in the provisions concerning Fundamental Rights and Directive Principles of State Policy. The Constitution provides various safeguards to Scheduled Tribes, which includes, social, economic, educational, cultural, political and services, which are briefly discussed below:

(a) Social safeguards
(b) Economic Safeguards
(c) Educational and Cultural Safeguards
(d) Political Safeguards and
(e) Service Safeguards

(a) Social Safeguards

Social Safeguards are contained in Article 17, 23, 24 and 25 (2) (b) of the Constitution. As per Article 17, untouchability is abolished, and its practice in any form is forbidden. The enforcement of any disability arising out of "untouchability had been made offence punishable in accordance with the Law." Two important legislations have been enacted to give effect to contents of this Article. They are, (i) The Protection of Civil Rights Act, 1955. This Act provides for punishment for preaching or practicing of untouchability and (ii) Scheduled Castes and Scheduled Tribes (Prevention of Atrocities) Act 1989. This Act aims to prevent the commission of offences against the members of Scheduled Castes and Scheduled Tribe's.[20]

Article 23 prohibits trafficking in human beings, and other forms of forced labour. In pursuance of this Article, Bonded Labour System (Abolition) Act, 1976, had been passed. This has led to framing special programmes for identification and release of bonded labourers.. According to a National Survey, more than two third (66 %) of forced bonded labourers belong to the Scheduled Castes and 18% of them belong to Scheduled Tribe's.[21] Other sources of the Planning Commission, estimate more than three forth (83%) of the total number of bonded labourers belonged to Scheduled Castes and Scheduled Tribes .[22]

Articles 24 deals with prohibition of employment of children below the age of 14 years in any factory or mine or other hazardous employment. The Child Labour (Prohibition and Regulation) Act, 1986. was framed to prevent child labour practices and providing relief to those engaged as Child Labour. Ironically, the large numbers of child labourers engaged in hazardous employment belong to Scheduled Castes and Scheduled Tribes. [23]

(b) Economic Safeguards

The provisions of Article 23, 24, and 46 form part of economic safeguards for Scheduled Castes and Scheduled Tribes.[24] Article 46 under the Directive Principles of State Policy provides that "the State shall promote with special care, the educational and economic interest of weaker sections of the people and in particular of Scheduled Castes and Scheduled Tribes and shall protect them from social injustice and all forms of exploitation."

It is in pursuance of this Article, that special programmes have been taken up for extending educational opportunities to Scheduled Castes and Scheduled Tribes..[25]

With efforts made by the State Government and Central Ministries, there is considerable improvement, in reduction in poverty over the years. Ironically, the poverty of Scheduled Tribes was twenty percent higher than general population in India. The below Figure reveals the economic conditions of Tribes in India.

Percentage of Scheduled Tribes and All Population Below Poverty Line

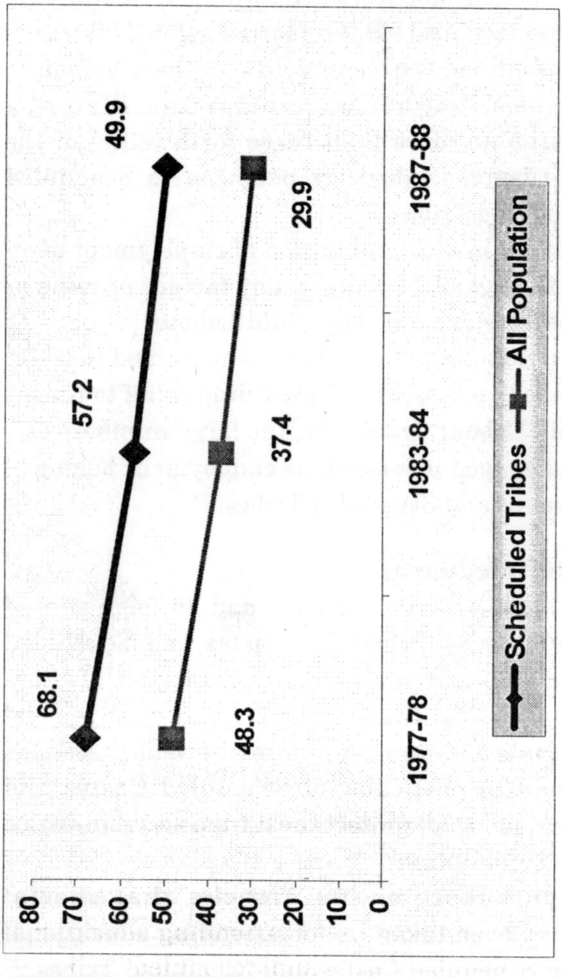

Sources: National Human Rights Commission, "National Seminar-cum-Public Consultant on Racism, Racial Discrimination, Xenophobia & Related Intolerance: A Report," New Delhi, 2001, p. 73

(c) Educational and Cultural Safeguards

Article 15 (4), empowers the State to make special provisions, for advancements of any socially and economically backward class citizens and for Scheduled Castes and Scheduled Tribes. This provision has enabled the State to reserve seats for Scheduled Castes and Scheduled Tribes in educational institutions. The following figure reveals the lower level of literacy status of Tribes in India from the year 1961 to 1991.

(d) Political Safeguards

Article 164 (1), provides that in the specific States there shall be a Minister in charge of Tribal welfare. Article 330 provides for reservation of seats for Scheduled Castes and Scheduled Tribes in Lok Sabha. In pursuance of this article, 41 seats are reserved for Scheduled Tribes in Lok Sabha. Under Article 24 (D), reservations of seats in Village Panchayat, Zila Parishads has been made for Scheduled Castes and Scheduled Tribes in proportion to their populations at respective level in direct elections. [26] It has also been provided that the reserved seats for Scheduled Castes and Scheduled Tribes shall be allotted by rotation to different constituencies in Panchayat at each level.[27]

(e) Service Safeguards

Article 16, which provides equality of opportunity for all citizens in matters relating to employment or appointment to any office, under the State and prohibits any discrimination on grounds of religion, race, caste, sex, descent, place of birth, residence...." It is through this provision that reservations in appointments and promotions for Scheduled Castes and Scheduled Tribes in matter of recruitment have been made..[28]

Tellingly, Scheduled Tribes representation is woeful lesser of in A and B, categories of posts increasing marginally only in the lower category jobs such as sweepers, peons and clerks.[29] The situation in Central Government services with the stipulated 7.5% reservation quota, may be seen in the following table:

Representation of Scheduled Tribes in Central Government Services
(As on 01-01-1996) Group

Central Government Services	**Central Public Sector**	**Undertakings**		
No. of Scheduled Tribe's				
Percentage of Scheduled Tribe. Employees	**No. of Scheduled Tribe's**	**Percentage of Scheduled Tribe Employees**		
A	1,891	2.89%	4,505	2.27%
B	2,913	2.68%	5,788	3.52%
C	1,33,170	5.69%	98,816	8.72%
D (including Sweepers)	79,722	6.54%	51,758	10.31%

Sources: National Commission for Scheduled Castes and Scheduled Tribes, Annul Report, 1996-97 & 1997-98

THE HUMAN RIGHTS ISSUES OF TRIBAL IN INDIA

This paper brings out the general problems /issues of human rights faced by Tribes in India are as follows:

(a) Recognized as Tribals not as Indigenous People

"Tribals are not the Indigenous people of India"! This is the official position regarding Tribes with the rider that most of them have been absorbed into the mainstream of Indian life.[30] The Constitution of India address them as only **"Tribes** and Tribal communities", (Article 342), and not as 'original inhabitants' or 'Indigenous People', which would entail important human rights implications.

In India the term "Indigenous" means "Scheduled Tribes", this has been declared by the World Bank on its own.[31] The studies prepared by the UN special Rapporteur, Martinez Cobo, a number of criteria were identified to determine "indigenousness". These included consideration of both objective and subjective elements, such as: ancestry, cultural aspects including religion, Tribal organization, community membership, dress and livelihood, language, group consciousness, residence in certain parts of the country and acceptance by the indigenous community.[32] As a corollary it would be referred that the Scheduled Tribes in India are Indigenous people.

(b) Linguistic identity not recognized

Another notable factor of the Indian Constitution is the exclusion of any Tribal language from the list of 14 official languages in the 8th Schedule. This has forfeited the right of Tribes not only to the official recognition of their long history and culture, and of their identity as a specific ethnic group, but also their right to avail of state patronage, funds and other facilities in the matter of developing and promoting their languages.[33]

(c) Tribal religion not recognized

The religions of the majority groups (Hinduism, Islam, Christianity, etc.) find due place in the National Census Reports. The Tribal religion is listed under the category of 'others', thereby receiving no specific identity and recognition. Failure to accept the unique character of Tribal religion, as substantively different from that of the established, organized religions is not only a gross denial of their religious identity, but also indirectly encourage Tribal to register themselves as members of the established and organized religions.[34]

(d) Discrimination in Scheduling Tribal Areas

The scheduling of Tribal area as per the mandate of the Constitution has also resulted in gross discrimination against the Tribals.:[35] Many Tribal contiguous areas have been left out in this scheduling process, such as Jammu & Kashmir, Assam, West Bengal, Uttar Pradesh, Karnataka, Kerala and in Tamil Nadu (Nilgiris and others) have been denied their right to special developmental benefits from the V and VI schedule of the Constitution. The new Panchayat Raj Extension Act, is one of the significant landmarks in the protection of Tribal people land and self -governance. Unfortunately, this Act has serious omission in that it has not considered the plight of Tribals in the unscheduled areas. [36] These limitations and omissions, issues and questions will form the agenda for future struggle by the Tribals in these States as well as in the rest of the country.

(e) Confusions in Identification and Classification of Tribes

Anomalies have arisen in the implementation of the Constitutional Provisions. The President of India, has to specify, which Tribe or Tribal communities are to include in the list of Scheduled Tribes of the concerned States and Union Territories. The problems includes: non Tribal group have been included; the same groups included in some areas have been rejected as Tribals in another area; some communities having similar surnames, but with dubious identities, have declared themselves as Tribals [37]and so on.

(f) Alienation and exclusion from forests and lands

Another blatant form of human rights violation relates to the use of rich natural resources of the Tribal areas for a variety of public purposed in the wake of national development. Wildlife Protected Areas, comprising of National Parks and Wild Life Sanctuaries, now constitute about 5 percent of the land area of India. Provisional estimates put the number of people living in and around protected area at around 4.5 million. According to a survey carried out by the Indian Institute of Public Administration (IIPA) in 1999-2002, 70 per cent of the sampled persons responding to a question of displacement stated that people had been relocated from their protected area.[38]

In fact, there is no proper data base on the displaced persons and project-affected persons (projects such as dams, mines, industries, etc). Studies on displacement 1951-1995 completed in six states and other research show that their real number 1947-2000 is probably around 50 millions. Some give such bigger number, Arundhuti Roy, for example, speaks of 56 million displaced by dam alone while Surijit Bhalla (2001) refers to a ridiculously low average of 1,360 displaced persons per large dam. Both depend on estimates because no official database exists. Based on the data provided by Government of India (1985) states that 40 per cent of the displaced persons and project-affected persons, during 1951-1990 were Tribals.[39] Ironically, instead of bringing hopes to Tribal society the development projects like dams, mines, industries, and sanctuaries have caused massive displacement. The forests being substantially taken away, the Tribals had no other alternative for their survival..[40]

(g) Denial of Dispersed Tribal Rights

About 30 percent of Scheduled Tribes are dispersed. They broadly comprise (i) migrants, migrant labourers and displaced persons, some of them get settled in new areas; and (ii) original inhabitants whose territories have been inundated by outsiders. Bulk of the dispersed Tribes is resourceless with concomitant loss of social status worse than even untouchables. Forced labour and debt bondage are rampant. The general poverty alleviation programmes do not address these vital needs. Violation of human rights of all descriptions is normal state of their existence.[41]

The various Constitutional safeguards, legislative provisions for the well being of Tribals, during the past sixty years of independence notwithstanding, the Constitutional promises of justice, liberty, equality and fraternity for Tribes have never been fulfilled.

References

1. Robert L. Maddex,(ed.,) **"International Encyclopedia of human rights: freedoms abuses, and remedies,"** CQ press, Washington, c2000, p.179.
2. **"Encyclopedia of Human Rights issues since 1945,"** Langley, Winston, (eds.,) Greenwood Press, Westport, 1999, p.151. also see S.J.Anaya, **"Indigenous Peoples in International Law,"** Human Rights Quarterly (HRQ), (1996); J.J.Corntassel and T.H.Primenu, **"Indigenous 'society' and International Laws"**; Human Rights Quarterly (HRQ), Vol. 17 no.2 (1995).
3. Jonathan Crowther, (ed.,) **"Oxford Advanced Learner's Dictionary of Current English,"** Oxford University press, New York, fifth edition, 1999, p. 1275.
4. Jacob Thundyl and K. Krishnan, (eds.,) **"Creating Voice for Indigenous people,"** National Advocacy Council for Development of Indigenous People (NACDIP), Chennai, December 2002, p.116.
5. European Convention on Human Rights, **"Report on equality and Non-Discrimination: Minority Right"**, by Strasbourg 1990, p.15, quoted by Joe.L.Washington, "United Nations Human Rights Apparatus for the Protection of Indigenous People",(WebLink: http: home.um.edu.mt/laws/test/mjhr/washington.html
6. James R. Lewis, Carl Skutsch, (eds.,) **"The Human Rights Encyclopedia,"** - Armonk, Sharpe reference, New York, c2001, Volume III, pp.761-66.
7. Joe.L.Washington, **"United Nations Human Rights pparatus for the Protection of Indigenous People,"** (Web Link: http:

home.um.edu.mt/laws/test/mjhr/washington.html), also see, Burger, ***"The Gaia Atlas of First Peoples: a future for the Indigenous world,"*** Gaia Books Ltd, London (1990); Richard Griggs, ***"The Meaning of 'Nation' and 'State' in the Fourth World,"*** Center for World Indigenous Studies (CWIS) Occasional Paper, o,p., No.18, 992, p.1.

8. A Panel of Legal Commentators (eds), ***"Law Relating to Human Rights,"*** 8th Edition, Asia Law House, Hyderabed, 2002.
9. United Nations, ***"International Instruments of the United Nations: a compilation of Agreements, Charters, onventions, Declarations, Principles, Proclamations, Protocols, Treaties, adopted by the General Assembly of the United Nations, 1945-1995,"*** United Nations ublication, New York, 1997. p.441.
10. Azim A. Khan Sherwani, ***"Human Rights of Indigenous Populations,"*** Legal News & Views, September 1998, p.3.
11. James R. Lewis, Carl Skutsch, (eds.,) ***"The Human Rights Encyclopedia,"*** op.cit: p.764.
12. Martinez Cobo study, ***"Conclusion, Proposals and ecommendations,"*** UN. Doc. E/CN-4/SUB-2/1983/21. Quoted by J.K.Das, in "Indigenous People and Human Rights," Ganga Kaveri Publishing House, Varanasi (India), 1997, p.43.
13. James R. Lewis, Carl Skutsch, (eds.,) ***"The Human ights Encyclopedia,"*** loc.cit.,
14. In Australia, an aboriginal land Containing important mineral resource has been leased to private companies for exploitation. Indigenous Peoples' Centre for Documentation, Research and Information, **(Weblink: http//www.docip.org)**
15. Scott Leckie, ***"Another Step towards Indivisibility: Identifying the Key Features of Violations of Economic, Social and Cultural Rights,"*** Human Rights Quarterly, The Johns Hopkins University Press, Baltimore, Vol.20, 1998, p.82
16. Azim A. Khan Sherwani, op.cit: p.4.
17. Peter Jones, ***"Human Rights, Group Rights, and Peoples' Rights,"*** Human Rights Quarterly, The Johns Hopkins University Press, Baltimore, Vol.21, 1999, pp.95-106

18. ***"Pathways to Self-determination: Canadian Indians and the Canadian States,"*** L.Little Bear, M.Boldt, J.Long (eds) quoted by Azim A. Khan Sherwani, "Human Rights of Indigenous Populations," op.cit: p.3.
19. K.S. Singh, ***"The Scheduled Tribes,"*** Peoples of India, National Serious Volume II, Anthropological Survey of India, Oxford University Press, Delhi, Bombay, Calcutta and Madras, 1994, pp.8-14.
20. National Human Rights Commission***"Report on Prevention of Atrocities Against Scheduled Castes,"*** New Delhi, 2004, pp. 9-13.
21. V.V. Giri National Labour Institute, ***"Bonded Labour in India: A Manual on Identification, Release and Rehabilitation,"*** NOIDA, 1997, p.70
22. National Human Rights Commission***"Report on Prevention of Atrocities Against Scheduled Castes,"*** op.cit, p.14.
23. Sujata V. Manohar, ***"Human Rights and Judiciary,"*** art. cited in ***"Studies in Human Rights,"*** V.T.Patil & T.S.N. Sastry (eds), Poni Rani Publications, Delhi, 2000, pp. 106–110.
24. A.R.Desai (ed), ***"Violations of Democratic Rights in India,"*** Sangam Books Limited, London, U.K., 1986, p.41.
25. National Human Rights Commission, ***"National Seminar-cum-Public Consultation on Racism, Racial scrimination, Xenophobia & Related Intolerance: A Report,"*** New Delhi, 2001, pp.69-74.
26. National Human Rights Commission, ***"Report on evention of Atrocities Against Scheduled Castes,"*** loc.cit.,
27. Dr. Mahendra Mohan Verma, ***"Tribal Development In India : Problems and Perspective," art. cited in " reating Voice for Indigenous people,"*** Jacob Thundyal, K.Krishnan (eds.,), National Advocacy Council for Development of ndigenous People, Chennai, 2002, p.25.
28. Sujata V. Manohar, ***"Human Rights and Judiciary,"*** loc. cit
29. Dr. R.K. Kshirsagar, ***"Constitutional Safeguards for the Scheduled Castes,"*** *in* ***Scheduled Castes and Scheduled***

Tribes in India: A Socio-Economic Profile," Anmol Publications, New Delhi, 1991, p.51

30. Vikas Adhyayan Kendra, ***"Myths and Facts about the Adivasis,"*** art., cited in ***"Creating Voice for Indigenous People,"*** Mr. Jacob Thundyl and K. Krishnan (ed), op.cit: p.96.
31. J.K. Das, op.cit: p.34.
32. Martinez Cobo Study, UN.Doc.E/CN.4/sub-2/1986/7/Add.I, pares. 1-398, also see Das J. K, ***"Indigenous and ribal People: The position in International Law,"*** Cited in A Quarterly Research Journal on Tribal Life and Culture, VI, 1995, p.51.
33. Aloysius Irudayam S.J.,(et.al.,) "Atrocities against divasis in Tamil Nadu," Peoples Watch, Madurai, 2002, p.99.
34. ***"Scheduled Tribes Not Governed by Hinau Marriage Act: High Court,"*** The Hindu, April 13, 2000, p.4.
35. Minority Rights Group International Report (98/4) ***"The Adivasis of India,"*** U.K., 1999,p.12
36. ***Indigenous and Tribal People Centre***, Weblink: **http://www.itpcentre.org/**
37. Information gathered from the Conference – ***"Towards life affirming Resources of Adivasi,"*** August, 2003, (Adivasi Cultural Programme and Conference was organized by NGO's on International Indigenous people day of August 9, 2003, at Salem, Tamil Nadu. Around 27 different groups of Tribes from various districts of Tamil Nadu participated and shared their views)
38. Asmita Kabra, ***"Displacement and Rehabilitation of an Adivasi Settlement,"*** Economic and Political Weekly, July 19, 2003, p.3073.
39. Walter Fernandas, ***"Rehabilitation Policy of the Displaced,"*** Economic and Political Weekly, March 20, 2004, pp.1191- 1192.
40. National Commission for Scheduled Caste and Scheduled Tribes, ***Annual Report 1996 –97, 1997–98,***. Vol.I, government of India, Loknayak Bhawan, New Delhi, pp.156-157.
41. B.D.Sharma, ***"Rights of Tribals,"*** Journal of the National Human Rights Commission, National Human Rights Commission, New Delhi, Vol.1, 2002, p.103.

7

Promotion of Human Rights Culture in Higher Education

R. Subramani

Indroduction

Human rights and fundamental rights allow us to develop fully and use our human individuality, our intellect, and our capacity and principles and to persuade our spirituality and other means and needs of our life... All of us have fundamental rights to live our lives with dignity, have our food with pride, and hold our opinions free from arbitrary force, Demand our education as a fundamental legislative right, and protect our shelter.

All these freedom and rights has been guaranteed by Universal Declaration of Human Rights. More than 55 years after the declaration of Universal Declaration of Human Rights on December 10, 1948 by the United Nations, the idea and the concept of Human Rights has still not been planted into the minds of the individual. But guarantying this right in the society or a county need to promote and build a culture of Human rights among people.

The Constitution of India integrating various provisions and dimension of human rights in its preamble. Part III and the Part IV of the constitution deal the exclusive right of the individual in the form of fundamental rights and Directive Principles of State Policy. Both the parts are descriptively dealt the individual basic rights .The constitution aims to bridge the structural changes in the heterogeneously scatted and divided society of India due to caste, class, region, religion, gender and so on.

The Indian Constitution directed the State in the context of basic rights of the individual in an authoritative tone. Article 38 of the constitution says: The state shall strive to promote the welfare of the people by securing and promoting as effectively as it may a social order in which justice, social, economic and political, shall inform all the institutions of the national life. In the incorporated 44th Constitutional Amendment added additional colour in the same article, it further reads, The state shall, in particular, strive to minimize the inequalities in income and Endeavour to eliminate inequalities in status, facilities, and opportunities, not only amongst individuals but also amongst groups of people residing in different areas or engaged in different careers. It also emphasizes the freedom of expression, freedom to hold opinion, freedom to practice business, freedom to form trade union, Right against Exploitation, Freedom of Religion etc. Despite all Articles 29 and 30 elaborately deal the Cultural and Educational Rights of the citizen, it clearly reiterating the individual cultural and religious rights.

Across the world Human rights can be operated at various height of our life. It has strong attachment with the values in the social system it sketch out our social relationships, our work relationships, our religious beliefs, and domestic relationship. The first level of relationship with family in the context of human rights needs to be addressed. The second level of human rights have direct link with the society or a community When we started the interaction with the community in various stages of the society we may encounter human rights issues. People who belong to the underprivileged community can unite together and organize themselves and demand for their human rights. Groups of people can resist government policies and actions that undermine their human rights. The next level of human rights is with the law at local, national and international levels. The United Nations treaties and accords have codified the rights of the human being across the world with out any discrimination. Even though many Human right organizations and practitioners are active in the field, millions of us around the world are experiencing the bitter taste of the convention.

Human rights culture and education

The definition for Human rights culture or the culture of human rights has not been prescribed visibly and also the term "culture". Dictionary Definitions describes that culture is "the total range of activities and ideas of a Group of people with shared traditions which are transmitted and reinforced by Members of a group" or "the artistic and social pursuits, expression, and tastes valued by a society or class, as in the arts, manners, dress etc

The phrase "culture of human rights" stirs up many different meanings in different people. One person's definition of "culture" will eventually fluctuate from another person. According to the perception of the individual the definition of culture will be defined. Similarly the word "human rights" also interpreted subjectively. Culture is defined as "a type of civilisation", Civilisation is defined as an "advancement beyond the primitive, savage state," a state marked by a sophisticated, self-controlled, fair and enlightened environment.

The 1993 Vienna Declaration ropes the view of universality of human rights in the context of diverse cultures. The Article 5 of the declaration, stated as follows:

"All human rights are universal, indivisible and interdependent and interrelated. The international community must treat human rights globally in a fair and equal manner, on the same footing, and with the same emphasis. While the significance of national and regional particularities and various historical, cultural and religious backgrounds must be borne in mind, it is the duty of States, regardless of their political, economic and cultural systems, to promote and protect all human rights and fundamental freedoms."

Besides that international and regional instruments protect a number of key rights relating to culture. The key points of the instruments revolving the following points:

Right to culture this includes a variety of components:

Right to take part in cultural life, Right to enjoy the benefits of scientific progress

Right of individual to benefit from the protection of the moral and material

Interests resulting from any scientific, literary or artistic production of which he is the author,

Right of the freedom from the interference of the state in scientific or creative pursuits.

When I try to codify the concept of human rights culture, many of the human rights activists still continue their debate on the definition. Here I would like to state some of the meaningful definitions of human rights culture.

Human rights culture is a lived awareness of Human rights principles found in Universal Declaration of Human Rights and Human Rights documents following are ones mind and heart dragged into ones everyday life.

Human rights culture means that where every one respect principles, norms and values of Human rights.

Culture of Human rights as a way of life to respect Human dignity

Human rights culture promotes both individual freedom and equality

A culture of Human rights is one in which the people create and obey legal institutions that respect protect and fulfill Human rights

A practical acceptance to mutually co-exist with other

The culture of Human Rights could promote the standard of the individual and the values of the society. It can be used as a tool for the social transformation in the society and country. Human rights education in schools and the higher education of

Asian countries initiative have started soon after the 1965 DOWA education policy and stress the importance of equality and lay path not in favor of the discrimination. The word DOWA consists of two Chinese characters and it was coined by japans government during the world war time. The government of japan wanted to eliminate the differences between the village soldiers and non village soldiers in the army. Now DOWA education policy means a set of educational strategies for democratizing the whole society and to reach equality.

A dedicated program for the teaching of human rights is being existed in Srilanka since 1983. In 1987, the teaching of human rights in schools became mandatory in new Philippine Constitution. In India, human rights education gradually taking its real face and materials for human rights education in schools was developed. In the year of 1993 Protection of Human Rights Act was enacted and as part of the act National Human Rights Commission was constituted. Soon after the formation of commission awareness and the education of Human Rights has initiated .Across the country eleven Degree programme, ten certificate programme, Fifteen Diploma programme are offered by various institutions. School textbooks are being reviewed to eliminate portions that erode human rights principles and introduce new portions and issues discussing human rights. Human rights education in India is already being taught in the curricula of many schools but it has confined in to social science.

African universities are offering peace education in its region and followed by the UNESCO initiative, the same exercise has carried out in other regions. In addition to the general modules, specific courses also introduced in post graduate level Refugees studies; conflict prevention and management are some of the important courses. These courses have designed as a post graduate level and one year programme. Through their course, teaching, research and outreach programme in the universities in Africa has give a hand in developing a culture of peace by ensuring the society development and attitude of tolerance and understanding.

In India 1968 and 1986 Policy on Education emphasis to eliminate obscurantism, religious fanaticism, violence, superstition, and fatalism and promote some core principles such as India's common cultural heritage, egalitarianism, democracy, secularism, equality of sexes, observance of small family norms and inculcation of scientific temper, etc. All these core values are integrated in the school curriculum.

The Indian education system has followed a 'Value and Awareness Model' of human rights education, there by, human rights are not taught as a individual subject and individual course, but ingredients of the human rights have been integrated in all subjects and in all stages This basic standard has been accepted and reproduced through all the Curriculum such as National Council of Educational Research and Training (NCERT).

The 1988 curriculum emphasizes that "the curriculum as a whole should help in promoting development in the pupils of a deep sense of patriotism, non-sectarian attitudes, capacity for tolerating differences arising out of caste, religion, region, languages, sex, etc. and ability to choose between alternate value systems, all directed to the sustained pursuit of unity and integrity of the country." It further says that "The Curriculum should reflect some of the major issues facing the world today such as disarmament, avoidance of nuclear war, prevention of violation of human rights, etc. The school curriculum while enabling the pupil to root oneself in the abiding national cultural traditions and value frame should also enable him/her to learn and appreciate the richness and to see himself/herself as a member of the new and emerging international community of humankind." Both the Curriculum Frameworks of 1988 and 2000 reiterate and included the core components acknowledged by the NPE.

Human rights education (HRE) in school is a major instrument to shape and design the society...Students need to be imbedded with a sense of mission to realize human rights. Human rights should be seen as an inherent element of human well-being. HRE therefore helps students, teachers and others in the community to become better human beings. Human rights culture should be planted in the minds of the young people. India is a pluralistic in nature, the culture of human rights could resolve the conflict, reduce the magnitude of intolerance

All the Asian human rights organizations and non governmental organizations are having meaningful dialogue in the context of diverse cultures and traditions in the field of human rights education. At the onset HURIGHTS OSAKA has conducted a south Asian training workshop on Human Rights education in school at bankok on June 2000 that work shop discusses and develop new dimension in the human rights education. Those workshop key objectives are

To develop social competence and responsibility towards greater empowerment of young people by embracing human rights culture for a sustainable future,

To develop young people's capacity to intervene with the appropriate human rights mechanisms, government, NGO's and civil society organizations,

To empower young people to develop their personality and senses to focus on human dignity and respect on the basis of equality,

To promote understanding, tolerance, gender equality and friendships amongst young people, indigenous young people, racial, national, ethnic, religious minorities and linguistic groups and finally, and

To strengthen leadership of young people and identify concrete and practical intervention techniques to issues concerning young people.

Human rights education aims to imparting the values and attitudes of the individual and knowledge which are essential to generate a world with out Human right violation, it attempts to popularize the Human rights culture into higher education curricula is best way to disseminate and develop the ideal philosophy of Human rights to the future generation.

Promotion of human rights culture in higher education

Higher educational institutions are playing a vital role in the promotion of Human rights and the production of young trained professionals and dynamic leaders through specific educational programme. In Asia our experience with human rights education has not marching towards the destination. It has stayed behind a minor educational activity and it needs tremendous planning and work force to device material and human resource for the educators. International guidelines and project reports, initiatives have not yet been far and broadly implemented in many countries; many of them are lying as a project reports.

More over, one of the major impediments to human rights education in schools is the lack of opportunities for teachers to study and practice new ideas in teaching human rights. In Africa, culture of peace curricula has introduced in higher education. The course aims to ensure the development of the society and attitude of tolerance and understanding, free from prejudices and misconceptions.

African colleges and institutes are devised the curricula address local, regional and international issues and problems of peace, and human rights. After this basic frame work appropriate peace modules are included in existing courses in various fields such as political science, international relations, history, Sociology, Social work, religious studies, management studies, education, law, communication studies, psychology, anthropology etc. They put in the peace element in each one of the designed courses. Alternative conflict resolution has incorporated in the law courses; Preventive diplomacy has included in political sciences; Inter ethnic Coexistence has integrated in sociology. Peace content and modules have been invariably designed in all the courses in the university including science and engineering. The University of Turban –Westville offers peace related courses and African centre for the constructive resolution of disputes. The offered curriculums and courses across the world prove the eventual changes in the education field. Developing countries are focusing on the human rights education they are very keen to device curriculum and incorporate human rights as a tool of social transformation.

Suitable teaching techniques are required for teachers, students, Researchers, NGOs, activists, field workers, government officials and institutions. The purpose of Human Rights education is to disseminate awareness of rights and responsibility, and to enforce a particular right of a specific group or class or institution. The universal superiority of human rights is based on the faith that human rights are natural characteristic of human beings Human rights cannot be seen and applied for certain contexts and the validity is derived from the especially source of their reality,. The socio-economic-cultural and political conditions of peoples do not classify human rights. In the globalize scenario Human rights could be incorporated invariably in all the division of the education.

In India we are experiencing a number of factions among the community. Because of the existing religion, caste, language, gender conflict we are struggling to maintain peace in the region. Across the country the magnitude of the conflict is not acceptable quantity. Apart from legal means, this is high time to revamp our culture of tolerance and universality through proper education.

Conclusion

Human Rights culture is a way of life and it can create a very cohesive environment to break the traditional misbelieves and misconceptions and help in contributing national values in concurrence with universal human rights values and principles. The world is on the process of redesigning the concept of universality and culture. The diverging views of States on the nature of human rights and the cultural differences of societies should be eliminated through a systematic approach. Human rights culture could be taught as a tool for social change. Education is the only way to build and mould the future generation. There is no deficient of ideas to initiate the human rights principles in the education. Single formula and individual theory is not sufficient to solve the problems of all societies like India, but some basic principles can applied with true letter and sprit. Individual freedom and dignity of the person should be protected and there is an urgent need to transfer the basic principles to the large scale of masses. Educational institutions have immense role to form public opinion, need to develop and introduce specific programme through curriculum and co curricular activities dedicated to Human rights culture.

End Notes

1. An Agenda for Peace in Africa. Information published by ACCORD, University of Durban-Westville, South Africa.
2. Culture of peace; A Declaration of culture and peace UNESCO, 1999
3. Darren J OByrne, 2005, Human Rights-An Introduction, Pearson Education Limited
4. Janusz symonides –Vladmir Volodin, 2004, A Guide to Human rights, UNESCO
5. Goolam Mohamedbhai, The role of Human rights in developing a culture of peace in Africa, United Nations publications, 2003
6. Moolchand sharma, Human rights education in Indian Universities and colleges, HURIGHTS OSAKA, 2003
7. Saroj pandey, Human rights education in schools: The Indian Experience, HURIGHTS OSAKA 2006-2007
8. Seafin A.arviola.J R Teaching Human Rights as a Tool for social transformation, HURIGHTS OSAKA, 2003
9. Students Need Education for Justice and Peace". ACCORD, University of Durban-Westville, South Africa
10. Report of south Asian training workshop on Human education in schools, Bangkok, June 23-24, 2000
11. Culture of Human rights Discussion available at.www.hrea.org/lists/hr.edu posted on 07 Sep 2006

12. Teaching Human Rights Practical activities for primary and secondary schools 2004 United Nations publications
13. Human rights education in schools, HURIGHTS OSAKA, 2003 www.hurights.or.jp
14. Human rights education in Asian schools, HURIGHTS OSAKA, 2007 www.hurights.or.jp

8

Humanity in Thirukkural

Prof. S.P. Guruparan

Humanity is the mother of freedom, equality and human rights. Inhuman activities are rampant in the present day world and the violation of Human rights comes under this category. We talk about civilization, where is civilization when man kills man on the basis of caste, creed, race and sex.

No country can euologise its culture and civilization if there exists any treatise that insists hatred and animosity between man and man. The Varanasrama system and Apartheid are the outcome of the barbaric thinking of man but there exists noble thinking too!

Thirukkural is the best example of it.

Thirukkural is written by Thiruvallaluvar whose wisdom is combined of both divine and rational thoughts, It is an elixir, and a panacea for all. It is a healer of human ills.

Thiruvalluvar insists Equality very much,

He says: *Pirappu Okkum Ellaa uyirkkum Sirappu*

Ovvaa

Seithozhil Vaetrumaiyaan -Kural [972]

People by birth are the same. Greatness and disgrace are due to the difference among vocations.

Maelirunthum Mael'allaar Maelallar Meezhirunthum Kerzhallaar keezhallavar.

Though people belong to high status they are not high if they possess quality low. And though people belong to lower status they are high if they don't possess quality low.

Thiruvalluvar insists Love very much.

He says: *Anpirkkum un'do Ataikkum Thaazh Aaarvalar*
Pun Kanneer Poosal Tharum -kural[71]

Does love have a bolt to shut?.

The tear that is shed would reveal the love one has

Love is a must for all
If not all will fall
Love is the basis for creation
And also it is the mother of compassion
Spontaneous flow of tear will be there
If one the healing love could bear
Nothing could block the flow of tear
When the lovable one's peril one sees near

He also says: *Anbin vazhiyathu Uyir Nilai Ahuthilaarkku*
Enpu Tho'l Por'ttha udampu.-kural[80]

The body with love is the body with life

And the body without love is nothing but skin covered bone without life!!

The meaning of our existence lies in rendering love
Love should be the teacher of our life
Life sans love is body without soul
Buddha, Jesus, Prophet Mohamad
GuruNanak; Kabir; St. Vallalaar;
Naarayana Guru-all these noble souls
Insisted love, love, love and only love!!

Where there is true divinity there will be urbanity and civility; Where there is rationality there will be refined humanity; and where there is refined Humanity there wouldn't be any kind of social atrocity

Freedom, equality and fraternity will blossom with the fragrance of equal rights when Humanity is based on divinity and rationality.

In Thirukkural LOVE and HUMANITY have been given importance along with VIRTUE.

Humanity is the breeding centre of human rights. Human rights make man's thinking bright, If man claims he is cultured, then he should adore Natural Law which insists equality and equal rights.

If you have faith in God you should accept that God is not partial, and he doesn't create people high and low.

If you claim you are a rationalist you should accept that it is irrational to Classify people into high and low.

If you insist that there should be inequality you are neither an atheist nor a rationalist. You are not a humanbeing at all.

9

Human Rights Perspective and Media: With Special Reference to Broadcasting

Dr. N. Madavan

Introduction

The fundamental freedoms of right to seek, receive and impart information forms the basis of broadcasting. The Principles require governments to extent no trivial amounts of broadcasting freedom to individual and organization. They Act as the base line to judge particular rules and regulation. The Indian Constitution, Supreme Court of India and International Human rights Treaties ratified by the Indian Government all affirm some form of the right to seek, receive and impart information. Article 19 of the Indian constitution states that, "All the citizens shall have the right to freedom of speech and expression". The Hero Cup decision says that "The right to freedom of speech and expression" also includes the right to be educated informed and entertained. The International covenant on civil and Political rights states that everyone shall have the right to the freedom of expression – this right shall include freedom to seek, receive and impart information and ideas of all kinds, regardless of frontiers, either orally, in writing or in print, in the form of art, through any other media of his choice.

However, when coming to the Broadcasting Bill of 1997 of Government of India, it is widely argued that the legislation does not take in to account or for that neither matter nor even consider the basic human freedoms of right to seek, receive and impart information. Hence it has generated a comprehensive discussion of the meaning of these fundamental rights and the values in this piece of legislation. Human rights activities have been not so active on this issue rather being concerned with the traditional; violation civil and political rights such us extra – judicial killings and preventive detentions. Hence the paper tries:

- to explore the maladies of the human rights violations that have been attracted in the context of the media particularly under broadcasting with special reference to India.
- to define the areas of human rights and limit the boundaries of human rights within the broadcasting arena.
- to provide suitable recommendations from the point of view of incorporating human rights ideals and values in broadcasting arena.

The Issue and Debate:

But those concerned about civil and political rights should make their own arguments and should comment on this proposed legislation themselves. First their interests are not always aligned with those of the broadcasters and cable operators. Commercial telecasters generally want to maximize diversity and amount and quality of content. Because human rights advocates have a different intellectual approach to the issues, they may identify problems with the proposed legislation which the broadcasters and others may overlook but which may affect the common interests of all parties. Second, politicians and public may discount the arguments of the satellite broadcasters because of the broadcaster's financial interests or because of the foreign ownership of some leading operators. The economically disinterested voice of the human rights groups will have more credibility in these political debates.

What is clear, then, is that there is a need for a sophisticated human rights perspective on the Broadcasting Bill specifically and media and telecommunications in India generally. As stated previously, this perspective should rest primarily on a rigorous discussion of the practical meaning in the ICCPR and the freedom of speech and expression in the Indian Constitution.

A human rights perspective does not answer question about the form of the new broadcasting authority or the structure of the media sector. Human rights instruments are better at listing lofty goals and setting minimum standards of treatment than at giving specific instructions about the form that a particular right is to take in a society.

Under many theories about the role human rights, states have wide latitude in defining what these rights entail. For example, different societies are likely to have different conceptions of 'public morality' and 'public order'. Different countries have different histories, demographics, laws and domestic and international interests; their judges may countries. Different legal systems may allocate property rights differently; what is owned and controlled privately in one country might be owned and controlled by the collective in another, and one's right to use or to direct what is owned by the collective may vary from society to society.

Despite these failings, a human rights perspective does have value in this debate. Whether or not the human rights treaties give clear guidance on how to resolve competing values, they do identify issues for examination and consideration – issues that most parties in the debate have not discussed publicity.

A human rights perspective leads one to ask why the proposed legislation criminalizes the reception of 'unauthorized' signals. Section 21 of the draft Bill states:

A person who in contravention of the provisions of this Act........... Receive any broadcasting service which is neither a licensed service nor a permitted service ... shall be guilty of committing An offence of illegal broadcasting and on conviction, shall be punishable with imprisonment which may extend upto five years, or with fine which may extend upto rupees ten lakhs (US 28,000) and in second and every subsequent offence such fine may extend to rupees fifty lakhs (US 140,0000), or with both.

Positive Aspects of Human Rights:

One see three positive aspects of a human rights approach to broadcasting legislation;

- First, human rights treaties establish fundamental values: the freedom of speech and expression is generally positive, restrictions on the right to seek, receive, and impart information are generally negative.
- Second, one can construct a positive vision of the role of the broadcasting authority and the structure of the media sector by attempting to maximize these principles with a mixed approach in which there is a role for private broadcasters, private citizens, and the government.
- Third, these principles provide tools for analyzing the proposed legislation to determine the extent to which it jeopardizes these values.

Conclusion:

Just because human rights instruments have their limitations does not mean that they are worthless. Just because there are contradictions in some of their principles does not mean that their values are insignificant. If one judged laws solely on the basis of internal logical or moral consistency, one would reject many laws and most constitutions. Instead, societies work with the texts that they have in order to govern themselves.

The freedom of speech, expression, and broadcasting is of vital importance to individuals and to society. It is necessary for the development of a free conscience and self-fulfillment. It is essential for academic inquiry and artistic expression. It is fundamental requirement for people to participate in democratic decision making. And it helps individuals and society determine the correct course of action.

Human rights activists have been remiss not to focus on these issues or to contribute their position to this debate. These issues merit their attention now. A mixed system maximizes the values contained in these treaties, ensures fundamental freedoms, minimizes imposition on the right to seek, receive and impart information, and addresses concerns about the dominance of any group of persons or the government. Those who care about civil and political rights can take the arguments listed here and lobby based on them.

References:

1. Agarwal, S.K, *Media and Ethics* (New Delhi: Shipra Publications, 1993).
2. Agarwal, Hema, *Society, Culture and Mass Communications: Sociology of Journalism* (Jaipur: Rawat Publications, 1995).
3. Gupta, V.S, *Third Revolution in Indian Perspective: Contemporary Issues and Themes in Communications* (New Delhi: Concept Publications, 1995).
4. Rao, N. Bhaskar and G.N.S.Raghavan, *Social Effects of Mass Media in India* (New Delhi: Gyan Publications, 1996).
5. Thomas, T.K (e.d), *Autonomy for Electronic Media: A National Debate on the Prasar Bharathi Bill* (New Delhi: Konark Publishers, 1989).

10

Human Rights and Bonded Labour

G. Gowthaman

Human Rights are of Universal importance. They are common to all regardless of caste, colour, religion, race etc., Human Rights are related to civil, political, economic, social, cultural, educational and Judicial Rights. Now a day, human rights has become an important topic of global concern. To safeguard, protect and promote human rights at all levels, knowledge of human rights is a must. To live with honour and dignity an individual should be allowed to enjoy human rights without any restrictions. The present day world witnesses the violation of human rights at large scale. In a democracy, its value could be analyzed only through the rights that are being enjoyed by its citizens. Giving freedom to others is the real freedom. One's rights and freedom should not affect that of others. It is the duty of each and every state to respect human rights and provide guarantee for the safeguards of human rights.[1]

Meaning of Bonded Labour

Bonded means put into bond or a tie or an agreement. Labour means work. The labour may either be physical or mental. By this, one toils under his employer. Bonded labourers are the persons who are bound to perform certain forced labour. A bond is between two persons one is an employer and the other is a worker or labourer. Serfdom also is brought under this system. The labourer or the tenant is bound to live and labour on the land belonging to another person. They have no freedom of movement and are forced labour especially in agriculture. The landlords or the money lenders are the masters. Poverty makes them to borrow money which in turn makes them to become bonded men. The landlords or the money lenders force the underprivileged people to work free or for very meager wages on their lands. The rate of interest for the borrowed money is abnormal. The debtor could not repay the borrowed amount with interest and it is compounded in due course. This makes him to work only for clearing the interest. As the debtors are illiterates, they are cheated by the money lenders. The debt could not be cleared during his life time.[2]

For an individual's debt his whole family enters into compulsory or forced labour on the lenders land. Accordingly, they lost their freedom of seeking other employment. Low wages also pose a threat to the daily survival of the labourers. They are not treated like human beings and are treated as commodities. This paved the way for selling or mortgaging the bonded labourers. Poverty makes him to accept bonded labour or forced Labour.[3]

Justice Bhagwati stated that where a person is suffering from hunger or starvation, where no employment is available to alleviate the rigour of his poverty, he would have no choice but to accept any work that comes in his way, even if the remuneration offered to him is less than the minimum wages. Both bonded and forced labour are traced as synonym.[4]

The Supreme Court of India held the view that where a person provides labour or service to another for remuneration, which is less than minimum wage, that labour or service provided by him clearly falls within the scope and ambit of the word forced labour. Thus the bonded labour is a person who provides or is providing or has provided labour or service to other person in lieu of an advance or consideration, which is less than minimum wages. Bonded labour system means the systems of forced labour. This system divests one's life blood and deprives his personal, liberty.[5]

International Bonded Labour

The problem of bonded labour prevails since ancient period. It is present in countries like India, even after her independence. It was referred as slavery through not in the name of bonds in ancient Greek, and Roman society. The greed of the landlords, money lenders and usurers provided opportunities for the growth of slavery. Slavery was in existence in Germany, Latin America and Britain. The slaves were from various tribes. Slavery was also existed in Middle East countries too. Debt bondage and serfdom are also forms of slavery in ancient societies. Huge numbers of human of slaves were engaged by the Upper classes and large estate owners. This resulted in the development of agricultural slavery. Subsequently, there prevailed the plantation slavery and debt bondage. The slaves under went frightful abuses and cruelties and almost they lost their human dignity. They were either paid no wages or very low wages. They were at the bottom of the heap. Thus, the real slave was in bondage. Liberty, richness and peace are not known to a slave. In England, slaves were openly sold in auction. Mostly the Negroes were sold as slaves. During the time of American war of Independence of 1776 many people had realized that slavery was wrong. At one stage prohibition of slavery was tried at. In due course, a large number of people in North America felt that slavery was an evil practice and it should be eradicated through out the state. This led to the passage of Slaves Emancipation Act in 1863 by Abraham Lincon.[6]

Bonded Labour in Pre-Independent India

The system of bonded labour existed in India in various names such as slavery, bondage, forced labour and exploited labour. In India, its existence could be traced from the period of Indus Valley Civilization. Due to the coming of Aryans in India, the caste system came into force. Sudras, the last cadre of society, were treated as slaves and untouchables. The Buddha Jataka Stories, were speaks about slavery. The Epics and Arthasasthra mentions that a man could be a slave either by birth or by profession. Further evidences are available of forced labour during the period of Guptas and Harsha. The Chola period in South India speaks about vettian, a sort of forced labour. Domestic slaves also were in existence. Qutbudin Aibek himself was a slave. During wars, slaves were utilized at the maximum level by the rulers and commanders of army. During the period of Mughuls slavery increased. Though Akbar tried to abolish slavery he could not succeed in his attempt. The bondage of agrestic slavery originated in Bengal and Bihar during the eighteenth century.[7]

Many, in order to survive during the famines in various parts of India, borrowed from the money lenders, Zamindars. When they failed to repay the loans, they were sold as slaves. Trafficking slaves had become a profitable trade in India. The slave trade was intensified in the latter part of the eighteenth Century. During the British period, the Slavery Abolition Act was passed in 1843. Then there came the forced labour. The Indian Penal Code prohibited forced labour in 1860. On the abolition of slavery, the vested interests called it in a new name to evade the provision of the above said Acts. Thus came the name of bonded labour.[8]

Different Names in India

The bonded labourers are called in different names in different states of India.

Table-1
Different Names of Bonded Labour in States in India

Sl.No.	*Name of the State*	*Name for Bonded Labour*
1.	Tamil Nadu	Izhava or Puleva, Holiya, Peadiyal,
2.	Kerala	Cherumar
3.	Andhra Pradesh	Bhagela., Jassigulla
4.	Central Indian States	Harawal, Barasaila
5.	Orissa	Gothi
6.	Karnataka	Jeetha
7.	Gujarat	Hali
8.	Bihar	Kamiya, Jonour

The bonded labourers were mostly belonged to the Depressed Classes, aboriginal people and Scheduled tribes.[9]

Bonded Labour in Post-Independent India

At one stage, Zamindari system was abolished in India. The Annual Report of the Commission for Scheduled Castes and Scheduled Tribes give a complete picture of bonded labour. As per the survey conducted by the National Labour Institute of 1978, it was estimated that there were about 13,00,000 lakh bonded labours in India. Almost every State in India has bonded labourers. In 1984, more than 1,00,000 lakh bonded labourers were set free from the clutches of landlords or other well off leaders in society. Various studies reveal that in many parts of India, the practice of bonded labour still continues. It was reported in ***Hindustan Times*** on 8 February 1991, that about 3000 bonded labourers are subject to exploitation. There is no reliable official data available about the exact number of bonded labours in India.[10]

Bonded Labour in Different Occupations

The right to live with human dignity is once for all forgotten. Neither the Government of India nor the State Governments have the right to take any action that may deprive a person from enjoying the basic rights as envisaged in the Directive Principles of State policy and in the articles of 39, 41 and 42 in the Indian Constitution.

Bonded labourers, even after 50 years of Independence, are found in various occupations.

Table-2
Bonded Labour in Various Occupations

Sl.No.	*Name of the Occuapation*	*Nature of the Labour*
1	Agriculture	Bonded
2.	Industries	Bonded

Sl.No.	*Name of the Occuapation*	*Nature of the Labour*
3.	Stone Quarries	Bonded
4.	Brick Industries	Bonded
5.	Building, construction sites	Bonded
6.	Power loom centers	Bonded
7.	Match Industries	Bonded
8.	Knitwear Industries	Bonded
9.	Mines	Bonded
10.	Jewel manufacturing centers	Bonded
11.	Diamond and Gem Cutting Industries	Bonded
12.	Carpet Industries	Bonded
13.	Hotels and Other establishment	Bonded [11]

UDHR and Bonded Labour

Article 23 says

(a) Every one has the right to work, to free choice of employment to just and favourable conditions of work and to protection against unemployment.

(b) Every one, without any discrimination has the right to equal pay for equal work.

(c) Every one who works has the right to just and favourable remuneration

ensuring worthy of human dignity and supplemented if necessary by other means of social protection.

Article 24 says

Every one has the right to rest and leisure, including reasonable limitation of working hours and periodic holidays with pay.

Covenant on Human Rights

The International Covenant on Human Rights views that safeguarding children and youth against social and economic exploitation would guarantee for the peaceful life. The child labour can be eradicated by punishing those who put the children in employment and those who preventing children to get education. Signatories are to follow these rules compulsorily.[12]

Indian Constitution and Bonded Labour

The articles 23 and 24 deals with the right against expoiltation. Article 23 prohibits forced labour. It is designed to protect the individual not only against the state but also other private citizens. It embodies two declarations. The first declaration is that the traffic in human beings and other similar forms of forced labour are prohibited. The second declaration is that any contravention of the provision shall be an offence punishable according to the law. Nothing in this article shall prevent the state from imposing compulsory service for public purposes, and in imposing such service the state shall not make any discrimination on grounds only of religion, race, caste or class or any of them. Article 24 provides that no child below the age of 14 years shall be employed to work in any factory or mine or engaged in any other hazardous employment[12]

Measures against Bonder Labour

The Government of India initiated measures against the bonded labour through the Constitution and by enacting much legislation in this regard. The noteworthy among them are

(1) Aticle 23 of Indian Constitution
(2) Mines Act of 1952
(3) Contract Labour Abolition Act of 1970
(4) Contract Labour Regulation and Abolition Act of 1970
(5) Bonded Labour System Abolition Act of 1976.
(6) Equal Remuneration Act of 1976
(7) The Interstate Migrant Workmen (Regulation of Employment and Conditions of Services Act 1979)
(8) Child Labour Prohibition Act 1981.

The Supreme Court of India is doing yeoman service to liberate the bonded labourers. It has directed the Central and State Governments for the release of bonded labourers, and to take steps for their rehabilitation. As per the direction of Supreme Court, the Tamil Nadu Government rehabilitated about 10,000 bonded labourers in 1997. A State wide survey identified 25.008 bonded labourers.[14]

Bonded Labour in Tamil Nadu

The bonded labour in Tamil Nadu is being identified in district wise. In Tamil Nadu a considerable number of Scheduled Caste and Scheduled Tribe people are living and the practice of untouchablity is prevailing. They are treated as bonded labour.

Table-3
Bonded Labour in Tamil Districts

Sl.No.	*Name of the District*	*Number of Bonded Labourers*
1.	Coimbatore	5499
2.	North Arcot	3448
3.	Perambalur	3003
4.	Chengleput	2794
5.	Erode	450
6.	Pernambattu	32
7.	Sslem	851
8.	Tiruchirappalli	8000
9.	Kancheepuram	40.000

Bondage prevails in a traditional worker- employer relationship in India. The parents need the money perhaps to pay for the costs of an illness, perhaps to provide dowry to a marrying child, or perhaps as is often the caste to help put food on the table. Approximately fifteen million children work as bonded laborers in India. Two players create the debt-bondage arrangement. The making of beedi, cigarettes is one such bonded-labour industry. The average advance in the beedi industry is 1500 rupees. The average number of bonded child labourers rolls in a day is 1500 for an average daily wage of nine rupees. Industries that do allow for gradual repayment of the original debts do not provide an easier escape from bondage. Poverty is inextricably linked to bondage and the combination of poverty and the lack of access to credit is another essential factor behind bonded labour.

In 1978 the Ministry of Labour launched a scheme that specified a "Rehabilitation allowance" in order to assist State Governments with rehabilitation. Under this scheme, the Central Government contributes half of the rehabilitation assistance allowance to free every bonded laborer, and the State where the bonded labourer resides pays to other half the allowance determined by a Ministry of Labour Planning Commission, was originally set at 4000 rupees. It has been raised to 6250 rupees in 1986. More than 3,25,000 child labourers are in the beedi industry, mostly in Tamilnadu. The city of Salem, Tamilnadu has been a major producer of domestically-consumed silver jewelry.Since 1980, 1,00000 child labourers are working in Salem district. An estimated 10000 Child labourers are working in Silver works. Gem cutting and poishing is a traditional cottage based industry where also child labour prevails. It as an estimated 1,00000 of the 1,60000 workers in this industry are believed to be bonded. Bonded child labourers in synthetic gem industry are in numbers in between 8000 and 10000. Nearly all of them are members of the Scheduled Castes. Synthetic gemstone are cut and polished in two districts of Tamil Nadu, namely, Trichy and Pudukottai Most bonded workers earn about 50 percent of the free market wage rate.[15] Generally non-school going children are regarded as Child Labourers who works in hazardous conditions or other wise.[16]

It has been estimated that some two million families in Pakistan are still victims of bonded labour. In 1992, the Government of Pakistan enacted laws against bonded labour.[17s]

Child Labour in Different Category

In 1998 the United Nations Organisation underlines the child labour which falls under several categories. They are

1. forced and bonded labour
2. Commercial and Sexual exploitation
3. Industrial Work
4. Agricultural Plantation work and related activities.

5. Street work
6. Domestic servants
7. Family and girl's work [18]

Active Child Labour in South Asia

Child labour is prevailing in South Asian Countries. For economic reasons a number of children involves in labour workd. The following table shows the economically active chld labourers in South Asian Countries

Table-4

Child Labourers in South Asia

Country	*Male Children*	*Female Children*
Bangaladesh	34,30,000	22,47,000
India	61,89,834	50,95,515
Indonesia	11,30,221	7,92,589
Nepal	2,18,979	3,12,856'
Pakistan	14,67,00	4,39,000
Sri Lanka	18,628	9,987 [19]

Even after a hundred years of child labour legislation and fifty years of Independence, Child labour is a common phenomenon in India. Today their numbers exceed these of any other country.[20]

Bonded Labour remains one of the most neglected human rights issues of our time. Bonded labour is the major cause of child abuse and exploitation in many parts of the world.[21]

There are 50,000 to 60,000 silk handlooms in Tamil Nadu. In Kanchipuram from 40,000 to 50,000 children work in bondage on the Silk Handlooms. Most silk looms are crowded together in dark, damp, and poorly ventilated rooms or buildings. There are 3,00,000 children are working to produce India's Fine carpets. Ninety percent of these children or about 2,70,000 are bonded labourers. Bonded labour was not abolished by law until 1975, when a Government ordinance called for its immediate eradication. Accordingly, the Supreme Court viewed that duty of the State is to identify, release and suitably rehabilitate the bonded laborers. Itis not only mandated by the Bonded Labour System Abolition Act, but is also required by the Indian Constitution.

The failure of State government to comply with their legal obligations, under the Bonded Labour System (Abolition) Act particularly the formation and adequate functioning of the district level vigilance leads to the continuing high prevalence of bonded labour.

The statistic problem is as a cute in the bonded labour context as it is in the child labour context. According to credible estimate, the number of bonded labourers in India is approximately sixty five million, representing slightly more than 7 percent of the country's total population. Certain individual states alone are estimated to have bonded labour population of one to two million people.A report from Tamil Nadu based on extensive research conducted at the direction of the Supreme Court, concluded that there were 10 Lakhs (One million) bonded labourers working in that State.

At the national level from 1990 – 1993, 537 inspection were carried out under the auspices of Child Labour. These inspections turned up 12303 violations. At the state level, the year 1990 –1993 produced 60, 717 inspections in which were 5060 violations. 1596 cases were filed against employers. The central government figures from 1994 – 1995 shows that there were 2, 51,424 bonded labourers. 24 NGO's and right groups estimate that over 15 million children are part of the bonded labour work force and between 50 – 120 million children are part of India's labour force.[22]

Estimated figures in between 60 and 115 million working children in India is the highest number in the world. Three types of bonded labour exist in practice around the world. (a) The first type involves a child inheriting a debt carried by his or her parents. (b) Another form of bonded labour occurs when a child is used as collateral for a loan. (c) A parent facing a usually large or urgent expense would use this method to obtain necessary money.

Estimate of the Ministry of Labour state that the figure 1317 million out of which 2 million are engaged in hazardous occupations. Today India has an estimate of 78 – 80 million child labourers. Over 85% of this child labour is in the country's rural areas, working in agricultural activities.

In April 1998, as many as 851 bonded labourers have been identified in Salem District, Tamilnadu, India. Efforts were taken to find out whether the elimination of bonded labourers was going on properly as per the Act of 1976 and whether the released bonded labourers were given immediate relief and assistance for rehabilitation. An official press release stated that among 851 bonded labourers 106 were from other states. NGO's and other interested personnel were appealed to take efforts to eradicate the bonded labour system in country.

Identity cards were issued to 474 bonded labourers who were rescued from different parts of Tamil Nadu. The cards entitled to them to claim benefits under the various rehabilitation measures to be initiated for them. They need not repay the money that they had borrowed from their former employees. They could report to the nearest police station. Each one of the rescued was eligible for a financial grant of Rs.10,000/- Housing facilities also are arranged for them through the Block Development officers. Arrangements are also made to provide jobs under the Employment Assurance Scheme. Priority would be given in all training schools under Training Youth for self employment. Besides the arrangements made for the enrolment of their children in schools.[23]

While rehabilitation measures were taken for the benefit of the former bonded labourers, the administration also launched action against the agents who employed the bonded labourers by filing cases against them. 212 persons were arrested under the Bonded Labour Abolition Act. The rescued should earn their livelihood without getting into debt and again falling into the hands of unscrupulous money-lender employers.

It was poverty which drove people to bonded labourers. In poor families the men were addicted to liquor, smoking and films which took away a sizeable chunk of their earnings and force them to enter into bond. Unless they cut down their expenditure on such evil practices, they could not build up their future on the right path and lead honourable life.

The enactment of the Bonded Labour Abolition Action 1976 had not solved the problem because of the failure of the authorities in invoking the provisions of the Act to put down the evil practice. Steps should be taken to identify the bonded labourers in various parts of the country and initiate legal action against the culprits, who kept the innocents in bondage. The role of NGO's is superb in identifying the bonded labourers.

A case beedi worker who was a bond said he was working as a bonded labourer for the last five years to repay a loan of Rs.4,000/-which he had taken from his employer who cut 50% of his wages by way of recovery of the loan dues and added that the employer asked him to work till he repay the loan. It is a surprise that some bonded labourers did not keep track of the wages cut by the employer and were unaware of the balance amount they owed or whether they continued to work even after their employer had fully recovered the dues with interest.

Another case reveals that an employer charges 5% interest for the loan of a worker who had taken and he had been working for the loan for the last five years to clear the loan. The poor labourer was getting only Rs.3700/- as his annual wage. It is quite unfortunate that most employers not known that bonded labour iss a crime while the bonded labourers also do not know they need not repay the amount to the employer as per the Bonded Labor Abolition Act.[24]

Various legislations which prohibit bonded labour are not successfully put in to force. The reason is quite simple. Unless the poverty is eradicated and employment opportunity is provided and compulsory education is made it is impossible to solve the Bonded Labour problem .The establishment and protection of human rights depends upon the eradication of bonded labour system.

End Notes

1. Sivagami Paramasivam, ***Human Rights a Study,*** Sri Ram Publication, Salem, 1998, p.2.
2. Lal. A.K., ***Bonded Labour in India,*** Delhi, 1976, p.17.
3. Sivagami Paramasivam, ***op.cit.,*** p.127.
4. ***Ibid.,*** p. 128.
5. ***Idid.,*** p. 129.
6. Patil Sharad, ***Problem of Slavery,*** New Delhi, 1976, p.41.
7. Kumar.C.A., ***Slavery in Bengal Presidency,*** G.E. Publishing House, London, 1977, p. 59.
8. Lal.K.A., ***op.cit.,*** p.61.
9. ***Ibid.,*** p.130.
10. ***Hindustan Times,*** 8 February., 1991, p. 10.
11. ***Ibid.,*** p.12.
12. Robertson, A.H., ***Human Rights in the World,*** New Delhi, 1972. p. 25.
13. U.N.General Assembly Resolution, 217.F.(iii), 10 December 1948.
14. International Government on Economics Social and Cultural Rights Articles. 2-18.
15. Mahajan, V.D., ***Select Modern Governments,*** Chand Company, New Delhi , 1988, p.76.
16. Goyal. P.K., ***Street Children and the Child Labour,*** Vista International Publication, Delhi,. 2005. p.70.
17. ***Ibid.,*** p. 90.
18. Mamta Rajawat, ***Child Labour the Indian Perspective,*** Kilaso Books Publication, New Delhi, 2004. p. 2.
19. ***Ibid.,*** p.3.

20. Srinivasa Reddy, B., and Ramesh.K., ***Girl Child Labour A World of Endless Exploitation,*** Dominant Publishers, New Delhi. 2002, p. 3.
21. ***Ibid.,*** p. 13.
22. Helen.R.Sekar, ***Child Labour Legislation in India, A Study in Retrospect and Prospect,*** V.V. Giri.
23. *Ibid.*
24. *Ibid.*

11

Right to Clean Environment with Special Reference to Water

B. S. Selvakumar

Introduction

Environment refers to a complex of surrounding circumstances, conditions, or influences in which a thing is situated or is developed.[1] The biological perspective of environment as well includes vital things like the Water we drink, Land we dwell and Air we breathe. Environment is the external force indispensable for every living things. Eversince the inception of Modern Age, the environment has undergone a rapid change, triggers fears about the future milieu in the minds of environmentalists, policy makers, scientists, social workers and citizens.

The severity of the environmental problem has been a major threat to human life. The meaning of protection of life under various national and international documents was only eradication of poverty but later years it also encompasses the clean environment for human being[2]. Rapid degradation of our environment in the pretext of national development and projects have caused a great problem to the existence of human life. The right to Environment implies the right to clean or healthy environment. Clean environment has been the pre-requisite to human life and it is universally accepted as a human right.Therefore, right to healthy environment is natural, inalienable and fundamental right of the people. The right to life is another potential instument of realisation of environment right. The United Nations conference remarked that "man is both creature and moulder of his environment which gives him physical sustenance and affords him the opportunity for intellectual, moral, social and spiritual growth. In the long and tortuous evolution of the human race on this planet a stage has been reached when through the rapid acceleration of science and technology, man has acquried the power to transform his environment in countless ways and on an unpreceedented scale. Both aspects of man's environment, the natural and the man made, are essential to his well being and to the enjoyment of the basic human rights, even the right to life itself"[3]

Every woman, man, youth and child has the human right to a safe and healthy environment, and to other fundamental human rights linked to and dependent upon a healthy environment. The *Universal Declaration of Human rights*(UDHR), Article 25 says, Everyone has the rights to a standard of living adequate for the health and well-being of himself and for his family, including food, clothing, housing and medical care and necessary social services[4]. Article 1 of *International Covenant of Economic, Social and Cultural Rights*(ICESCR) and *International Covenant of Civil and Political Rights*(ICCPR) say; All people may, for their own ends, freely dispose of their natural wealth and resources without prejudice to any obligation arising out of international cooperation, based upon the principle of mutual benefits, and international law. In no case a people be deprived of its own means of subsistence.[5]

The Human Rights at Issue, According to the *People's Movement for Human Rights Education* (PDHRE)[6], the Human Rights relating to the environment are set out in basic human rights treaties and include:

The human right to a safe and healthy environment.

The human right to the highest attainable standard of health.

The human right to ecologically sustainable development.

The human right to an adequate standard of living, including access to safe food and water.

The human right of the child to live in an environment appropriate for physical and mental development.

The human right to full and equal participation for all persons in environmental decision-making and development planning, and in shaping decisions and policies affecting one's community, at the local, national and international levels.

The human right to safe working conditions, including adequate safeguards for pregnant and lactating women.

The human right to freedom from any type of discrimination.

The human right to education and information, including information relating to links between health and the environment.

The human right to share in the benefits of scientific progress.

Environment perspective in the Indian Constitution

Mere declaration of environment a human right at the floor of United Nations was not enough. In consonance, the nations have to take some objective steps in this larger issue of mankind. India in 1976, have brought many constitutional amendments in one go, through which environment as a whole is placed at the position of human rights. Originally, constitution of India did not contain any provisions having a direct bearing on environment. However, some of the provisions do make tangential reference to the problem like article 47,48 and 49 contain directives to government. India was one of the few countries that has provided constitutional safeguards to preservation of the environment. Article 48-A, 51-A(g) and entries in three legislative lists are inserted in the constitution.

These provisions contain a clear mandate to the citizens to protect and improve the environment. Therefore, they continue the basic policy framework for all the legislative and executive programmes in this regard[7]. India has declared the year 2007 as water year and the common minimum programme of the United Progressive Government has given priority the state of water, both quality and quantity.

The *preamble* of the Indian constitution now characterize India as Sovereign, Socialists Secular, Democratic, Republic. Though, India has always been following the ideal of socialist pattern of society, yet it was for the first time this ideal was given a constitutional recognition by 42nd Constitution amendment Act 1976. The problem of environment Pollution is a social problem and the state, being a socialistic pattern, is obligated to address such issues.

The *Directive Principles of State Policy* article 47 says that the state shall regard the raising of the level of nutrition and the standard of living of its people and the improvement of public health as among its primary duties. This article provides for the improvement of the public health as one of the primary duties of the state and it could very well include by implication of the protection and improvement of the environment, for the control and prevention of environmental pollution necessarily and primarily comes within the concept of the improvements of the public health.

New insertion of articles 48-A says that the state shall endeavour to protect and improve the environment and to safeguard the forests and the wildlife of the country., has directly intervened to casts an obligatory duty on the state to endeavour to protect and improve the environment. To make it effective few insertions are made in the legislative lists enshrined in the seventh schedule of the constitution.

Addition of IV-A of fundamental duties in the constitution has proved deep concern of the state to protect and preserve the natural environment. Article 51A(g) enjoins that, it shall be the duty of every citizen of India ...to protect and improve the natural environment including forests, lakes, rivers and wildlife, and to have compassion for living creatures.

In accordance with National Policy for Environment, state has promulgated environmental laws to deal environment directly. Those are the Water(prevention and control of pollution) Act 1974, the Air(prevention and control of pollution) Act 1981, the Environment (protection) Act 1986[8].

Thus, the Concern for Environment protection is vivid in the Directive Principles of State policy and the Fundamental duties of the Indian Constitution. Its is no denying fact that clean environment forms a base for the cardinal principle, right to live. Article 21 of the Fundamental rights, Article 3 of the Universal Declaration of Human rights (UDHR) and Article 6 of the International Covenants on Civil and Political rights (ICCPR) enshrine the Right to Live. A narrow view of 'Right to Live' may refer to the protection of life and eradication of poverty, but also a broad view would encompass clean environment as well. The severity of environmental problems has now proved a major threat to human life and polluted Water,in particular, is posing a serious hazards to the survival of the flora and fauna of the ecosystem.

Right to clean Water

Water, an important factor of the environment is considered as the Elixir of Life, has been in neglect for a long time and now, at all levels of governance. In the 21st century, water is the converging and meeting point of the world community. Water is our common present nd future. "It is the invaluable heritage of our children[9]. The greatest challenge that humanity faces include responding to the world's current need for water, foreseeing their consumption requirements and ensuring food production without harming the environment. At least 400 million people live in regions where water is severely scarce[10]. Millions of people across the globe still do not have access to clean water, by 2025 there will be water shortage affecting millions of people covering as many as 52 countries. The worlds 38 poorest countries are located near areas that lack ample water supplies. Dirty water has become the world's most dangerous killer. At least 25,000 people die every day and diarrhea alone kills 4.6 million young children every year.

The UN water development report says that nearly 6000 people, mostly children, die of water-related causes every day. Owing to Man's unmindful actions, hazards to the flora and fauna are rampant. Countries in order to emulate developed nations are in the process of rapid, unplanned and disproportionate industrialization, takes heavy toll on their water resources. The vast quantities of carbon dioxide and other green house gases released by vehicles and industrial smokestacks were trapping the earth's heat, this will have dire consequences including acute water shortage. Even the so called developed nations, the United States for example are refused to be governed by the Kyoto protocol, to cut down the emissions.

India suffers from zonal and regional water shortages, there exist stiff opposition among states over water sharing, and schemes are narrow enough to have regional jurisdiction as scope. The Inter-linking of rivers is opposed by water dominant states and the delay and shortage of monsoon rain adds the woes of people. The Supreme Court of India, in the *Dehradun Quarring* case, held that, "we are not oblivious of the fact that the natural resources has got to be trapped for the purpose of social development but one can not forget at the same time that tapping of resources have to be done with requisite attention and care so that ecology and environment may not be affected in any serious way...It has always to be remembered that these permanent assets of mankind and are not intended to be exhausted by one generation"[11]. Scientist say that owing haphazard growth of polluting industries have led to increase in global temperature, acid rain, green house effect, ozone hole, deforestation etc., all these gross blunder have ill effect in our eco-system. This in turn affects the natural water cycle. Inspite of all said constitutional and legislative provisions the pollution of water sources and water bodies continues, in the pretext of religious rituals and deveopment. "Millions of people on the banks of the river Ganga are heading towards an environmental catastrophe. The water of the river of Kanpur consisted 29.200 units mg/ml of iron when the maximum limit is 0.3 units, and manganese was found to be 0.900 mg/ml when the WHO limit is 0.5 mg/ml. Seventy percent of all the available water in India is polluted"[12]. India faces challenges in the water sector in the form of declining per capita aqvailability of water over exploitation of ground water resources leading to lowering of ground water table in certain pockets, deterioration in the water quality, cost and time over-runs in the completion of irrigation and multi-purpose projects and poor maintenance of the existing systems. Of course, the most important challenge is to appropriately address the natural disasters related to water, like flood and drought. The water availability for the country as a whole has been assessed as 1869 billion cubic meters(BCM). However, it is estimated that only about 1123 BCM can be utilized which includes 690 BCM of asurface water and 433 BCN of replenishable ground water resources[13]. On an average for the country as a whole, the present position is better than many other countries. Most of the water resources of the country are generated from the rainfall during the monsoon period and that too, from a few spells of intense rainfall. As a result, the country suffer from flood-drought-flood syndrome. It is necessary to create infrastructure and adopt practices to augment the utilizble water resources and improve the efficiency of created facilities. At present the per capita storage capacity in India is only 207 cubic metres as compared to 1111 cubic metres in China[14]. As a result of growing population the per capita water availability of india is declining every year. The projected water demand in India, according to the Central Water Commission is as shown below.

The projected water demand in India

Year	*Population*	*Food grain*	*Requirements In million tons Irrigation*	*Drinking*	*Water demand in cubic km Industry*	*Total*
1992	860	175	460	25	15	500
2000	1000	250	630	33	30	693
2025	1530	400	770	52	120	942

Source: central water commission, Govt. of India, New Delhi, 1991.

Like air, water is a necessity of life, and is integral to life. It promises a commodity for business in the 21st century what oil was to the 20th century. Keeping in mind the business potential the world is moving towards water wars. Profit motive is obvious in the privatization of water, puts life of the poor at stake. Many major corporations have been moving into the water market, privatization of water supply has been high on the poltical agenda after the developing countries accepted General Agreements on Trade in Services. The water situation in India is so grim that, what once given to strangers by every house hold and found in cold earthen pot on the road side absolutely free, has become scarce and an economic entity, replaced the pots are multinational refrigerators selling the same as packaged drinking water. Villages devoid of clean water facilities has become the target of multi national corporations to sell their packaged water and soft drinks.

Suggestion

In the context of human rights, the gravity of the environmental situation in general and water in particular, calls for a concrete strategy incorporating modified local, state, national and global water management policies in the realm of conservation and management of water, for which the following suggestions may be useful

1. Recognising Human right to clean water and No privatisation of water sector
2. Creating sound infrastructure and maintenance of existing systems.
3. Creating evironment awakening among stakehoders
4. Government Commitment and must evoke people's participation
5. Advocating Efficient use of water.
6. Make the polluters pay for their actions
7. Making Rain Water Harvesting (RWH) compulsory
8. Regulating and adherene to the plan for constructions

9. Encourage civil society involvement in conservation and management of water
10. Government assuming the whole responsibility and accountability.

Conclusion

The irony is that, the fourth World Water Forum(WWF) held in Mexico City in March 2006, has missed a major opportunity to empower one billion people who are without a source of clean water, by failing to declare water as a basic human right[15]. Millions of poor people of the world take plain water as a meal. Water a free gift from our natural environment, over the years has become scarce and an economic entity. Therefore, Clean potable drinking water has been a distant dream of the poor and thus, they are deprived and not in a position to afford it. Millions of people across the globe still do not have access to clean water. The deprivation of clean water to the poor and future generation is tantamount to depriving the right to live and right to environment. The Andhra pradesh high court construed the right ecological balance as " It would be reasonable to hold that the enjoyment and fulfillment guaraanteed by Art. 21 of the constitution embraces the protection and preservation of nature's gifts without (which) life cannot be enjoyed. There can be no reason why practice of violent extinguishment of life alone should be regarded a violence of Article 21 of the constitution. The slow poisoning by the polluted atmosphere caused by environmental pollution and spoilation should be regarded as amounting to violation of Art. 21. of the constitution.[16] Therefore, in the context of human rights, it is imperative to utilise, conserve and manage water in an efficienct manner by all the stakeholders. However this cannot be achieved until the first step, in this regard is taken at all levels of governance; recognizing and declaring ***Clean water, a basic human right***. Thus, to respect and care for water today is to respect and ensure life tommorrow.

Reference

1. Aftah Alam, "Human Rights in India, Raj Publication", Delhi-9, 2000.
2. Bajwa.G.S., "Human Rights in India", Amol Publication P.Ltd, New Delhi-2,1997.
3. Basu.Durga Das, "Introduction to the Constitution of India", Wadhwa Company, Nagpur,1999.
4. Jaswal. Paramjit & Jaswal. Nishtha "Human Rights and the Law", A.P.H.Publishing Corporation,New Delhi-2, 1996.
5. Jayapalan.N., "Human Rights", Atlantic Publishers and Distributors, N.Delhi-27,2000.
6. Jaya shree Gupta," Human Rights and working women", Aravali Printers and Publications P.Ltd.,N.Delhi-1,1999.
7. Jitendra Mohan & Meena Sehgal," Drug Abuse among child Workers", Abhijeet publications, New Delhi-94,2004
8. Johari.J.C,.Principles of Modern Political Science," Sterling Publishers private Limited",New Delhi-16,1995
9. Mehartaj Begum.S, "Human Rights in India", A.P.H.Publishing Corporation,New Delhi-2, 2000.
10. Narasimhan.R.K., "Human Rights and Social Justice", Commonwealth Publishers, New Delhi-2, 1999
11. Dr.Ponnaian and others, "Human Rights for the Third Millennium", M/s.pon Rani publications, New Delhi-9, 2001.
12. Sharma Vinod, "Human Rights Violation", A.P.H.Publishing Corporation,New Delhi-2, 2002
13. People's Reporter, August-September 2006 & January 2007,Mumbai
14. The Hindu, 16,19,22,29march 2006.Chennqi edition.
15. The Frontline April 21, 2006.

End Notes

1. Environment,Encyclopedia, Wikipedia.com
2 Mohiuddin Ahamad Farooqui, Human rights in India issues and challenges Edited by Aftab Alam(Healthy Environment: A human right), Raj Publications, New Delh-9,2000.p.275.

3. Encyclopedia, United Nations, p. 780.
4. Article 25, The Universal Declaration of Human Rights, 1948.
5 Article 1. International Covenants on Economic, Social, Cultural Rights & International Covenant on Civil and Political rights, 1966.
6 The People's Movement for Human Rights Education www.google.com
7 Mohiuddin Ahamad Farooqui, Human rights in India issues and challenges Edited by Aftab Alam(Healthy Environment: A human right), Raj Publications, New Delh-9, 2000.p.277.
8 Ibid, p. 279.
9 Vicente Fox Quesada (Mexican President), Fourth world water forum, 16march 2006.
10 WWF News, people's Reporter,25 March 2006, p.1.
11 Aftah Alam, Human Rights in India, Raj Publication, Delhi-9, 2000, p. 257.
12 Ibid, p. 280.
13 Water year, People's Reporter, January 10-25,2007, p.7.
14 Ibid.
15 Making water a basic right, The Hindu, 29 marh 2006, p.10.
16. Goyal.P.K., ***Street Children and the Child Labour,*** Vista International Publication, Delhi,. 2005.p. 70.
17. ***Ibid.,*** p. 90.
18. Mamta Rajawat, ***Child Labour the Indian Perspective,*** Kilaso Books Publication, New Delhi, 2004. p.2
19. ***Ibid.,*** p. 3.
20. Srinivasa Reddy, B., and Ramesh.K., ***Girl Child Labour A World of Endless Exploitation,*** Dominant Publishers, New Delhi. 2002, p.3
21. ***Ibid.,*** p. 13.
22. Helen.R.Sekar, ***Child Labour Legislation in India, A Study in Retrospect and Prospect,*** V.V.Giri National Labour Institute, New Delhi, 1997, p.2.
23. Shukla.C.K., and Ali, S., ***Child Labour and the Law,*** Sarup and Sons, New Delhi, 2006. p. 3.

24. Goyal, P.K., ***Street Children and the Child Labour,*** Vister International publishing. Delhi.2005.p.80.
25. Prafullah Padhy, ***Social legislation and Crime,*** Ishal Book Publication, Delhi, 2006. p.72
26. Mahajan, V.D., ***op.cit.,*** p.20
27. Sivagami Paramasivam, ***op.cit.,*** p.133.

12

Hunger – A Human Rights' Issue

R. P. Pankaja

It is generally believed that economic growth and development will reduce poverty as it provides for empowerment in amenities and increase in comfort levels. The conditions of living like proper housing, sanitation facilities, per capita consumption of water and electricity, increasing enrolment in schools and low child mortality, adult literacy, life expectancy are some of the basic indicators by which the economic growth of a country may be gauged. The process of urbanization in India for becoming an industrial modern society has revealed a growing list of problems marked by poverty, unemployment, etc. One of the most important causes of poverty is the population increase that has severe pressure on housing and deteriorating quality of life seen in the form of the lack of basic amenities, proliferation of slums, lack of safe drinking water and unsatisfactory means of waste disposal.

Besides, the ramifications of poverty are more prominently seen in the non-availability of food. Shortage of food has led to suicides in several states. For instance, the state of Maharashtra has been unable to stem the tragic loss of lives of farmers in spite of the Rs.5.75 crore package given to it by the centre. During the formative years, it is absolutely necessary that a child has nutritive food and healthy surroundings. Sadly enough, these are not easy to come by as a recent survey by the World Food Programme estimates that nearly 18,000 children die everyday due malnutrition and hunger. "Hunger" thus seems to be the most demanding of challenges and hence has been considered to be the focus of this paper.

In the rural areas, a large number of people are involved in agriculture and related jobs. Most of them earn only wages. With the development of agricultural sector, no doubt, wages increase but this increase lags behind the growth of agricultural incomes. It could be argued that the agricultural terms of trade have improved. But this has benefited only the big farmers and not the small laborers or marginal workers. Consequently, the cost of living for the latter is high.

A study by the Punjab Agricultural University on farm incomes in Punjab for the year 1987-88, found that 64% of a farmer's expenditure goes towards food, 9% on clothing, 2% on education etc,. He spends less than 1% on fruits. How is the picture today? The rise in price of every commodity is unabated. And prices are going out of control. For instance, the price of *moong dal* increased 118%, from Rs. 22.50 to Rs. 49/-, *urad* up 82%, *atta* is up 44%. Perishables are doing no better. Eg., Onion prices increased 186% before stabilizing to weeks back. The urban folk may voice their anger but what a bout the rural folk who spend more than 60% on food? The upshot of the above is that by a hike in food prices, not only the laborers in the rural areas but the wage earners in the urban areas also are the worst hit.

It could be argued that the price rises are only seasonal. But as in the grains, it has a structural issue. The lack of effective distribution links and processing leads to nearly 16million tonnes of vegetables and 40 million tonne of fruits being wasted. Too many middlemen are involved so much so the consumer pays nearly six times what the farmer gets paid for his produce. Thus both the consumer and the farmer are denied affordability.

Though it may seem paradoxical, it is essential that the state has to intervene to help those not assured of regular incomes. The Green Revolution has created new acreage in cultivation and has invested in new technology to such an extent that India is considered to be the second largest producer of food grain. But it is nowhere when it comes to the international norms in yield per acre. The present crisis gives clear indication of what needs to be cultivated, what may be exported or imported. At the same time the need to empower people has to be a core strategy so that they will respond to issues that affect their lives. There are several instances where justice is delayed or denied to them. Further, they also lack access to justice since they do not seek any form of justice to protect their rights, including their fundamental right to food.

In this regard, Jean Dreze and Amartya Sen observe in "Hunger and Public Action:": "The point is not much that there is no law against dying of hunger. That is, of course, there and obvious. It is more that the legally guaranteed rights of ownership, exchange and transaction delineate economic systems that go hand in hand with some people failing to acquire enough food for survival...... In seeking a remedy to this problem of terrible vulnerability, it is natural to turn towards a reform of the legal system, so that the rights of social security can be made to stand as guarantees of minimal protection and survival". This highlights the urgent need of all governments to tackle hunger. With the acceptance of economic, social, and cultural rights as enforceable human rights, recognition of hunger as a human rights issue is as much acceptable too. In the Indian context, it is as much relevant rather than being a mere political objective.

At the UN Millennium Summit held in Sept.2000, the world leaders of the 191 member nations decided to establish time bound measurable goals to combat poverty, hunger, disease, discrimination against women, illiteracy, environment degradation etc.. Called the Millenium Development Goals, hunger and poverty top the list. The member nations also agreed to achieve this by 2015. How far this will be a reality, we will only have to wait and see.

However, **strategic steps** based on a human rights approach, if undertaken, would make it possible, for,

(i) people will then be proactive to issues that directly concern them, including, hunger;

(ii) governance will then be suitably reformed.

To make this a reality, the member nations of the U.N. have to firstly, make the right to safe drinking water, a balanced diet and primary healthcare, a basic human right. Secondly, developing countries may be enabled to improve small farm productivity. Thirdly, by encouraging industrial nations to launch a special drive to increase their agricultural produce by acceptable methods, it would certainly be possible to produce the required quantity of food grains.

The World Food Programme can draft a special charter for achieving freedom from hunger. Those technologies which can contribute to enhance nutrition and health security may be utilized protecting their intellectual rights. At the same time care should also be taken to see that the livelihood of the locals is not affected. This will ensure that their income security is maintained.

It is in this context that the legal framework and the notion of legal empowerment of the poor through and law and institutional reforms becomes significant. In a democracy like ours, the focus of a rights-based approach to development is

- to ensure that the government is made accountable to the citizens and the international community about their progress;
- to integrate the norms, standards and principles of the international human rights system into the plans, anti-hunger (and anti-poverty), in this context;
- to define human rights, goals and objectives specifically providing for indicators and measurements to monitor progress within a given period in the specific area of

improvement, namely, food, clothing, shelter etc. so that the society is not affected.

Judicial intervention: A wrongful act becomes valuable for judicial space when it is recognized as a violation of human rights. Thus it makes it mandatory for the enforcement for its directives for the implementation of remedial measures. Viewed thus, the antipoverty measures undertaken by the government will undergo an attitudinal change so that the abolishing of poverty is no more a mere policy but is constitutional and human rights imperative. Institutions like the Human Rights Commission will then have an important role.

To conclude, the involvement of the civil society is absolutely essential for any policy to be implemented well. If hunger is recognized is recognized as a human rights issue,

(1) the domestic and international civil societies will have to take an active part. This will create an empowering dimension in the work of the civil society in ensuring a hunger and poverty-free governance as a principle of administration;

(2) a political consensus can be achieved on the ways and means of achieving the same;

(3) objectivity can be maintained in the implementation of policies relating to fighting hunger and poverty so that resource allocation and targeting of areas and people suffering from extreme poverty is not based on biases and prejudices. This is important for the resources allocated may not reach the beneficiaries. To avoid this problem, recognition of hunger as a human rights issue will broaden the scope of implementation without discrimination and bring about internationally developed principles for good governance.

13

Human Rights and the Children

A. Sethuramasubbiah

The Phenomenon of Child labour, widespread and rampant as it is, owes its existence to socio-economic and cultural forces and so can not be seen in isolation. It has, in recent years, received attention from NGOs, trade unions, employers' organisations and research institutions. The strategy of sequential and progressive elimination of child labour has gained the attention of the wider public and underscores the validity of India's legislative policy with respect to child labour. However, great deal remains to be done. "Children of India, have you any human hope? Are we a nation without shock and shame,"- Hon'ble Justice V.R.KrishnaIyer asked with poignant aghast. Why? Not because of the many grave sins of injustice and corruption the Administration commits in many dimensions but because every child in tears suffers in silence the daily trauma of bonded labour. The Constitution forbids this crime against children. Legislation bans this inhumanity. International instruments provide with sensitive compassion and global obligation the need for childhood to be defended against the culpable violation of the rights of infant innocence.

The Universal Declaration of Human Rights, the International Covenant on Economic, Social and Cultural Rights,

The International Covenant on Civil and Political Rights constitute a trinity often called the MagnaCarta of humanity. The vistarama of varied categories of human rights, versatility of protection to vulnerable sectors of people and the sensitive methods to ensure enjoyment of human rights by everyone may show astonishing advance. A quick run-down of the topics touched upon by the United Nations organs is instructive.

A compassionate catalogue where the United Nations shows concern for human rights may well begin with the right to self-determination, at least for sub national identity often repudiated by colonial powers and apartheid cultures. The list of Human rights, which every human being has, a right to enjoy includes:

- The right to life;
- Abolition of slavery and suppression of the slave trade;
- Abolition of forced or compulsory labour;
- Freedom from torture;
- Freedom from arbitrary arrest, detention or exile;
- Equality in the administration of justice;
- The right of everyone to leave any country, including his own, and to return to his country;
- The right to a nationality;
- Freedom of thought, conscience and religion;
- Freedom of opinion and expression;
- Freedom of association;
- The right of everyone to take part in the government of his country;
- The realization of economic, social and cultural rights;
- The right to work;
- The right to education;
- The right to health;
- Freedom from hunger;
- The right to participate in cultural life;
- The right to a clean environment;
- The right to adequate shelter and services

The universality of the above rights does not detract from the special concern for the rights and welfare of members of vulnerable groups. These categories cover:

- Children;
- Mentally retarded persons;
- Persons belonging to ethnic, religious or linguistic minorities;
- Persons born out of wedlock;
- Indigenous populations.

Child Labour: Denial of Child Rights

It is unfortunate that even today the problem of child labour is prevalent to a great extent in our country and in the world. The latest statistics show that about 250million child workers exist in the age group of 5-14 all over the world. A recent survey conducted by the international Labour Organisation (ILO) states that out of these 61 per cent are in Asia, 32 per cent in Africa and 7 per cent in Latin America. India has the largest number of child labourers. It is also true that child labour in India is more of a rural phenomenon with more than 90 per cent children working in agricultural and allied activities in the villages. Children are important assets of any nation as they are the future citizens. The destiny of a country depends directly on how well its children are looked after.

According to the convention of the rights of the Child (CRC) child labour may be regarded as a denial of child right. Under this right come rehabilitation, protection of child workers and improvement of their working conditions. Hence regulation of these aspects of child labour is felt essential. Right to education and access to recreation and to childhood itself is associated with the rights of the child.

The concept of childhood is relatively of recent significance particularly in the context of children's rights. For the first time the French Revolution in 1789 led stress on equality, fraternity, and dignity of the human being from whom the rights of the man have emerged. In the 19th century, the children were not given any special importance rather their ignorance and weakness led to all kinds of torture, operations and misuse of their labour and comfort. It was taken for granted that child labour is due to poverty. But it is found that child labour has been due to the negative attitude of parents and of the society in general. Some argue that "work is experiential learning and good for the child". Children were suffering from various deficiencies and ailments and adequate care was not taken by the poor parents and the society. Hence, declaration of the rights of the child in 1959 is taken as a significant step in the "Best interest of the Child". Now-a-days ILO, UNESCO and other international agencies take interest in safeguarding the child rights particularly in relation to the exploitation of child labour.

The CRC in fact devotes much greater attention to civil rights than to the economic, social and cultural rights. The implementation of economic, social and cultural rights is made subject to the availability of the resources while civil and political rights have corresponding obligations and progressive implementation of economic, social and cultural rights. A country's richness is judged by the norms like "maximum extent of utilisation of valuable resources" in order to address child labour more effectively.

With this background, child labour is now considered in a humanitarian as well as human rights approach. Child labour is taken as a violation of civil and political rights or a violation of economic, social and cultural rights. However, all these rights are interacted and immediate steps need be taken for taking all these aspects or effectively breaking a point in the vicious circle. Of course, we cannot resolve the problem overnight, but no time can be delayed for taking adequate action in the matter. Under the CRC, there are various requests relating to child labour—discrimination, abuse, encroachment to privacy and recreation impeachment on the child's education and safety and security of the child.

Child labour is attributed mainly to exploitation, discrimination, powerlessness, caste and gender operation. There are various attitudinal factors, which are responsible for taking children to hazardous jobs on dignified services and insecure and indecent life-callings. Even the World Bank is imposing restrictions on the misuse of child labour. It is estimated that that the greater productivity of those children who remain in primary schools for reasonable time will enable them to earn over six times the cost of giving them the additional education. Primary education, says the bank in the largest single contributor to the economic growth rates of high performance. Although a number of legislations have been enacted to regulate child labour, it has not yet been possible to bring child labour even to the minimum or to a reasonable standard. It is, therefore, insisted that there should be a constitutional amendment to transfer the subject of education from a Directive principle of State policy to a Fundamental Right so that the Government will be bound to provide minimum standard of education to every child. Various NGOs are now active to control the quantum of child labour and reduce its harmful reactions and repercussions. Government has also set up a few committees to deal with child rights in its various sections of the society. Government have also set up a separate commission for protection and safeguarding children's rights.

India has tremendous armoury of legislations, regulations and statues, which call for the protection of the rights of children. The Directive principles of State policy embedded in the constitution of India seek compulsory primary education for all children. This is one of their basic rights and a goal still far from realization. India is also a party to save international conventions regarding protection of children's rights. India has also ratified CRC in December 19992 which states in Article 32 "State parties recognized rights of the child to be protected from economic exploitation and from performing any work, i.e., likely to be hazardous or to interfere with the child's education or to be harmful to the child's wealth or physical, mental, spiritual, moral or racial development.

In ratifying this Convention, India has assumed yet another obligation to bring national laws and practices into conformity with international standards.

The UNICEF has identified the following causative factors relating to inequalities and abuse of child's right in the context of children's labour. These are:

(i) bonded to pay up debts to landlords incurred by their parents;
(ii) working in situations in which their parents are unemployed; and
(iii) not paid the minimum wages and prone to physical, mental and sexual abuse by employers.

Human Rights Commission has recently perceived that there is a growing recommendation in the senior-most policy-making circles of the country of the need for ending child labour, supporting with those employed in hazardous industries. This had led to the approval of series of constructive measures by the Central Government. Even the State Government has allowed the suit and has implementing a number of restricting legislations. In India, Government has taken steps to constitute a National Authority for the Elimination of Child Labour (NAECL) and also a National Child Labour Project (NCLP) which is being undertaken in 12 different areas of the country. The commission is also most respectful of the fact that the Department of Education has deliberated on this matter carefully and that instead of All India Legislations on Child Labour, it has chosen to adopt a different strategy to achieve the goal of the universalisation of elementary education.

UNICEF in India is implementing programmes against child labour and trying to abolish child labour in a phased manner. It has stated its policies as follows:

- all forms of child labour should be eliminated to comply with agreed child rights;
- as seen in other countries the enactment and enforcement of legislation to make primary education compulsory as a pre-requisite for the elimination of child labour;

- while poverty alleviation is clearly relevant, it is not necessary nor desirable to await economic developments as a means of eliminating child labour;
- motivation and enforcement of existing legislation of child labour is necessary as a supportive measure for the elimination child labour;
- in addition to continuing support for government programmes on child labour, UNICEF would seek to strengthen NGO alliances which are proving effective in drawing public attention; and
- while advocating for an end to child labour, UNICEF would focus on programmes of rehabilitation of children released from labour into the educational system and to improve their livelihood.

Thus the specific objective to combat child labour would be:

- to promote compulsory primary education as the fundamental strategy for elimination and prevention of child labour by enrolling and retaining the students in schools;
- to advocate for revision and reinforcement of legislation for prohibiting child labour particularly in hazardous occupation and industries; and
- to assist in central and state governments to develop and implement programmes and action plans for the release and rehabilitation of children from labour in various industries and occupations.

Thus to conclude,

"The day will come when nations will be judged not by their military or economic strength nor by the splendour of their capital cities and public buildings but by well-being of their people; by the levels of health, nutrition and education; by the opportunities to earn a fair reward for their labour ; by their ability to participate in the decisions that affect their lives, by the respect that is shown for their civil and political liberties; by the provision that is made for those who are vulnerable and

disadvantaged and by the protection that is afforded to the growing minds and bodies of their children".

Reference

1. ***"Childlabour Law -An overview"**, (1998) V.V.G.N.L.I, Noida, UP.*
2. ***"Human Rights and Inhuman Wrongs"** (2004) V.R. KrishnaIyer.*
3. ***"Social Legislation and Social Change"** (1998) Dr. K. Shanmugavelayudam.*
4. ***Human Rights Watch** (1996), The Small Hands of Slavery: Bonded Child Labour in India, Human Rights Watch, New Delhi.*
5. ***International Labour Organisation** (1991), Still so far to go – Child Labour in the World Today, ILO, Geneva.*

14

Child Labour and Legal Legislation

N. Anandhi & Dr. S. Suresh Kanan

Introduction

The problem of child labour in underdeveloped and developing countries is quiet high and abnormal. Children of various age groups have been employed in large number in industries, hotels and other places on account of poverty. They are deprived of education, proper health, fundamental rights have no meaning to them. At a young age, they are driven to work in difficult and hazardous fields simply to sustain their own lives and that of the family which entirely depends on them.

Background

The significance and the importance of the child lies in the fact that the child is the universe. If there was no universes without humanity. Today's children will be the leader who will hold the country's banner high and maintain the prestige of the nation. If a child goes wrong for want of proper attention, training and guidance, it will indeed de a deficiency of the society and of government of the day.

Both at the national level and the international level great interest is being shown in the matter of welfare of children.

Children need special protection because of their age, Physique and mental facilities. They are a "supremely important national assets" and the future well-being of the nation depends as to how children grow and develop.

It is estimated that by 2000 A.D. 25 per cent of the world's population will be children and 40 percentage of the entire global labour force will be below the age of 15 years. In developing countries 40 percentage of the total population under 15 years and 75 percen are employed as child labour.

ILO in a study concluded that in Asian Countries 70 to 80 per cent of children are either working or simply wasting their lives away. Employment of vhildren has continued therefore o be a problem.

Child labour is the major cause of child abuse and exploitation in many parts of the world. No one knows for certain how many children are working. Child employment is illegal and there is often an attempt to conceal it.

Child Labour In Various Countries

Child labour is increasing world wide because of economic and non-economic factors in SouthAsia and Africa. In many countries more and more poor families are leaving the country side for cities. In Brazil, Child Labour is very high and 2 million street children are found in Rio alone. Among the developed countries, U.S.A. has highest child labourers. One million Mexican children are sold at Bangkok railway station. In south Africa 6,30,000 children work on white owned farms and are subjected to racial exploitation. These children are given punishment sometimes resulting in death of the children or permanent disability.

Child Labour In India

ILO has estimated the total work force of children in the world as 52 million, of these, 38 million are estimated to be in Asia or one fourth of all working children in the world are in

India. An exact number of working children is difficult to know due to unorganized nature of activities, multiplicity of concepts etc.

The census of 1961 gave the figure of child labour of 14.50 million. In 1971 the reported figure was 10.74 million which is 4.66 per cent of the total population and 5.95 percent of the total labour force. In 1981, 11.17 million were reported to be child workers, particularly because child labour is not often taken on full time and work by a child is often treated as a secondary activity. Therefore the census figures considerably under – estimate the magnitude of child workers in India. As per the 1991 census, there are 14 crores working on full time basis.

The national sample survey data not only indicates a higher number of child workers but also emphasized that it has gone up over a period of time. It estimates the figures to be 17.36 million. Operation Research group Baroda mentions 44 million as the figure for working children. Concerned for working children (CWC) of Bangalore indicates the figure as 100 million. Nearly 6 crores of children are working in organized and unorganized sectors in India. So India is in second place of the world.

Child Labour in Tamil Nadu

Tamilnadu for a large proportion of children employed in the vast un-organised sector, informal and unregulated sectors. Tamilnadu ranks seventh in the country with reference to childlabour.

North Arcot, Salem and Madurai districts account for a higher proportion of childlabour. In the state Kanyakumari, Thiruchirapalli, Dharmapuri and south Arcot districts have similar distribution of working children. In Chennai, Niligiris and Pudukkattaqi Districts the proportion of child labour is low. In Thanjavur and Chengalpattu districts, the child labour proportion is relatively low.

North Arcot, Dharmapuri, Salem, Erode, Madurai and Cooimbatore together accounrt for 68% of total of child labour force in agriculture. The number of female children working in the unorganized sector is higher compared to the number of male children in Thirunelveli, Ramanathapuram, Madurai, Coimbatore and Erode districts.

Nature of Problem

Child labour is not a new phenomenon to our age. What is new however is its perception as a social problem the world over. There has been a distinct change in recent past in the values and attitudes of the legitimizing groups of society is vis-à-vis child labour because of some new developments.

regions of childhood employment result in a permanently weakened and damaged labour force. Child labour involves the use of child labour as its point of lowest productivity. Hence it is an inefficient utlisation of labour power. The argument that employment of children, increases the earnings of the family and keeps children away from mischief is misleading. It glasses over the fact that child labour deprives children of educational opportunities minimizes their chances for vocational training, stunts their physical growth, hampers their intellectual development and by forcing them into the army of unskilled labourers or blind alley jobs, condemns them to low wages of all their lives.

A great majority of these children work in agriculture and the unorganized sector like all commercial establishments and shops or quasi family undertakings. 79 per cent are employed as cultivators or agricultural labourers, 8 per cent in livestock, forestry, plantations, etc., 6 per cent in households and other services the rests in trade, commerce and transport.

Various surveys conducted by the labour bureau reveal that children are employed to do light job, such as helping in the field, in factories for packing, pasting of labels, etc., and in match factories, tea factories, tea estates, bedi manufacturing, printing, number of children as domestic servants, works in hotels, restaurants, canteens, wayside shops, newspaper selling, coolies, shoes-shine boys, vendor, etc.

Though Indian law does not pro hibit the employment of children in cottage industries, family, house-holds, restaurants, or in agriculture yet it is quite evident that the working conditions of the children in these small organization is far inferior of those of large factories.

Meaning of Child labour

A generally valid definition of child labour is presently not available either in the national or international context. Any definite turns upon the precise meaning we attach to two components of the term "child labour' (i.e.) "child" in terms of his chronological age and "labour" in capacity. Child labour however, can broadly be defined as that segment of the child population which participates in work either paid or unpaid.

The term "child labour" is commonly interpreted in twodifferent ways first, as an economic practice and second as a social evil. In the first context it signifies employment of children in gainful occupations with a view to adding to the total income of the family. It is in the second, sense that the term child labour is now more generally used.

Causes of Child Labour

- Poverty
- Cheap availability
- Illiteracy
- Over population
- Large size of family
- Rural migration
- Economic compulsion - only earning member of the family
- Unemployment/underemployment
- Scarce schooling facilities
- High rate of non-school going children – high magnitude of Child labour
- Unorganised sector: Agriculture
- Casual nature of employment
- Unequal distribution of land
- Social customs and beliefs

- Belief that children would do ———effectively
  ———quickly
  ———learning

  Child Labour is the work which involved some degree of exploitation i.e., physical, mental, economic and social.

Preferrance of Child Labour.

- Child Labour is cheap
- Children are most amenable to discipline compared to adults.
- They are efficient, quick workers in repetitive work
- They are more suited for some types of jobs
- Children are honest and sincere

LEGAL FRAMEWORK

Acts Related To Child Labour

- Children (Pledging of Labour) Act 1993
- Employment of Children Act 1938
- Minimum Wages Act 1948
- Plantation Labour Act 1951
- Mines Act 1951
- Merchant Shipping Act 1958
- Motor Transport Act 1958
- Motor Transport Act 1961
- Apprentices Act 1961
- Atomic Energy Act 1961
- Beedi and Cigar Workers (condition of Employment) Act 1960
- Shops and Establishments Act in various States and Union Territories
- Child Labour (Prohibition And Regulation) Act 1986
- Factories Act 1948.

The Role of International Labour Organisation (ILO)

The ILO was deeply concerned about the protection and promotion of the interests of woeking children right from its very inception in 1919.

The protection of children as an essential element of social justice, is a part of the preamble to the constitution of the ILO. In fact at the turn of the century, child labour in the industrializing countries was of such urgent public concern that it was an important stimulus in the creation of the ILO itself. The Philadelphia Declaration of the International Labour Conference in tis meeting in 1944 recognised that it was the duty of the ILO to promote the programmes relating to child welfare among the nations of the world. Convention No.138 of the conference of the ILO in 1973, entitled "MINIMUM AGE OF ADMISSION TO EMPLOYMENT" came into force on June 19, 1976 and is now the major instrument regarding child labour.

International Programme for Elimination of Child Labour (IPEC)

This is an Action Programme which has been established by the ILO commencing work in 1990. The ILO entered into an agreement with the Government of Germany in December 1991 for implementing the programme over a period of five years with an assistance of DM 50 million. In 1992 Belgium also became a donor in the programme. India was one of the first countries to join the programme which is now under implementation in 10 countries.

Indian Constitution and Child Labour

ARTICLES	*PROVISION*
15(3)	Enables the state to make special provisions for children
23	Prohibits the traffic in human beings and forced labour
24	Forbids employment of children below of 14 years in factories, mines and other hazardous occupation

39(e)	Directs the state safeguard the tender age of children from entering into jobs unsuited to their age and strength forced by economic necessity.
45	Directs the state to provide free and Compulsory education to all children upto the Years of age.

Legislative Provisions for Child Labour

Protection of children is offered under many labour laws. The Governmant has enacted several laws to promote proper growth and development of children and has made provisions for their proper care, protection, maintenance, welfare, training, education and rehabilitation. A brief mention of these laws is given below

Assistance to Voluntary Organisations

During 2004-2005 financial assistance was given to 20 voluntary organizations in the field of child labour for implementation of continuing as well as new projects for the welfare of the working children and to provide non-formal education supplementary nutrition, health care and vocational training.

Child Labour Action and Support Programme (CLASP)

This progaramme is aided by the Government of Germany. It aims at strengthening the country's capabilities for climination of child labour. Assistance taken under this programme is used for the purpose of supporting on-going activities under the National Policy of Child Labour. The total allocation un der the programme which is started in 1992 is US $0.83 million and upto December 1994 the expenditure incurred to an extent of US $0.24 million.

The Supreme Court has ordered the setting up of a corpus fund with a Rs.2500 contribution by the employer for every child employed in a hazardous industry.

Every offending employer will have to pay Rs.20,000 as compensation for the violation of the child labour act 1986.

The Supreme Court also asked the states to ensure that an adult member of the working child's family gets a job in the place of the child. In case this was not possible Rs.50,000 be contributed to the fund for each child.

Committees and Commission on Child Labour in India

Some of the observations and the findings of various committees abd commissions which have investigated the conditions of the labour in general and of the child labour in particular in India from time to time are as follows.

- The Royal Commission on Labour 1929
- Labour Investigation Committee 1944
- National Commission on Labour 1966
- Gurupadaswamy Committee 1979

Conclusion

The educationstatus assessment found that while the majority of the children had been entrolled in primary school most had dropped out at the primary level to enter the labour force.

Multified aspects of inaction plan required in four areas identified areas are:

- Houuse hold economy and Area development
- Enforcement and legal frame work
- Education
- Communication and Social Mobilisation.

15

Child Labour : Indian Prospective

G.Subramanian

"Any work done by children in order to economically benefit their family or themselves directly or indirectly, at the cost of their physical, mental or social development".

- Tahir Hussain (1991) about 'Child Labour'

Children are the future citizens of a country. It is duty of individual in a society to see that the dreams and rights of a child are fulfilled. As per the latest International Labour Organization (ILO) 2003 survey, "Child Labour between the ages of 5 and 14 figures astounding to 256 million, out of which Asia accounts for 153 million working children"[1].

The problem of child labour continues to pose a challenge before the nation. Government has been taking various pro-active measures to tackle this problem. However, considering the magnitude and extent of the problem and that it is essentially a socio-economic problem inextricably linked to poverty and illiteracy, it requires concerted efforts from all sections of the society to make a dent in the problem. India has the world's largest child labourer population. In 2001 census, there are 1,26,66,377 working children in India [*See annexure for State wise working children in India]*. But, the United Nations

Children's Fund (UNICEF) estimates that there are more than 35 million such children, accounting for 14 per cent of the children in the 5-14 age group. Other unofficial estimates are much higher, ranging between 60 and 125 million child labourers. In Tamil Nadu, according 2001 census, 4,18,801 working children are there. One more data from Tamil Nadu Sarva Siksha Abhyan Report, 2004 records that more than 25,000 Child Labours are in Vellore, Virudhunagar, Tirunelveli, Tuticorin, Dharmapuri, Namakkal, Salem, Erode, Trichy, Kancheepuram, Dindigul and Chennai District.

In Indian Constitution, Article 21A [Right to Education], Article 24 [Prohibition of employment of children in factories, etc.] and Article 39 [Securing working children], provides protection to Child Labour. The Supreme Court in Unnikrishnan J.P. v. State of Andhra Pradesh (1993) SCC 645 is a landmark judgment which declared that every child up to 14 years of age has a fundamental right to primary education.

Legislative provisions prohibiting and regulating employment of Children as per the Child Labour (Prohibition & Regulation) Act, 1986. As per the latest amendment of this Act, which came into force in 10th October 2006—children who are employed in 15 hazardous industries including domestic sector and restaurants, kids must be freed from child labour and returned home. Hazardous and exploitative child labour has a profound negative impact on a child's physical, emotional, mental, spiritual, moral, and social development. In many cases, children engaged in labour suffer poor health, a lower IQ, physical harm and abuse, low self-esteem, little or no education, and deprivation of adequate support systems.

In consonance with the above approach, a National Policy on Child Labour was formulated in 1987. Government has accordingly been taking proactive steps to tackle this problem through strict enforcement of legislative provisions along with simultaneous rehabilitative measures. State Governments, which are the appropriate implementing authorities, have been conducting regular inspections and raids to detect cases of violations. Since poverty is the root cause of this problem, and enforcement alone cannot help solve it, Government has been laying a lot of emphasis on the rehabilitation of these children and on improving the economic conditions of their families.

There are various issues with child labour and education. One is the cultural implication in the various regions of the country; the other is special education for children who have been through the aggressions of child labour- linked to rehabilitation. The measures taken by the government for the release of children, from hazardous occupations are significant through the formulation of National Child Labour projects (NCL projects). This was an attempt towards visualizing education as one of the basic ingredients of child welfare services, with main areas such as:

>>Stepping up enforcement of child labour laws
>>Non-formal education
>>Income and employment generations
>>Special schools
>>Sensitising public on child labour issues
>>Survey and evaluation.

This has made it possible for a large number of children to come out of their cruel surroundings and deprivation. However, inherent flaws in the Child Labour Act (Prohibition and regulation), 1986 has failed to provide relief to the large number of children, who are engaged in work situations outside those listed industries.

The Indian policy and lawmakers are clearly working with contradictory initiatives, half planned policies, and generic mechanisms when it comes to fighting child labour. Unfortunately, there is a lack of mechanisms, which are capable of attacking the underlying problem of poverty – and actual reasons for violations of child rights. The Indian scene of child labour is dominated with various cultural impacts where education alone cannot work to complete the rights chain. Each state, and each district have varied cultural impacts and cannot be addressed through a national scheme alone. Similarly, issues of rehabilitation and mental health considerations cannot be addressed until the size of the problem is acknowledged.

At a policy level there is a long way to go. The first step would be to step out of the denial phase, the second to realise the country's cultural diversities towards children, and the third to understand the needs of a child who has been rescued from child labour.

(This paper is prepared by the Executive Director, Manitham - Human Rights Organisation, 274-GC, Avvai Shanmugam Salai, Royapettah, Chennai-14. E-mail: manitham@gmail.com ; website : www.manitham.net)

Glossary

1. International Labour Organization (ILO) 2003 survey.

16

Rights of Disabled Persons-Where Are We in India?

P.Anathakrishnan

Introduction

UN General Assembly by resolution 3447 (XXX) of 9 December 1975, while Declaring the Rights of Disabled Persons and call for national and international action, to ensure that it will be used as a common basis and frame of reference for the protection of these rights in the following terms:

- The term "disabled person" means any person unable to ensure by himself or herself, wholly or partly, the necessities of a normal individual and/or social life, as a result of deficiency, either congenital or not, in his or her physical or mental capabilities.
- The rights shall be granted to all disabled persons without any exception whatsoever and without distinction or discrimination on the basis of race, colour, sex, language, religion, political or other opinions, national or social origin, state of wealth, birth or any other situation applying either to the disabled person himself or herself or to his or her family.
- Disabled persons have the inherent right to respect for their human dignity.

- Disabled persons have the same civil and political rights as other human beings; paragraph 7 of the Declaration on the Rights of Mentally Retarded Persons applies to any possible limitation or suppression of those rights for mentally disabled persons.
- Disabled persons are entitled to the measures designed to enable them to become as self-reliant as possible.
- Disabled persons have the right to medical, psychological and functional treatment, including prosthetic and orthetic appliances, to medical and social rehabilitation, education, vocational training and rehabilitation, aid, counselling, placement services and other services which will enable them to develop their capabilities and skills to the maximum and will hasten the processes of their social integration or reintegration.
- Disabled persons have the right to economic and social security and to a decent level of living. They have the right, according to their capabilities, to secure and retain employment or to engage in a useful, productive and remunerative occupation and to join trade unions.
- Disabled persons are entitled to have their special needs taken into consideration at all stages of economic and social planning.
- Disabled persons have the right to live with their families or with foster parents and to participate in all social, creative or recreational activities.
- Disabled persons shall be protected against all exploitation, all regulations and all treatment of a discriminatory, abusive or degrading nature.
- Disabled persons shall be able to avail themselves of qualified legal aid when such aid proves indispensable for the protection of their persons and property.
- Organizations of disabled persons may be usefully consulted in all matters regarding the rights of disabled persons.

2. Overview of the issue of human rights of persons with disabilities at the international level

21. Fundamental human rights of persons with disabilities

The principle of the right to equality, addressed throughout the normative standards set out by the international human rights instruments is the foundation of the rights of individuals with disabilities. In order that the rights of persons with disabilities may be further realized, contemporary international law has increasingly recognized the need for all states to incorporate human rights standards into their national legislation. Although the means chosen to promote full realization of economic, social and cultural rights of persons with disabilities may differ among countries, there is no country exempt from the need for improved policies and laws for individuals with disabilities.

2.2 International Norms and Standards relating to the rights of persons with disabilities

Research has indicated that the consequences of disablement are particularly serious for women. Women with disabilities are discriminated against on two grounds: gender and disability, and often they have less access to essential services such as health care, education and vocational rehabilitation.

The Convention Against Torture and other Cruel, Inhumane, or Degrading Treatment or Punishment may be utilized to ensure that appropriate state action be taken for those who have become disabled as a result of inhumane treatment as well as to promote prevention.

The Convention on the Rights of the Child is an example of a human rights instrument that specifically and generally addresses the rights of children with disabilities. In addition to the general international human rights instruments, disability-specific instruments concerning the rights of persons with disabilities have been adopted at the international level. These include the Declaration on the Rights of Mentally Retarded Persons, the Declaration on the Rights of Disabled Persons, the World Programme of Action concerning Disabled Persons, the Principles for the Protection of Persons with Mental Illness and the Standard Rules on the Equalization of Opportunities for Persons with Disabilities.

3. Issues concerning a special instrument on the rights of persons with disabilities

3.1 Historical Overview

1980s: The first initiative emerged in the Global Meeting of Experts to Review the Implementation of the World Programme of Action concerning Disabled Persons at the Mid-point of the United Nations Decade of Disabled Persons.

1990s: In May 1990, the Economic and Social Council authorized the Commission on Social Development to consider establishment of a working group, funded by voluntary contributions, to elaborate the Standard Rules on the Equalization of Opportunities for Persons with Disabilities.

3.2 New initiative for an international convention on the rights of persons with disabilities

The United Nations General Assembly adopted the resolution 56/168, which established an Ad Hoc Committee to consider proposals for a comprehensive and integral international convention to promote and protect the rights and dignity of persons with disabilities, based on the work done in the field of human rights and social development.

4. Recent developments concerning the broad human rights framework to promote the rights of persons with disabilities

The United Nations conducted a comprehensive comparative study of global disability policies and programmes in 1997. The report of the Secretary-General, "Review and appraisal of implementation of the World Programme of Action concerning Disabled Persons" indicated that a broad human rights framework must be further developed and established for disability policies and programmes to promote social, economic and cultural rights as well as the civil and political rights of persons with disabilities, the need for the rights of persons with disabilities to be recognized, a broad human rights framework..

5. Overview of the issue of human rights of persons with disabilities in India

5.1 Disability types:

Disabled people do not form a homogenous group. They may be, the physically disabled, mentally retarded, the visually, hearing and speech impaired, those with restricted mobility or with so-called "medical disabilities" and learning disabilities. They can broadly be classified as Physical and Communication, Mental, Learning and Medical disabilities.

5.2. Constitutional Framework in India

The Constitution of India applies uniformly to every legal citizen of India, whether they are healthy or disabled in any way (physically or mentally) and guarantees a right of justice, liberty of thought, expression, belief, faith and worship and equality of status and of opportunity and for the promotion of fraternity. To safeguard the interests of the disadvantaged sections of the Society, the Constitution of India guarantees that no person will be denied 'equality' before the law (Article 14 of the Indian Constitution). Relevant Articles in Indian Constitution providing constitutional guarantees to all including disabled are:

Article 15(1): It enjoins on the Government not to discriminate against any citizen of India (including disabled) on the ground of religion, race, caste, sex or place of birth.

Article 15 (2): Access to shops, public restaurants, hotels and places of public entertainment or in the use of wells, tanks, bathing places (ghats), roads and places of public resort maintained wholly or partly out of government funds or dedicated to the use of the general public.

Article 17: No person including the disabled irrespective of his belonging can be treated as an untouchable. It would be an offence punishable in accordance with law.

Article 21: Every person including the disabled has his life and liberty guaranteed.

Article 23: Forced labour is prohibited and the same is made punishable in accordance with law.

Article 29(2): The right to education is available to all citizens including the disabled.

Article 32: Every disabled person can move the Supreme Court of India to enforce his fundamental rights and the rights to move the Supreme Court.

5.3 Legal Framework for Disabled:

i. Design Act 1911: It deals with the law relating to the protection of designs any person having jurisdiction in respect of the property of a disabled person .

ii. Succession Act, 1956: It provides that physical disability or physical deformity would not disentitle a person from inheriting ancestral property.

iii. National Building Code of India 1983 with proposed Amendments: Main features are: "Every building should have at least one access to main entrance/exit to the disabled which shall be indicated by proper signage.

iv. The Mental Act, 1987: Under this Act mentally ill persons are entitled to the following rights:

· A right to be admitted, treated and cared in a psychiatric hospital or psychiatric nursing home or convalescent home established or maintained by the Government or any other person for the treatment and care of mentally ill persons Mentally ill persons have the right to get regulated, directed and co-coordinated mental health services from the Government, Government hospitals and nursing homes either as in patient or on an outpatients basis.

· The police have an obligation to take into protective custody a wandering or neglected mentally ill person, and inform his relative, and also have to produce such a person before the local magistrate for issue of reception orders.

· Where mentally ill persons own properties including land, which they cannot themselves, manage, the district court upon application has to protect and secure the management of such properties by entrusting the same to a Court of Wards, by appointing guardians of such mentally ill persons or appointment of managers of such property.

· The costs of maintenance of mentally ill persons detained as in-patient in any government psychiatric hospital or nursing home shall be borne by the state government concerned unless such costs have been agreed to be borne by the relative or other person on behalf of the mentally ill person and no provision for such maintenance has been made by order of the District Court. Such costs can also be borne out of the estate of the mentally ill person.

· Mentally ill persons undergoing treatment shall not be subjected to any indignity (whether physical or mental) or cruelty. Mentally ill persons cannot be used without their own valid consent for purposes of research, though they could receive their diagnosis and treatment.

· Mentally ill persons who are entitled to any pay, pension, gratuity or any other form of allowance from the government (such as government servants who become mentally ill during their tenure) can not be denied of such payments. The person who is in-charge of such mentally person or his dependants will receive such payments after the magistrate has certified the same.

· A mentally ill person shall be entitled to the services of a legal practitioner by order of the magistrate or district court if he has no means to engage a legal practitioner or his circumstances so warrant in respect of proceedings under the Act.

v.The Persons with Disabilities (PWD) Equal Opportunities, Protection of Rights and full Participation Act, 1995:

It is a significant step, which ensures equal opportunities for the people with disabilities and their full participation in the nation building. The Act provides for both the preventive and promotional aspects of rehabilitation like education, employment and vocational training, reservation, research and manpower development, creation of barrier-free environment, rehabilitation of persons with disability, unemployment allowance for the disabled, special insurance scheme for the disabled employees and establishment of homes for persons with severe disability etc.

vi. The Rehabilitation Council of India Act, (RCI Act 1992): It prescribes that any one delivering services to people with disability, who does not possess qualifications recognized by RCI, could be prosecuted. This Act provides guarantees so as to ensure the good quality of services rendered by various rehabilitation personnel.

6. Issues related to elaborating the rights of persons with disabilities in India

a) The present constraints and potential for adjudication of the human rights of persons with disabilities have not yet been fully explored either by legal experts or advocates for the rights of persons with disabilities.

b) General problems of accessibility to the institutional resources for utilizing legal, administrative or other official procedures to adjudicate the rights of persons with disabilities.

c) The access and the use of the domestic (national) judicial system and the issue of underutilization of international law in the domestic courts.

d) Empowerment of the disability community as well as the community at large - the issue of capacity building in the disability community as well as non-traditional sectors of society to address issues of concern to them in the existing judicial and administrative for and through promoting general awareness and education to inform both the disability community and society as a whole about the human rights of persons with disabilities as a critical human rights issue.

e) Mainstreaming of disability in a broader policy and legal discourse - networking among the disability community and their advocates, the supporting non-governmental community, academic institutions, legal experts and practitioners to forge a sense of integrated community to prioritize the agenda for protecting and promoting the rights of persons with disabilities.

7. Support required by Disabled-A revelation from Survey: Survey was done with both disabled and the NGOs to spell their perception of requirements for the disabled.

v Chennai-Suburban Region, June 2004- August 2004

S. No	*Services Required*	*Percentage*
1	Healthcare, supply of Aids and Appliances and medicines	85
2	Inclusive education for disabled after special schooling in pre-primary/ primary level. Integrating with mainstream education; Remedial free coaching for disabled persons	75
3	Friendly social atmosphere from community	80
4	Self-Employment or employment in government/private sector; Equal opportunities in employment without any prejudice against the disability; Specialized vocational training	83
5	Financial support for self-employment at nominal interest rates	81
6	Transport services specially for impaired persons	75
7	Residential homes and free care for homeless disabled persons	85
8	Income support in terms of regular pension to the families whose bread earner is disabled	78
9	Priorities in all poverty alleviation programmes especially support to women.	68
10	Dissemination of information through media. Press and other methods regarding the government schemes and concessions for disabled persons.	85

Source: Field survey conducted in 2004 by Vishvodayaa Trust

The loss of job or change of job is one of the major psychological and mental problems associated with the onset of disability. Significantly 60% of these working people lost their job after the disability. Another 15% had to change their job due to the onset of the disability. Only 13% disabled persons continued with their jobs even after the onset of disability.

7.1 "Barriers" creating problems for disabled:

- Environment - this includes inaccessible buildings and services, inaccessible communication and language
- Attitudes - this includes stereotyping, discrimination and prejudice
- Organisations - this includes procedures and practices, which are inflexible.

These barriers 'disable' people with impairments. If these barriers are taken away or reduced the disabled people will be able to take a full and active part in society.

7.2 Good Practices Initiatives

Following were identified in the survey:

- Community Awareness
- Education Related Strategies
- Poverty alleviation and Income Generation Strategies
- Social Services and Health care Strategies
- Research and Documentation

8. Conclusions-Options for future action to promote the rights of persons with disabilities

- Adoption of legislative frameworks by Governments that reflect international standards relating to disability that advance rights of persons with disabilities;
- Commitment by policy makers, programme planners and technical experts to broaden policy dialogues with regards to the incorporation of international norms relating to disability as well as specific legislative mandates that emanate from the disability legislation in their respective countries;
- Involvement of civil society in a broad discourse on law and disability policies; how to incorporate international norms in domestic legislation and policies.

Organization of innovative forums in which legal and policy professionals, academics and civil society can exchange knowledge and experience as well as obtain technical guidance and advice on development of disability-sensitive policies and laws.

Human rights for persons with disabilities encompass human rights in all spheres of life. The future work of the disability community has the potential to integrate the resources of "traditional" human rights communities, focusing on political and civil rights and "non-traditional" human rights communities, focussing on economic, social and cultural rights, as well as civil society organizations that have not yet focussed on issues concerning persons with disabilities. Together newly emerging disability-sensitized communities would work toward the goal of a society for all in promoting economic, social and cultural rights from a disability perspective, to achieve a society accessible for all.

End Notes

1. "Informal Consultative Meetings on International Norms and Standards for Persons with Disabilities." (9 February 2001), Division for Social Policy and Development of the United Nations Secretariat.
2. General Assembly resolution 54/4 of 15 October 1999, United Nations.
3. General Assembly resolution 54/263 of 26 June 2000, United Nations.
4. General Assembly resolution 2200 A (XXI) of 16 December 1966, United Nations.
5. General Assembly resolution 2856 (XXVI) of 20 December 1971, United Nations.
6. Patrick Flood, "The Effectiveness Of The United Nations human Rights institutions", Westport, Conn.: Praeger Publishers (1998).

7. Caroline Dommen, *Claiming Environmental Rights: Some Possibilities Offered by the United Nations' Human Rights Mechanisms*, 11 Georgetown International Environmental Law Review 1(Fall 1998).
8. Thomas Buergenthal, International Human Rights Law and Institutions: Accomplishments and Prospects, 63 Washington Law Review 1(1988).
9. David Weissbrodt, The Role of International Organizations in the Implementation of Human Rights and Humanitarian Law in Situations of Armed Conflict. 21 Vanderbilt Journal of Transnational Law 313 (1988).
10. Benedetto Conforti, Enforcing International Human Rights In Domestic courts (1997).
11. Edith Brown Weiss, International Compliance with Nonbinding Accords, Studies in Translational Legal Policy No.29, The American Society of International Law (1996).
12. Paragraph 26 of General Assembly report A/54/388, United Nations.
13. "Education For the Disabled Children", National Council of Educational Research And Training, New Delhi.
14. Bupinder Zutshi, "Disability Status in India- Case Study of Delhi Metropolitan Region", project report.
15. Vishvodayaa Trust, Field survey, June 2004-September 2004.

17

Human Rights Issues and News Media Coverage

C. Velayutham

The term "human rights" refers to universal rights of human being, regardless of legal jurisdiction or other factors such as ethnicity, race, nationality, and gender. The situation of the human rights in India is a Complex one, as a result of the geographical size of the country and tremendous diversity, its status as a developing country, and its history as a former colonial territory. Hence, the Indian media have a crucial role in safeguarding human rights and promoting social justice. Journalists can help in the promotion of human rights by:

(a) Doing microscopic analysis on the issues rather than mere reporting the facts

(b) Investigate the causes of problems and providing possible solutions

They can create mass awakening about human rights and help to form public opinion.

Press Freedom and Human Rights

The Indian media has been by history and tradition a fairly independent voice, linked prior to independence to core struggles of emancipation and mobilistion. The journalists, whose pride was offended in the subjugation of the country by a foreign power, vehemently wrote against the British colonial rule. Once the British left, journalists were left with nothing to fight for. They should have given their attention to frequent human rights violations in independent India which still remains highly stratified in terms of caste, gender, and class even now. But since most journalists then hailed from the upper strata of society and they did not undergo sensitisation in human rights, they lacked social concern. Freedom was the driving force during the independence struggle.

Such a Zeal for the freedom of the press got revived during the imposition of the eighteen month emergency during 1975-77 which curtailed the freedom of expression with censorship measures by the union government. It would not be an exaggeration to say that the emergency turned out to be a blessing in disguise for the print media in the country, as it definitely helped them to reshape the definition of 'Investigative journalism' in the post emergency era.

1980-90's were still the years when Indian journalism believed that like the judiciary, it is an arm of democracy that has an important role to play in ensuring social justice and in the task of nation building. Despite the many constraints it faced, primarily from money-minded newspaper managements, Indian journalism struggled to provide widespread coverage of news, and support it with background, critical thinking, insightful analysis and writing of a fairly high order.

The maiden instance of Human rights violation reporting

The Bhagalpur Blindings provide a lesson in the crucial contribution that journalistic research can make in creating public awareness of human rights, more so in a society which has numerous deep-rooted abuses is likely to be overlooked. Over three years, from 1979 to 1982, policemen blinded 33 criminals in Bhagalpur Jail using acid. Codenamed Operation Gangajal, a report carried by The Indian Express, the incident became a national scandal and 14 policemen were suspended.

Of the 14 policemen, 13 were acquitted and reinstated in service. When The Indian Express brought the issue into national focus, the Supreme Court accepted it as a writ petition. The Mainstream media took a sustained campaign on the rights of prisoners along with the impact of the pictures of the blinded men to touch the public conscience. Later, human rights movement gaining prominence in the recent decades, but still rights issues appear only as features in mass media, though rarely as hard news.

Changing media scenario

According to Ganesh K. Sovani (2003), the print media has played a significant role during last twenty five years or so in reporting the violation of human rights issue. However off late the print media is been receiving a tough competition from television with the advent of several news channels such as NDTV, Star News, Zee News and Aaj Tak. This healthy competition between print and electronic media has compelled them to carve out a new kind of readership /viewership in other areas such as fashion, cuisine, healthcare, real estate, and sports. The media industry may justify this trend by saying that it caters for the demands of its so called 'Target audiences'. But this modernisation resulted by pushing the human rights issue to the back seat.

A study conducted by Viewers forum and Centre for advocacy and research on the 24X 7 News channels for nine weeks, to find out the focus of the coverage - was it on human development issues or was it more about Lifestyle? The findings clearly show that the priority list of the News Channels:

Coverage of Development Story as Main Subject:

Development Story	*Frequency (%)*
Local Self Governance	1.13%
Development	0.45%
Water	0.21%

Development Story	*Frequency (%)*
Agriculture	0.15%
Infrastructure/Civic Amenities	0.15%
Poverty	0.12%
Human Rights	**0.07%**
Drought	0.06%
Employment/Unemployment	0.06%
Electricity	0.04%
Women related stories	0.28%
Women's Rights*	**0.12%**
Women's Reservation	0.08%
Women-others	0.06%
Women- Girl Education	0.02%

There has been perhaps no period in human history when societies were not faced with conflicts. However, when the print media made its appearance in the 17th century, its potentiality as mass communicator, informer and propagator was realized and soon converted into a weapon. It is an often- repeated saying that 'militants thrive on the oxygen of publicity" and they have successfully used media as a powerful weapon to manipulate public opinion and to gain sympathy or concern and also supporters.

In the 1990s in the State of Punjab and Jammu and Kashmir, When military was at its peak in these two states, the credibility of the media and threats to their free functioning also came to the forefront.

In Punjab, the press was under threat from militants who had imposed a crude form of censorship on the local press by enforcing publication of their dictates so as to perpetuate the fear psychosis, the stronghold of terrorists.

In Kashmir, human rights excesses by army and the Para-military forces had invited international concern and criticism. The role and the plight of the press also came under scanner. The result of inquiry into the report of human rights excesses was astonishing.

The Coverage on the seven states located in the north-eastern part of the country is the Classic example, of typical media chauvinism. The violence centric coverage of this region has created a negative image resulting in the Lack of development of these states. Due to this, this region is totally cut-off from the rest of the country, both socially and economically.

On the other hand, Media experts, caution the electronic media in particular against the glorification of the terrorist as a celebrity and exploitation of the experiences of people affected by their acts. This is perhaps violation of the human rights by the media at its worst. In the matter of terrorism and insurgencies, the media whether print or electronic, should be guided by the compulsion of self imposed restraint and anxiety to prevent further violation of human right and loss of more life on account of media reporting. Therefore, role of media in organizing public opinion against terrorism is very important.

Minority rights and media

Post 9/11 scenario has completely tarnished the image of Muslim in India. Especially the Television news channels have created a distasteful image of the Muslims. Negative Media depiction has indeed have caused the syndrome of hatred and suspicion towards Muslims.

Following the July 11 bomb blasts in Mumbai the media, especially television, came in to sharp criticism. Repeated images of police round-ups of youth in minority dominated areas created the public impression that dozens of Muslim suspects were being interrogated. These raised questions about the ethics of television channels that actively contributed to creating a public image of who the guilty are, but then remained silent when the answer proved indecisive. A specific case related to a prominent Hindi television channel. The channel broadcast an inaccurate report relaying that after the bomb blasts firecrackers were burst at Padgah village, near Mumbai. The fact was that the village is minority dominated and that it is home to persons allegedly accused of participating in earlier terror attacks, added spice if not truth to the broadcast. Agitated residents protested this coverage to the village *sarpanch* and registered an oral complaint with the police (who refused to register a first information report, FIR). A meeting was thereafter held with various members of the *mohalla* committee condemning the coverage. Several *sarpanches* and gram panchayat chiefs attended the meeting. However, the said channel carried no correction in its subsequent telecasts.

Zahira Sheikh, a young woman from a poor and illiterate family who has been in the centre of media attention ever since she became the public face of the Godhra riots. For the media, it has been Zahira vs. the State of Gujarat, for some time to counter Narendra Modi. This young Muslim woman received enormous support and sympathy which then turned into hatred and disbelief when she changed his stance in court. The media had decided to take Zahira to the gallows much before Supreme Court delivered its verdict. This issue is the 'evident' of media exploitation.

Media's double standards on minority related issue can be once again explained through another example. On one side, Media is campaigning against Capital punishment but on the another side, the repeated telecast of the hanging footage of former Iraqi dictator Saddam Hussein has created havoc in Iraq, killing hundreds of civilians. In India two children on seeing the repeated visuals on television, hung themselves to feel the pain of Saddam. Who is to blame for this? Even the way in which Mohammed afzal's capital punishment issue is being handled by Indian media was proved bias.

My Coverage of Female Infanticide as TV journalist

Female infanticide in TamilNadu was first highlighted in 1985 by the leading newsmagazine India Today which reported the existence of the practice in Usilampatti, in Madurai district of southern Tamil Nadu. This report shocked the general public because women in Tamil Nadu are known to be better educated and to have a greater degree of autonomy than their counterparts in northern India.

From 1990 onwards, continuous reports of female infanticide in Salem district in central Tamil Nadu were published, initially in the Tamil media and later in the English language newspapers. When I started my Prelimilinary Research, for my Special news analysis on the issue in Salem, Dharmapuri, Namakkal district in 1996 and also based on field reports of local NG0s, I concluded, that female infanticide was occurring in many parts of Tamil Nadu and not just in the selected pockets identified. So, I planned to investigate.

My first encounter as a journalist on the practice of female infanticide was accidental in Edappadi, in Salem. I had never even dreamt of its existence when I was planning to do an in-depth Special feature in Salem, Dharmapuri, districts of Tamil Nadu. When I brought the situation to the attention of my Vice-president- News, he refused to take my observations seriously. These incidents continued and went unnoticed by local authorities and the Government till that time.

Later after convincing my Vice President - News, on the condition that I have get interviews from the Mothers who actually killed their own infant girl, I was allowed to proceed with the Coverage. {The Sirappu Parvai was a sponsored weekend news slot which rated Top TRP among Prime time slots in SUN TV}. The people in these districts refused to allow me inside their village and after continuous efforts,{ Keeping Strict deadlines in my mind and capitalizing on their ignorance} I managed to convince them and started my Exclusive coverage. }.I struggled a lot to bring the truth out of the people, as it was considered normal practice among the locals. It was really a challenging task for me to investigate this issue in getting the details and interviews. I was able to do an elaborate the story with interviews from the mothers who actually killed their own infant girl. We even decided to not to mask the interviews to project the channel's genuinity and credibility. When the story went on air it caught the attention of the public and the Government.While doing this story the my main intention was to break the story with exclusive interviews of the mothers and to sensationalize the issue.

Many of my others stories on the old age homes, child sex abuse highlighted the gravity of the issue visually with supporting case studies and interviews. While covering Old age Homes and the living condition of the neglected senior citizen of my state I was asked to cover on several case study .The pathetic visuals of senior citizens sheltered in an unhygienic old age homes had a great impact on audience. We received many phone calls from the audiences who came forward to extend financial support to the old age homes.

Child sex abuse is the human rights issue I covered .In this news story we had about eight cases of child sex abuse incidence which happened over the period. Since, ours is the visual medium we decided to carry the interviews of the abused girl child narrating the incident. We carried the interviews without masking the identity of the victims. This is the issue of journalistic ethics and self regulation comes.

Human rights and Media Activism

Media is known as the Watchdog of the society. Television news channels, which constitute the mainstream media, have played the role of observers, reporters and even analyzers of news. But the latest role of 'Activist' taken by the media has created a new dimension to coverage of social and human rights issues. The media have started taking upon it individual cases and mobilizing mass public campaigns. With such support from the public, the media goes a step ahead to pass pre-judicial verdicts in certain cases. The recent example of this media activism is of the murder of Jessica Lal, Priyadarshini Mattoo rape and murder, and the Nithish katara murder issue which was taken up by NDTV, IBN-CNN through SMS and media orchestered candle light campaign. This campaign did have a great impact on the public and made the government machinery to function effectively. But at the same time, these incidents reported because it has an urban essence in it. The victim belongs to a upper middle class and the accused involved are either politician son or the Businessman. Media will not play the same 'activist' role on a Dalit women rape or murder issue. On September 29, 2006 a gang rape and mass murder at Kherlanjee in Maharashtra's Bhandara district left four members of a Dalit family brutally massacred with Bhaiyyalal Bhotmange, the father, being the lone survivor. The Maharashtra police indulged to suppress evidence of the crime during the primary stage of investigations itself. Will the media treat this case of human rights violation similar to that of Jessica Lal or Priyadarshini Mattoo?

The abysmal reporting done by News channels in the recent past brings us to a situation where media has failed its prime duties. In the Noida (Nithari) kidnappings & serial murders, the media has proved to be a farce. Until the accused were caught, this issue was never on the priority radar of the Noida based channels. This is because the victim belongs to the lower strata of the society.

Another recent Instance of gross Human rights violation is the, Police brutality on the villagers in Nandigram in West Bengal. Nearly a dozen were killed in firing and national media (electronic) was oblivious-discussing cricket world cup and Amir Khan's birthday celebration. Even on the minimal coverage, the insensitive anchors were busy discussing about Buddhadeb's politics and mamta's statement on land acquisition at Singur and Nandigram.But none of them questioned about police brutality on women.

Ethics, Victims, and Objectivity

Another problem for journalists is Professional ethics - It is always difficult to avoid taking sides when journalists receive most of their information from the alleged victim. It is only human to feel sympathy for someone brutalized by the military, but a journalist who aspires to be credible must strive to be objective and that requires a neutral and a detached approach.

Yet another difficulty in covering human rights is that if the violators belong to military forces, journalists reporting allegations against them risk appearing unpatriotic by casting aspersions on their own defense forces. This was seen in the United States when the Pentagon accused journalists of being an-American for reporting serious misdeeds by the military. This implies a duty of ethical journalists to be vigilant and aggressive in reporting on human rights, while recognizing the limits of what is realistically possible.

Another difficulty while covering human rights issue is that, only the dominant stake holder are given more prominence in coverage when it comes to caste or ethnic conflicts. The relative or complete absence of media coverage of issues arising out of Adivasi struggles in the states of Chattisgarh and Jharkhand is the classic example.

A survey conducted by the Delhi-based Media Study Group points out a distinct absence of caste diversity and a predominance of the 'upper' castes within the upper echelons of the Indian media, This was inferred on Reservation issue covered by 24X7 News channels recently. ("Media Pundits", CMS, July-August 2006).

Lesson learnt and future Challenges

The media devote very little space for human rights issues, particularly with their market-driven style of functioning in the recent years. They rarely follow up human rights stories, which they report with a greater zeal in the beginning.

Fundamental rights and Directive principles enshrined in the Constitution will make sense only if a person who studies them has human rights awareness. So mere teaching of the Constitution in academic programmes will not do. With the liberalisation in 1990s, social concern is on the decline. With the widening base of the middle class in the decades after independence, it has a great say in journalism. The middle-class dominated journalistic profile takes up human rights issues only related to its strata with ease. Media coverage of human rights, if done effectively, will help to remove narrow-mindedness and enhance cultural relativity and promote social harmony.

Media intervention in human rights issues can be creatively used for social mobilization. The best way of ensuring this is by having diversity in a news room. Recruiting journalists from different social classes particularly in terms of religion and caste, so that the problem of not understanding the class values of other people can be overcome. At the same time regular workshops / capacity building programme for sensitizing journalist on human rights issues will be another constructive step.

The media should continue to expose cases of injustice. Media bosses and journalists should also think in terms of positive media intervention {there should not be any urban-rural divide in coverage}.With each human rights violation get exposed in the media and someone set an example, several likely human rights violations will be averted. Good journalism is a constant process of seeking solutions.

References

1 Bushan, Chandra. 2003. Terrorism and Separation in Northeast India. New Delhi: Kalpaz publication.

2 Ramanujam, S.R. "Media meddling with justice?"

3 http://www.thehoot.org/story.asp? storyidWeb5917621177 Hoot20837%20AM2306&pn Sengupta, Subhajit "Role of media in recent dalit outrage http://www.thehoot.orgstory.asp?storyid= Web219652 3856Hoot31837%20AM2427&pn

4 Dua, H.K. Quoted by Prem Kumar in "Development and Communication: Partners in Same Process." *Vidura* Vol. 41, Issue No. 3, July-September 2004. pp. 47-49.

5 Sovani, Ganesh K. "The Media and Human Rights."

6 http://www.mediawise.org.uk/files/uploaded/Media %20and%20human%20rights%20in%20India.pdf Posted in 2003.

7 Ramakrishnan, H.2003. "Poverty Eradication and the Indian Media." *Media Asia* Vol. 30, No. 1. pp. 5-10.

8 Behara, Bijay Kumar, and Banchhanidhi Pani. Media as Upholder of Human Rights Plays Key Role in Sensitising Authorities and Public." *Communicator* Vol. XXXIV No. 1, January-1999. pp. 22-24.

9 Aram, I. Arul.2000. Human Rights Education for Mass Communication Students. Ed. R.M. Pal and Somen Chakraborty. *Human Rights Education in India.* Indian Social Institute, New Delhi pp. 212-217.

18

Safeguarding Human Rights Against Various Future Environmental Threats

S. Venkta Subramanian

Introduction:

Indeed it is after the Bhopal gas tragedy, Gujarat earthquake and 2002-2003 draught issue, the themes of environmental protection and natural resource conservation and safeguarding the quality of life of the people, have assumed greater significance in India. It has also become a major economic, political and social issue. During analysis of the causes of above quoted disasters, it was sound that not only the human negligence was responsible for these incidents but also an inadequate knowledge and traditional attitude towards "Human-environment conflict" and Natural resource conservation. We all know that, safeguarding or protecting human rights against future natural environment threats is not a one-way phenomena. It needs a combined, continuous and co-ordinate efforts claimed from human beings, centre-state government non governmental communities and the corporate companies. In this 21st century there will be a number of natural threats, like global warning ozone depletion climate change etc., which will be caused a serious impacts on the atmosphere and on our planet earth.

These inter related (or) inter linked natural problems will cause a serious impact on human health in the near future. To strengthen this view, the **"Vienna convention on preservation of ozone layer"** held in 1985, has warned the world nations "to take appropriate measure to protect human health and the environment against adverse effects resulting or likely to result from human activities, which modify or are likely to modify the ozone layer and atmosphere". In this part Indian Government has sole responsibility to protect the people from these grave threats. But, due to the negligent attitude, of our Indian government, has forgotten to give utmost importance in the policy level at the early stage. For the past one decade, government has taken some of the constructive steps to generate the awareness among the people and consumers about the importance to avoid the polyethylene and chloro- fluro carbon based products. The steps have also taken to reduce the pollution level in the industries and control vehicle's pollution. So far, we have not yet achieved the positive results. It is high time to take care of these issues. Because, we have already done a more damage to ozone layer. So that, to face these challenges, in 21st century, there must be an attitudinal change among the people and need a refined and improved government strategies to manage these issues. These improved strategies will be helpful to safeguarded the human life from the dreadful diseases and protect the right to life of our citizen. So that, the centre theme of this paper is centered around this problem. This attempt mainly highlights the role of individual, center-state governments, corporate companies and international communities to save this earth's atmosphere.

THE NEED FOR POSITIVE HUMAN RESPONSE OVER THE NATURAL ENVIRONMENT

Humanity should learn to use the eco-friendly products and controlling themselves from involving in unsustainable activities and injudicious utilization of natural resource. As an individual, every human being must take pledge to do some constructive and regenerative work for saving this earth from its complete destruction of natural resource. They must always use eco-friendly products and involve in various eco-regenerative activities like avoid using polyethylene bags etc. AS consumers they can be more aware and check whether the products we buy are likely to contain chloro-fluro carbon etc. When they have a choice, they could chose ozone friendly products e.g., conventional spray pumps for insecticides, rather than aerosols, while buying a refrigerator or Air conditioners, choose one with CFC- Free Technology. While getting a refrigerator which has CFC gas in the compressor repaired, ensure the gas is not released in to the atmosphere they can as for as possible, buy and use pillows and mattresses stuffed with cotton instead of foam. Let us not use Styrofoam glasses and cups, use leaf or reusable plates.

To strengthen these Ideas, the international governmental agency called Greenpeace released its eco-pamphlet it laid down 10 "rules" for its readers to follow: "use public transport when possible, use-energy-saving light bulbs, turn off electric gadgets at the wall, do not use a tumble dryer ...." etc. So that, to manage (or) to avoid climate change and ozone layer depletion, let's do our bit to save this atmosphere.

THE ROLE AND THE DUTY OF OUR INDIAN GOVERNMENT TO TACKLE THIS GLOBAL ISSUE AND PROTECT THE RIGHTS OF THE PEOPLE

Aside from maintaining, sovereignty, integrity and internal security, state continues to be responsible for management of crisis, particularly those precipitated by natural calamities. Our country is endowed with a rich experience of managing various natural calamities. Well established institutional arrangements, policy mechanisms have been evolved to deal with some of the natural calamities like seasonal draughts and floods at the national and sub-national levels and local. These mechanisms have two distinct and linked components (1) Early warning system (2) Monitoring system.

As the mechanisms to deal with these two aspects are broadly similar and inter-connected, the subject has been dealt with together where ever possible. At present, Draught and flood fore casting functions in the central government is carried out by the Indian Meteorological Department (IMD). This responsibility arises out of the duty to forecast on the IMD to obtain and compile rainfall data through out the country, over the years, IMD has evolved methodologies to forecast the probable intensity of south-west monsoon on a broad regional basis – IMD also compiles weekly rainfall summaries giving figures of precipitation at the district level. Based on this IMD determines occurrence of meteorological draughts and flood. Now the country has 36 meteorological sub-stations. Through these institutional mechanisms, our Indian government manages the seasonal flood and draught. Apart from these, there are some other institutions also function for managing the natural calamities, they are (1) Crisis Management Group (2) National Calamity Management Committee, functions with the financial help of Finance Commission. But, these institutions can function only in the initial and post-disaster stage. we still depend on various government organizations for the mitigation functions. There is no proper institutional mechanism to tackle this issue completely. Like wise to like Chinese change and global warming still we are in the long back. At the government policy level the master of climate change can global warming in at the bottom of the list of national priorities. There is no any proper institutional mechanism so far, working separately for managing these problems : still it is at research station level like Tsunami warning station, there is a head for separate institution at government level to manage the future issue. In this connection the government must get cooperation from international government and non governmental agencies like Tyndal Center, down to earth, green peace etc.,. These organizations are also working for controlling these problems genuinely.

THE ROLE OF INTERNATIONAL ORGANIZATIONS IN PROTECTION OF OZONE LAYER AND ACHIEEE

To contract these problems there are number of agencies, working separately for managing these problems. Among them the universal common agency like United Nations, UNDP are very much conscious of the world wide maintaining the environmental safe for human beings. Particularly, to control these two ecological problems, the member countries joined together to discuss about various measures to control the effect of these two ecological threats. At the initial step in 1983, Nations agreed in Vienna to take important measures.-... to protect human health and environment against adverse effect of ozone layer depletion. In September 1987, an assessment was reached on specific measures to taken in the Montreal protocol on substances that deplete the ozone layer to the signed.

In 1994, the United Nation's General Assembly proclaimed sep 16, the international day for the preservation of the ozone layer, commemorating the date of the signing, in 1987, of the Montreal Protocol. India has ratified the Vienna convention in 1991and Montreal Protocol in 1992. So, these multi-lateral agreements provide technical and financial assistance to move on to using ozone friendly replacements.

THE ROLE OF COOPERATE COMPANIES IN HALPING THE GOVERNMENT TO REPLACE THE ECO -FRIENDLY TECHNOLOGY

As manufacturer of consumer products, the corporate companies are also responsible for emitting the ozone depleting substances. Because, many of the consumer products like refrigerators, air conditioners contain the chloro-fluro carbons and Freon gas. The other manufacturing companies like fumigation producing companies, foam making industries, aerosol manufactures, fire fighting agents manufactures, cleaning agent industries, are constantly produced the ozone gas and other ozone depleting substances. These emitted substances destroyed naturally and reach the stratosphere and destroy ozone layer. These companies come forward and take responsibility in not producing ozone based products. In this regard, they must cooperate with government and international level agency to replace the eco – friendly or ozone free technology.

19

The Role of International Forums in Implementing International Human Rights Laws

D.S. Makkalanban

Whereas disregard and contempt for human rights have resulted in barbarous acts which have outraged the conscience of mankind, and the advent of a world in which human beings shall enjoy freedom of speech and belief and freedom from fear and want has been proclaimed as the highest of the common people,

Whereas it is essential, if man is not to be compelled to have recourse, as a last resort, to rebellion against tyranny and oppression, that human rights should be protected by the rule of law........

-2nd and 3rd paragraphs of Preamble of UDHR

Introduction

The law on Human rights is the outcome of the experience arising out of the political necessity and civilization, ultimately finding its place in most of the written Constitutions of the world community under the chapter heading as Bill of Rights (UK) in 1689, Fundamental Rights (USA) so on. The US declaration of independence from clutches of British Empire in 1776 and creation of French Republic in 1789 came out the "Declaration of Rights of Man". However, drawn heavily and primarily from the British unwritten Constitutional practice, and therefore this paper deals with the Human rights as it obtains in the International Law and in international enforcement forums which in turn finds incorporated in the National Laws of the recently born. states by virtue of their admission to United Nations and other international organizations. The paper is set with the twin objectives of:

- Firstly, to explore the historical roots and surface environments that necessitated for establishing international forums and international laws to protect human rights
- Secondly, to analyze the role of international forums and international laws to promote human rights.

Origin

The concept of Human Rights existed in Western thought for several centuries, atleast since the time of King John of England. The principles of human rights were reflected in the earliest known legal document called Magna Carta or Great Charter. The text was signed in 1215 as recognition made between King John of England and the people. As a result, the charter granted rights to the citizens of England and created limitations to the Kings authority.

Before this pact the idea of human rights is well reflected in works of Greek thinkers like works of Plato, where he based his whole theory in conception of 'justice' that his well reflected in his 'Ideal State' in his treatise "Republic". The concept of human rights rests in providing justice and providing amenities to equip one's own talent merely corresponding with natural law according to Plato.

Later, the viewpoint of natural law sustained in the works of the Roman Philosophers like Italian theologian philosopher, St. Thomas Aquinas works that involved divinity with natural law. In the 17th and 18th Century, philosophers had also begun to discuss the theory of "natural rights" that has developed from the idea of natural law. That is, human beings were born with certain rights that could not be denied by any authority as they were gifted by nature by birth. Medieval philosophers Jeremy Bentham's concept of utility, John Locke' theory of natural law, Jean Jacques Rousseau's concept of 'popular sovereignty' that is reflected in 'General Will' concept promoted the thought. Other early proponents of human rights were English philosopher J S Mill in his 'Essay on Liberty', and American political theorist Thomas Paine in his essay, 'the Rights of Man'. And also Thoreau in his treatise, 'Civil Disobedience'. Further, the theory of international law by Hugo Grotius added to its development in 17th century and it sustained to the present works of Jacques Maritain, Rawls theory of Justice etc, and finally got incorporated in the international treatise and international organizations. Through which it found ways to enter into national laws of member nations.

Its Growth and Impact

It is during the 19th century, the human rights came to be internationally recognized, though not directly and specifically. The major break through were the treaties relating to piracy and abolition of slavery. Since 17th century various developments can be traced in inter-national state agreements, expressing concern over the treatment of aliens and prisoners of war. General welfare and positive nature of individual subjects, witnessed the recognition of Human rights internationally resulting in a corresponding right of humanitarian intervention due to decline in value of life and values in member countries. (For example in the Armenian Genocide in 1915-1916, Turkish government killed one and a half million Armenians. Later, the Holocaust killing of 6 million Jewish people and left many more with the scars of human cruelty. The genocide of Cambodia between 1975 and 1979 led to the death of over half a million Cambodians by the Khmer Rouge. In 1994, the genocide in

Rwanda led to approximately 800,000 people being brutally murdered as the international community deliberated and struggled to find consensus for an "intervention force" in Rwanda. From the "ethnic cleansing" in Kosovo to the tortures at Abu Gharib prison in Iraq there have been human rights violations).

A smart beginning of the protection of Human rights by an international organization, started with the establishment of League of Nations in 1919.The 19th century peace agreements with Eastern European and Balkan states provided for the protection of minorities, essentially providing for equality of treatment and opportunities for collective activity and importantly part XIII of the Treaty of Versailles which created International Labour Organization ensuring right of Association and better standards of working condition, further strengthened the position. The revelations coming from the Nuremburg war criminals, the atomic bomb, and other horrors small in magnitude paraded the period.

As a rescue, No doubt later the UN Charter, UDHR of 1948 and other UN related instruments happened to be a source of inspiration for the protecting and promoting human rights. The charter of UN contains important human rights provisions in addition to containing the framework of the organization. It reaffirms, "Faith in fundamental human rights in the dignity and work of the human person," in the equal rights of men and women and of nations large and small". However it became one of the pioneers in promoting human rights in international sphere. The UNHR is the first international statement to use the term 'Human Rights' and has been adopted by human rights movement as a charter. The United Nations General Assembly unanimously adopted the Universal Declaration of Human Rights. It recognized the need to "promote and encourage respect for Human Rights and fundamental freedoms." The Declaration is a testament of our commitment to the basic principles of Human Rights. In brief, the declaration includes:

- Covenant on Civil and Political Rights: it includes the basic civil and political rights of the individuals and the nations.
- Optional Protocol to the Covenant on Civil and Political Rights: it adds legal force FOR Covenant on Civil and Political Rights by allowing Human Rights Commission to investigate and judge complaint of human rights violations.
- Covenant on Economic, Social and Cultural Rights: it includes the basic economic, social and cultural rights of the individuals and the nations.
- UN Convention on the Condition of the Wounded and Sick in the Armed Forces (I) or The First Geneva Convention: it includes rights of individuals, combatants and non-combatants, prisoners of war or enemy captives during war.
- Convention against Genocide
- Convention against Torture
- Convention on Elimination of Discrimination against Women and
- Convention on the Rights of the Child.

Further, The Council of Europe established in 1949 through its charter in Article1 and 3 of its statue upholds the human rights. Likewise The European Convention on Human Rights, The European Commission of Human Rights, and The European Social Charter, European Convention for Protection of Torture and inurning and Degrading Treatment or Punishment (1987) etc came into force for the same.

On the other side civil societies and Non-Governmental Organizations across the world from time to time uphold their commitment to protection and promotion of human rights. The Amnesty International, Freedom House, Human Rights Watch, Lawyers Committee for Human Rights etc play a vital role in international arena fighting for human rights and values. The impact has reached to the extent of protecting not only human rights but also for animal rights. As such there are innumerable NGO's fighting for animal rights across nations like Red Cross.

The major role played by international agreements, laws, organizations, civil societies and NGO's has necessitated the member nations to follow them and practice them as the international community recognized the growing importance of strengthening Human Rights Institutions. The impact of these has resulted in creation of National Human Rights Commissions with providing special powers. In the year 1991, a meeting of representatives of National Institutions was held in Paris. A detailed set of principles on the status of national institutions was developed. These are commonly known as Paris principles. These principles, subsequently was sanctioned by the UN commission on Human Rights and the UN General Assembly and have become the foundation and basis aspect for the establishment and operation of National Human Rights Institutions.

As a result, In India the establishment of an autonomous National Human Rights Commission reflects the obligation of Government for successful execution of Human Rights provisions under National and International Instruments. The commission is the first of its kind among the South Asian Countries. The commission came into effect on 12 October 1993 by virtue of the protection of Human Rights Act 1993. Fourteen Indian States have also set up their own human rights commissions to deal with violations from within their states. The act contains extensive provisions related with its functions and powers, composition and other related aspects. The composition of the commission includes a chairperson and 4 members and the chairpersons of the National Commission for Minorities, The National Commission for the Scheduled Castes and Scheduled Tribes and The National Commission for Women who shall be deceived to be the members of the commission for the discharge of functions specified in clauses (b) to (j) of section 12 of the act. There is a Secretary General who is the chief-executive officer of the commission. The headquarters of the commission is at Delhi.

Conclusion

Even though innumerable human rights agreements and charters exists, various human rights organizations and activist are there to protect the cause of human rights, there are gross violations of human rights all over the world. The need of the hour is to contribute to the creation of a Universal culture of human rights. According to UNESCO the areas on which Human rights development should take place are,

1. Promotion of knowledge on human rights through education
2. Training and dissemination of information.
3. Strengthening of co-operation.

With these

4. Global civil society should be mobilized in voicing their concerns and exerting pressure to end crimes against humanity.
5. Governments must be held accountable by their citizens to ensure the rule of law is applied impartially.
6. International organizations should disseminate human right issues and implement human right laws.
7. It is duty of each and every individual to strive to fulfill UN Millennium Developmental Goals of which: 'Freedom from Want' and 'Freedom from Fear' are much of relevance.

It has been rightly stated by the famous international jurist namely Kelson ash 'Human Welfare is the common root of all the laws". Whether international law or municipal law is not a matter at all. The soul object of the enforcement of international law as well as state law should be aimed at the promotion of human welfare. If not, it would be true what, Albert Einstein stated, *'I know not with what weapons World War III will be fought, but World War IV will be fought with sticks and stones'.*

References

1. United Nations Charter- 1945.
2. Universal Declaration Human Rights Charter – 1948.

3. The Council of Europe- 1949.
4. Jayapalan. N, *Human Rights* (New Delhi: Atlantic Publishers, 2000).
5. Johari .J. C, *Principles of Modern Political Science* (New Delhi: Sterling Publishers, 1995).
6. Mehartaj Begum. S, *Human Rights in India* (New Delhi: A.P.H.Publishing Corporation, 2000).
7. Viswanathan. V.N, *Human Rights {Tamil Version}* (Chennai: Pavai Publications, 2006).

20

Human Rights in Primary Education: The Indian Context

S.Jayakumar

Former President of India Dr. A. P.J. Abdul Kalam, popularly known as people's President asserted that he would meet 1.5 billion students during his tenure as President of India. At the first interaction with students of Anna University, Chennai, after his brief tenure as President of India to a question put forth by a student, whether he had met 1.5 billion students or not? He replied to that student, Where are you still, already it has been done. This interaction shows the love and trust of the foremost citizens of India have towards students and children's of India.

In Legal Texts

The constitution of India under Article 21 (a) assures that each and every child of age 6 to 14 must be provided free and compulsory education. Thus the right to education is made a fundamental right. With this, The Preamble, the other fundamental rights Article 24 and 25, the fundamental duties and the Directive principles of State Policies are the concrete steps towards the realization of education as a human right.

Drawing from the Indian constitution, human rights perspectives have dominated the formulation of educational Policies, The report of the various education Commissions and the statement of educational policies of India have articulated the importance of the right to education and education in human rights as part of the effort for the reform and the development of education in India. Apart from the above constitutional authorities the legislations such as: The National Policy on Education (NPE), 1986 has reminded as the guiding principles for formulating school curriculum, teacher education curriculum during the last two decades in India.

The international bodies and laws too have a major impact on education system in system in India. The Universal Declaration of Human Rights in 1948 assures free primary education to all its member nations (including India). The Conventions on Rights of the Child adopted on 1989 fights for the rights of child and especially for educational rights of the child. However, India was a signatory to this Convention only in 1992. The World Conference on Human Rights stated that human rights education, training and public information were necessary for the encouragement and success of steady and harmonious associations among communities and for nurturing reciprocated understanding, tolerance and peace. It also asserted that the States should strive to eradicate illiteracy and should direct education towards the full development of the human personality and the strengthening of respect for human rights and fundamental freedoms.

In Practice

The violation, promotion and protection of human rights in a plural society like India has its own background and specificity. In a complex country like India, social violation of human rights and violation at all levels have necessitated the introduction of Human Rights in Education at all level of school education. The standard examples in Tamil Nadu that would suffice the above arguments are:

1. Death of 35 schools girls with 36 persons, leaving 139 injured due to school building collapse on 04.04.1964 at Saraswathi Vidyalaya Higher Elementary School, Maninagaram, Madurai. [1]
2. A nursery school boy died because the roof fell on him at Thiruparakundram on 05.07.2006.[2]
3. A primary school boy died because the auto carrying him collapsed in a drainage hole in Karur on 12.10.2006. [3]
4. A girl child died at Thiruvaiyaru because wall collapsed and fell on the kid on 01.07.2006. [4]
5. The most heartbreaking and recent example that gathered the attention of whole nation is the Kumbakkonam incident on 16.07.2006 that took away 96 precious blooming kids life away in school building burning accident at Saraswati English Medium School. [5]

So where are the laws that is to be practiced, the quality of education that is to be given and required infrastructures that must be guiding the primary education of the country? The tragedies explain the human rights issues that are concerning the primary educational system in our country. Those are:

- Infrastructural facilities: that includes pleasant environment, proper health amenities, playground, classrooms, furniture's, toilets, sufficient teachers, maps, charts, water facilities, electricity, ventilation, entry and exit, fire extinguishers, transport conveniences etc.
- Quality in services: that includes standard syllabus, well equipped teachers, responsible management etc, and
- Social Interaction: teacher- student relationship and teacher- parent relationship.
- The government's role in enforcing the law and its vigilance.
- The role of civil society's vigilance towards the functioning of government as well as schools.

However, in practice these basic human rights facilities in education has been largely denied and the denial of these human rights in primary education has attracted and is been replaced by corruption and ignorance of these human rights. These has resulted in hefty loses and has compromised the quality of educational services and also failure in implementation of the international and national laws that have been enacted to protect and promote child's welfare. So one wonders:

- Will education, allow the human right to be served and saved?
- Will it be a stepping stone for the child's future?

Conclusion

It is clear of reservation that education has become a commercial service and the standard has become low. It definitely affects the society and civilization of a country. Merely speaking, it affects the basic rights of a citizen in a country to pursue right education. If there are no Human rights practiced in education – how can one teach human right education among schools and colleges? Unless human rights are observed in educational services, beyond doubt one can expect more of Kumbakkonam incidents in future. The appreciation of the values of Human Rights in education should move beyond declaration and teaching but become a way of life.

End Notes

1. *The Hindu*, Cover Story, 05.04.1964.
2. *The Daily Thanti* 06.07.2006.
3. *Dinamani* 13.10.2006.
4. *The Daily Thanti* 02.07.2006.
5. *The Hindu* 17.07.2006

References

1. The Conventions on Rights of the Child- 1989.
2. Universal Declaration Human Rights Charter – 1948.

3. Basu, Durga. Das, *Introduction to the Constitution of India* (Nagpur: Wadhwa Company, 2000).
4. Jaswal. Paramjit & others, *Human Rights and the Law* (New Delhi: A.P.H. Publishing, 1996).

21

Attrocities Against Dalits and Human Rights Violations in Tamil Nadu

R. Elangovan

Intorduction

From the time immemorials, the maladies of caste identity and atrocities against Dalits are deep rooted in Indian Society. Particularly, In Tamil Nadu, the attaricities against Dalits are on the Increased in the state. The raising trend in the atrocities in Tamil Nadu is closely associated with growing assertion among the Dalit in the State. These atrocities are brutal in nature leading to grievious hurt and murder of Dalits. They are aimed at generating scare, and fear psychosis, so that the Dalit would be forced to accept their subordinate status. These violent acts are, more often than not accompanied by a massive destruction of properties such as firing of the houses., breaking of house hold utensils and setting fire on crops in the lands owned by Dalits. The purpose behind most of the attrocities is to roots out Dalit resistance, socially, psychologically and economically. Even after the human rights and civil rights are talked much in India and at world wide, attrocities against Dalits are still followed in many places in the state. The purpose of this paper is also revolved around this matter and to make crtical anaylsis in the human rights point of view.

Caste Attrocities In India

There are number attrocities against religious minorities and between the various caste groups in India. There are many attrocities and social oppressions are, mostly aimed at Dalits people. Data collected by the government and its agencies highlight the scale of physcial aggression and oppression faced by Dalit communities. The 2005 Annual Report of the National crime Records Bureau (NCRB) under the Union Ministry of Home affairs states that a crime against scheduled caste communities is committed every 20 minutes in the country. It records that 26,127 cases of attrocities against S.C. Communities were reported 2 years back. In 2004, the recorded number of crimes against Dalits was 26,887. The 2005 report states that there were 1,172 cases of rape of Dalit women, 664 cases of murder, 258 cases of kidnapping and abduction and 3,847 cases of causing hurt, there were 2911 cases under the protection of civil rights Act and 8,497 cases under the SC and scheduled Tribes (Prevention of Attrocities) Act. Among these offenders, only few of them were convicted.

Types of Attrocities Committed against Dalits

Attrocities against Dalits range from verbal abuse to rape and forcing them to consume human excreta and urine, from dinial of access to public amenties such as drinking water, roads, bus stops, markets and temples to denial of civil rights; from physical harm to social boycots. In some of the places in a nation, police personnel often play a role in the violance against Dalits. There were many number of custodial rape and violince were among the most frequent forms of assault on the Scheduled Caste community

New forms of attrocities against Dalit in Tamil Nadu

There are many sorts of things invite attack on Dalits. An alleged "disobedience" of village caste-Hindus elders, refusal to perform "duties" such as conveying information about death, or a Dalit boy falling in love with caste-Hindu girl. Even the victory of a foot ball team of Dalit boys in a school match, or a Dalit bus drivers refusal to oblige a caste-Hindu by stopping the vehicle near his residence, (or) purchase the lands from the caste-Hindus, Dalit girl fallen, in love with caste-Hindu boys, refusal to come and work for any domestic or agricultural released work, have provoked attrocities against Dalit villages in the Tamil Nadu state.

Compartively, there were more number of incidenis occur against Dalits than other states. In this regard, The Dalit population inTamil Nadu continues to be denied their fundamental rights. They are subject to inhuman discreminatory practices. Most of the Dalits live in objtive poverty without basic amenities. The Dalits go through barbaric attrocities and violation. The following are some of major challenges that the Dalits encounter on Daily basis:,

Human Rights-Perspective of Dalit attrocities

Right to life and Dignity of Dalits is being denied Dalits, right to live with dignity has been systematically violated and sadly in most cases with the active support of the state apparatus. There are many number of incidents that have taken place releted with human rights violation, particulaerly, the right to life and dignity of Dalits. Among them,for the several decades, Dalits were denied entry by the vanniars (the dominant backward castes of Nothern Tamilnadu) in theAzheswar temple at Azhagapuram village, in the Ariyalore district . In this caste-ridden village, the "Two Tumbler" system is still active. In Tamil Nadu, the caste disparties, social and economic and caste-based attrocities are pertpetuated and propogated by all the social instituions like family, educational, religious institution, market and working places.

A few years ago, in a village called Echur, near Thirupporur, a young women who married a Dalit man was set on the funeral pyre and burn alive by her caste-maniac parents and siblings. The heart-rending cries of that sit drifted and subsided with in the dark cremation ground. The Dalit youth, who own in search of his wife, was also burnt on the same pyre. In some of the places, thecaste-hindu peple grouply involved and burns down the cheris (Dalit settlement set apart from the caste Hindu Village) In 1968, a caste-fanatic landlord, who burnt alive forty-four people in the popular vermani massacre. In other places, in the state, Dalits are unable to pull the cheriat, combinely with the other caste-hindus. From the many years, people of Dalits not allowed to touch the Kandadevi temple chariot. In the other Village called Alagapuram, Dalits are unable to enter the temple.

Apart from these attrocities, Dalits are not allowed to file a nomination papers for contesting in panchayat Institutions resorved for dalits. In many panchyats, government incapable of holding the election ever after 6 years.

In Erampatti, near Allanganallur village in Madurai District, the people living in the Cheri were chased out by the caste-hindus for celebrated Dalit leader"s Birthday.The Police attrocities against the Dalit people are also high in the State, in villages like Kodiyamkulam, Gundupatti, Okalur, Vandavasi the police continue to force their way into several cheris to carryout rampages. Even in most of Tamil Villages, two-tumbler system (Glass tumbler for upper caste and cocount shalls for untouchables) is still followed. The cremation ground is also located separately for the upper castes and the untouchables". A few years ago, near Kumbakonam, in Tanjavur district a murderous mob prevented Dalits from a carring corpse through a government-constructed bridge on public road.

The problems of Bonded labour among the Tamil Dalits.

Bonded labour is also an another "version" of castesim practiced in Tamilnadu. There are constitutional, legal provisions that prohibit the practice of bonded labour. The Article 23 of the Indian constitution and the bonded labour (Abolition) Act 1976are spcitically estatished for pronibitty all agreement and obligation arising out of system. In Tamilnadu, there were many number of bonded labour problems practiced. For example: The labours working in the manjolai tea estate had been working as bonded labours, for extremely long hours and they were paid very meagre wages. Therefore, the majorai Dalit worked decided to organize a rally against this attrocity and got permission from the government to conduct the rally. But due to some unfortunate happenings, these rally was turned into violence. There were number ralliest losed their life in the violence. This incident took place in 23 July 1999. Many number of Dalit people are still working as bonded labour in the various parts of Tamil Nadu, particularly in the districts of Coimbatoreand Theni, many Dalit families working in agricutural lands as bonded Labours.

Right to Land Denied

Land is central to the question of livelihood. Violation of the rights to land and related resources represents perhaps the most common form of attrocities against Dalits, articularly in Tamil Nadu. In this state, a huge hectares of other caste -Hindu Dalit lands (Now it is called Puncham Land) here illegally occupied and owned by the landlords her the megre aount. It sees the national level. Statistics, though, the Dalits in India account for 25% of the population, they one only 1% of the cultivable land. 8.6% of Dalit household remain landless and 49% of the Dalit population is agricultural labourers 25% of them are cultivators having very small land holdings. Although they are the backbone of the indianagriculture, a vast majority of them have no right over it, and has no share in it. Many efforts for land reform are scuttled and violently undermined by the landlords of the estimated 30 million accres of surplus lands only 5.42 million has reached the beneficiaries over a period of half a century. The dominant communtieis have aggressively reacted to any struggle by the dalits for a legitimate share in the land. This has brought enormous destrutation, pair and agomyto the Dalit community.

Conclusion

Human rights are one crucial aspects being prominently discussed these days., It is o critically conversed in the wake of growing attrocities against the historically deprived group. A Dalit human right now has become an International issue and organisation likes. Human rights watch, Amnesty International, Minority Rights Groups and Anti-Slavay International are making Dalit human rights a priority issue and are concieved to raise internationally in U.N. bodies, governments and the public at large, what ever the efforts might be, without changing of mind setting of Caste-Hindu people, no body can rectify these problem. The Sate government should educat them in proper maner and inculcate the value oriented education for the younger generation of various communities.

'Casteism-makes a human mad!
Humanism makes a human mature!

References

Thirumavalavan, Meena Kandasamy, Gail Omvedt, Vera Santhanam, ***Talisman, Extreme Emotions of Dalit Liberation***, Samya, 2004, 1-25.

Jha, Vivekanad 1975, ***Stages in the History of Untouchables***, Indian Historical Review, Vol.2.

Srivastava, S.N., 1980, ***Harijans In India Society***, The Upper India Publishing Housing Pvt., Ltd.

Jaiswal, Suvira, 1998, ***Caste***, New Delhi, Manohar Publication, 2000.

M. Kistaiah, ***Public Policy & Administration***, Sterling Publishers Pvt. Ltd., India.

G. Sreenivasa Reddy, ***Scheduled Caste and Public Policy***.

J. Michael Mahar Ed., ***The Untouchables in Contemporary India***, Tuscon, The University of Arizona, 1972.

Mishra, ***Exploitation and Atrocities on the Dalits in India 2006-2007***.

Michael, ***Dalits in Modern India*** 2006-07.

22

Dignity of Dalit Women

M. Elavarasi

Introduction

Globe is changing. Rights and values are being gained and Lost all over. The more you know the better able you to make a difference.

The word 'Dalit' in Sanskrit means the oppressed or downtrodden and is used to refer to that class of people who belong to the lowest category in the caste system of traditional Hindu Society. Referring to this class of society Mahatma Gandhi said "Socially they are lepers, economically they are worse than slaves, religiously they are denied entrance to places we miscall 'houses of God'. Although presently Indian society has moved far from the days of the "Untouchables" Dalits as a class still exist and atrocities against them are still happening.

Status of Dalit Women

Dalit women's are thrice discriminated outcastes, due to their caste, few, gender discrimination, being women and finally economic impoverishment due to unequal wage disparity with low or underpaid labour, According to Hindu Caste Hierarchy there are four caste namely (i) Brahmins (ii) the Kshatriyas (iii) The vaishyas (v) The shudras. Below this four tier caste ladder is another rung, who are called untouchables

(Panchamas). Among the untouchables the status of women is further eroded and closely linked to the concept of purity.

Books like the Manusmriti devide people into a stratified caste system and promotes in equality between men and women. Acc to Manusmriti, women have no right to education, Independence or wealth. It not only justifies the treatment of Dalit women as a sex object, and promotes child marriage but also justifies a number of indent atrocities on women as can be seen in the full verse.

Manusmriti (IX: 94) An man aged thirty years, shall marry a maiden of 12 who pleases him.

Manusmriti IX (3): Her father protects her in childhood her husband protects her in youth, and her sons protect her in old age. A women is never fit for independence even the killing of a Dalit women is justified as a minor offence for the Brahmin's equal to the killing of an animal. If the killing of an untouchable was justified as a minor offence you can imagine the treatment they received throughout their lives.

Position of dalit women - in view

Vulnerably positioned at the bottom of India's caste class and gender hierarchies, Dalit women, experience endemic gender and caste discrimination and violence is the outcome of severely imbalanced social, economic and political power equations. Their socio-economic vulnerability and lack of political voice increase their exposure to potentially violent situations, while simultaneously reducing their ability to escape. This situation exists in India today despite constitutional guarantees of non-discrimination on the basic of caste and gender article 15(1), right to life and security of life(Article 21) and the constitutional directive to specifically protect Dalits from social injustice and all forms of exploitation(Article 46).

The Hague conference on Dalit women's rights represented the next step in the struggle for the human rights &and dignity of Dalit women.

CONCLUSION:

The last 10 years have been significant in terms of initiatives and efforts that have been undertaken at various levels.

However there have been several road blocks and obstacles that have slowed the pace of women's empowerment in India. Whether it is a issue of Justice, Peace, human Rights or the destruction of the environment we need to work across the boundaries of caste, religion and cultures. Once our purpose and values are clear, conflicts between self-interest and social obligation find a moral balance between themselves. We become aware of when to take a stand. That is the time we start making the right decisions for long - term gain, rather than making the wrong decision for short - term gain. Wisdom and maturity lead to greater understanding of Major Issues.

To wind up

"Study as if you were to live forever.
Live as if you were to die tomorrow".

-M.K. Gandhi.

Index

C

D

E

Q

R

S

T